Designing and Delivering Training

David Simmonds

David Simmonds is a principal lecturer in training and development at the University of Westminster. He has over 25 years of experience in training and development.

The Chartered Institute of Personnel and Development is the
leading publisher of books and reports for personnel and training
professionals, students, and all those concerned with the effective
management and devlopment of people at work. For details of all
our titles, please contact the publishing department:
tel: 020 8612 6200
e-mail: publish@cipd.co.uk
The catalogue of all CIPD titles can be viewed on the CIPD
website:
www.cipd.co.uk/bookstore

Designing and Delivering Training

David Simmonds

Chartered Institute of Personnel and Development

Published by the Chartered Institute of Personnel and Development
151 The Broadway, Wimbledon, London SW19 1JQ

First published 2003
Reprinted 2004, 2006, 2007

Design by Fakenham Photosetting, Fakenham, Norfolk
Typeset by Fakenham Photosetting, Fakenham, Norfolk
Printed in Great Britain by The Cromwell Press, Trowbridge, Wiltshire

British Library Cataloguing in Publication Data
A catalogue of this publication is available from the British Library

ISBN-13 978 0 85292 992 6

Chartered Institute of Personnel and Development
151 The Broadway, Wimbledon, London SW19 1JQ
Tel: 020 8612 6200
E-mail: cipd@cipd.co.uk   Website: www.cipd.co.uk
Incorporated by Royal Charter.   Registered Charity No. 1079797

Contents

Dedicated to Rachel Grace Elizabeth Simmonds

Born 25 March 1983
Died 12 April 1983

You helped me to learn to live,
one day at a time

Acknowledgements

Many people have helped me in the process of writing this book.

I am particularly grateful to:

Ruth Lake at the CIPD, for her constant encouragement, particularly when I felt like giving up.

Robert and Joanne Hall, for letting me stay at their 'oasis' in Brittany
http://www.chateaudefretay.com

Karen Markham, for her tireless word-processing and advice.

Students on the MAHRM programme at the University of Westminster, for being the first recipients of this work, and for offering such useful feedback.

Many friends, including Cedric and Penny, Dave and Dori, Mike and Lesley, Tim and Judith, Mike and Alison, Carl and Eunice, Rob and Julie, Simon and Ruth, Ben and Judith, and others, for their prayerful support.

And especially my family, particularly, Janet, Paul, Mark, Chris and John, for their love.

All the errors that remain are my own.

David Simmonds
London
Easter 2003

The author and publishers gratefully acknowledge the following for permission to reproduce copyright material:

AMACOM: Fitz-enz, J., 2000, *The ROI of Human Capital: Measuring the economic value of employee performance*, AMACOM, New York.

ASTD: Reitman, A. and Williams, C., 2001, *Career Moves: Take charge of your training career now*, ASTD, Alexandria, Va.

Blackwell Publishing: Woodall, J. and Winstanley, D., 1998, *Management Development: Strategy and practice*, Blackwell Publishers, Oxford. Cripps, P., 2001, *The Blackhall Guide to Employee Development: Developing people to develop your company*, Blackhall Publishing, Stillorgan.

Butterworth-Heinemann: Hodges, T., 2002, *Linking Learning and Performance*, Butterworth-Heinemann, Woburn, Mass.

Chartered Institute of Personnel and Development: Darling J. *et al*, 1999, *The Changing Role of the Trainer*, IPD, London. Harrison, R., 2002, Learning and development, CIPD, London. Marchington, M. and Wilkinson, A., 2002, *People Management and Development*, CIPD, London. Martin, M. and Jackson, T., 2002, *Personnel Practice*, CIPD, London. Reid, M. and Barrington, H., 2000, *Training Interventions*, CIPD, London. Reynolds, J. *et al*, 2002, *How Do People Learn?*, CIPD, London. Stewart, J. and Tansley, C., 2002,

Training in the Knowledge Economy, CIPD, London. Wilson D., *et al*, 2001, *The Future of Learning for Work*, CIPD, London.

Kogan Page: Megginson, D., *et al,* 1993, *Human Resource Development,* Kogan Page, London.

McGraw-Hill Companies: Woods, J. and Cortada, J., 2002, *ASTD Training and Performance Yearbook*, McGraw-Hill, New York.

Pearson Education Ltd: Mullins, L., 2002, *Management and Organisational Behaviour*, Pearson, London. Stewart, J., 1999, *Employee Development Practice*, Pitman, London. Stewart, J. and McGoldrick, J. (1996) (eds.) *Human Resource Development: Perspectives, strategies and practice*. Financial Times, Pitman Publishing: London.

Perseus Books: Gilley, J. *et al*, 2001, *Philosophy and Practice of Organizational Learning, Performance and Change*, Perseus, Cambridge, Mass.

Productivity Press: Chawla, S. and Renesch, J., 1995, *Learning Organization*, Productivity Press, Portland, Oreg.

Random House: Handy, C., 1997, *The Hungry Spirit*, Random House, London.

Routledge: McGoldrick, J. *et al*, 2002, *Understanding Human Resource Development*, Routledge, London.

Sage Publications: Lynton, R. and Pareek, U., 2000a, *Training for Organizational Transformation: Part 1*, Sage, New Delhi. Lynton, R. and Pareek, U., 2000b, *Training for Organizational Transformation: Part 2*, Sage, New Delhi.

List of Tables

List of Figures

Introduction

To successfully develop human resources, an organisation must identify the skills it needs now and in the future. These skills must enable the organisation to achieve its strategic goals ... It may well be the case that larger firms have more funds available to invest in learning activities, and sufficient personnel to release some staff for formal training. Hence, the size of the organisation is likely to be important in determining its capacity to foster formal training ... smaller firms may need to find less formal approaches to engender learning by their employees.

Hyland *et al* (2000)

AS WE THINK AND ACT, WE LEARN

Not all learning generates new knowledge, since much of it strengthens and confirms what is already known. Equally, that learning may not transferable, or even desirable. Nevertheless, by undertaking workplace activities, employees constantly engage in goal-directed activities that can be the source of knowledge creation.

Training pays great dividends. Based on their research in the Australian hotel industry, Davis *et al* (2001) observed that:

- When the variable change in the quality of staff was compared, it was found that in two thirds of the enterprises that responded, staff quality had increased.

- Just over half (56 per cent) of respondent establishments had staff training and reported improved productivity.

- Of the respondent establishments, 90 per cent reported reduced turnover.

- There was no difference in the perceived level of staff commitment.

The survey of establishments in Western Australia raises more questions than answers. Of the three human resource functions discussed (performance appraisal, salary and benefit strategies, and training and development initiatives), only one of the functions indicates an improvement in quality and productivity, along with a reduced turnover of employees. *This was the function of training.* It is interesting to note that there appeared to be no increased commitment to accompany the other improvements.

So, how can we design effective employee training programmes? Adults learn more effectively when they are allowed to discuss the subject, relate it to their own experiences, and discover the value of the skills for themselves. However, this type of learning is also very resource-intensive. Many organisations regularly sacrifice long-term gains for short-term convenience. Many training sessions are lecture-based simply because of the resource commitment involved. Yet most employees do not learn very well when they are 'talked to'. They want to be more actively involved in the learning experience. Learner-centred training on the other hand, requires personal involvement, commitment, and experiential gains. This involves learning-by-doing. Many argue that competence, rather than knowledge, constitutes real power. Training really takes place when skills that can be defined are developed until the competence level is measurably enhanced. Training aims to provide employees with performance improvement. The outcomes of training, therefore, must be tangible, in that they should support and facilitate the organisation's strategic aims.

Successful development programmes result from conscientious planning and design. A great deal of attention must be paid to the desired outcomes. Problems will occur when there is a lack of planning regarding the purpose of the training and how those outcomes will be measured. If the learning event is not implemented in a logical, systematic and sensitive manner, it will be very difficult, if not impossible, to see sustainable change.

WHAT IS THE PURPOSE OF THIS BOOK?

In the summer of 2002, I started to design a new module as part of the University of Westminster's MA in Personnel and Development. When I became surrounded by – and nearly submerged in – a sea of journal articles and texts by a galaxy of writers, and I thought that instead this should be just one text that synthesised much of the essential knowledge in the area.

Consequently, *Designing and Delivering Training* has been written deliberately to provide much of the underpinning knowledge identified in the Professional Standards of the Chartered Institute of Personnel and Development (CIPD) for the specialist elective of the same name. This falls squarely in the identified and discrete cognate area called 'training and learning', along with four others:

- Learning and Development
- Management Development
- Managing Organisational Learning and Knowledge
- Managing the Training and Development Function.

However, it does not pretend to provide readers with all they should know, or indeed all there is to know. This is for two reasons. First, it would be arrogant in the extreme for me to suggest I could cover in one text the breadth and depth of understanding in this colossal body of knowledge. And, second, by the time you read this, some of it will already have been superseded by more recent research. Training is changing all the time. Therefore, you will need to take responsibility for your own learning!

Some Internet sites have been suggested both in the text and on the accompanying web pages. However, I'm sure you will find others as good, or better. You will almost certainly have experiences that are different to mine, and you may well know of research, articles or books that I have omitted. All to the good! I would be happy to hear from you at: simmond@wmin.ac.uk.

WHO IS THIS BOOK FOR?

This book is intentionally aimed at the needs of students undertaking studies for the Designing and Delivering Training specialist elective of the CIPD's Professional Development Scheme. However, I am aware that there could well be others who will also find much in it that will be of benefit to them. These could include:

- students undertaking other CIPD specialist electives
- students on the CIPD Certificate in Training Practice
- people working towards NVQs outlined by the Employment National Training Organisation
- students undertaking other postgraduate studies that include an element of human resource management in general or human resource development in particular.

Moreover, training practitioners, HR professionals, line managers and senior executives will also discover much here that will be to their advantage.

WHAT IS THE STRUCTURE OF THE BOOK?

Each chapter follows closely the learning outcomes and indicative content of the Professional Standard's ten operational indicators:

1. Analyse and interpret the broader organisational context and business environment in order to ensure that training meets business needs and achieves stakeholder support.
2. Use effective investigative and analytical methods to advise and assist clients in identifying needs, at all organisational levels, to which training is the most appropriate response.
3. Work with stakeholders to plan fair, accessible, effective and timely training solutions to meet those needs.
4. Collaboratively design training events (including formal programmes) that are securely grounded in principles of learning and make efficient and effective use of available resources.
5. Organise fair, accessible, effective and timely delivery of training.
6. Incorporate new technology as appropriate into the training and learning processes.
7. Advise on, and help to ensure, effective transfer of learning.
8. Carry out feasible, timely and cost-effective monitoring and evaluation of training programmes, and agree with stakeholders on any necessary changes to training provision and practice.
9. Manage, administer and market training activity, using new technology as appropriate.
10. Take responsibility for their own continuing professional development.

I have tried deliberately to fit the book and the chapters into a size and shape that would align with a normal teaching term or semester.

A *smörgåsbord* to delight every taste!

Within each chapter, there is a section devoted to an exploration of the theoretical approaches to each subject from a number of different perspectives. As far as possible, I have tried to include the latest thinking from a range of international authors. I have deliberately not overanalysed their input, but instead I offer them to you for you to critically evaluate each contribution in the light of your own experience and your other reading. Secondly, I have attempted to provide a section on the practical application of those theories based on empirical research, case studies, and relevant experience. Again, it has been left to you to determine to what extent such submissions truly reflect your own approach and the good practice you have encountered elsewhere.

Finally, by way of introduction, I offer you the wisdom of Rob Parsons (2002) and his seven laws at the heart of success:

> LAW 1
> Don't settle for being money-rich and time-poor
>
> LAW 2
> Believe that the job you do makes a difference
>
> LAW 3
> Play to your strengths
>
> LAW 4
> Believe in the power of dreams
>
> LAW 5
> Put your family before your career
>
> LAW 6
> Keep the common touch
>
> LAW 7
> Don't settle for success – strive for significance

Liverpool
Community
College

The organisational context and business environment

 The major challenge for leaders in the twenty-first century will be how to release the brain power of their organisations.

Warren Bennis

LEARNING OUTCOMES

■ Describe the business environment, the organisation's corporate goals and business targets, and the practical implications of these for the trainer.

■ Explain current and likely future skills imbalances across the external labour market and within the organisation, and their performance and training implications.

■ List types and choices of trainer roles to fit different organisational contexts.

CHAPTER OUTLINE

■ The organisational context of structure, corporate and organisational strategies, and work processes; human resource development policy and practice in organisations, and the opportunities and constraints they present for training impact.

■ Fitting specific training initiatives to wider organisational contexts; how training can aid planned change in the organisation's external and internal environments; issues for training in the change process.

■ How training roles are typified in research, and used in practice; choice of roles for training in different organisational contexts.

INTRODUCTION

In this first chapter, we will be looking at a wide range of issues on a very broad canvas. It is important for those working in the training function to be able to relate what they do both to organisational and national objectives. We will be exploring the links between training and change, and between development activities and organisational strategies. We will also discover the ways in which trainers' roles are shifting, not just to reflect the revolution taking place in work patterns, but also to enable those changes to become more effective.

THE ORGANISATIONAL CONTEXT AND BUSINESS ENVIRONMENT – IN THEORY

The business environment for training

Training and change are mutually dependent. For much of the last 50 years or so, training has too often been used as a short-term, involuntary response to the latest changes in the organisational context. How can we enable our people to utilise this new computer more effectively? In what ways can the employees from that other company be enabled to use our financial procedures, now that we've merged? Which staff will need to understand the new legislation on working-time practices in order to plan the shift rotas?

Leadbetter (2001) takes a somewhat jaundiced view of the changes around us at this time:

> Innovation, intangibles, information and intelligence are the driving forces for the modern economy … Innovation is at the heart of our society's cult of change. We invest systematically in change – through research, development, and innovation – to develop new ideas and turn them into new products more quickly than ever before, and then to spread these products around the world more quickly. We live in a culture constantly in transition, on the way to somewhere else. The next upgrade is always just around the corner.

However, I take his point. I was undertaking a consultancy assignment in a well-known UK biotechnology company in the early 1990s, and noticed a young man who seemed to do very little other than wander around the office all day, dressed in scruffy jeans and a T-shirt. When I enquired as to his role, I was informed that he was paid a very large salary, because about twice a year he would produce an idea that would make the company millions of pounds!

Change is here to stay! The only thing we can know for sure is that tomorrow is likely to be different from yesterday. This is true for our families, our friends, and ourselves. It is certain that there will be changes in our workgroups, our departments, and our organisations. But there has always been change, since the beginning of time. We can plot the amount of change over time (see Figure 1).

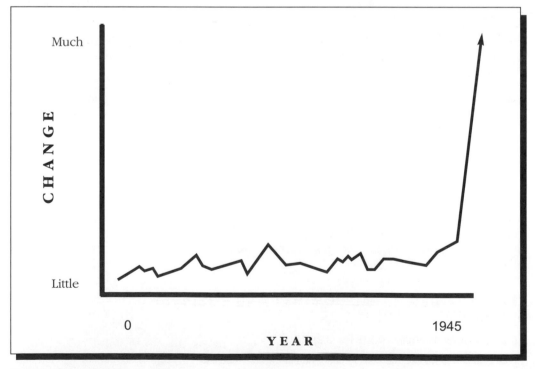

Figure 1: *The change graph*

What alarms many people is the rate of such change. It often seems that we are rushing out of control, as if somebody else has got their foot on the accelerator! There has been more change in your lifetime than all the other changes in the history of civilisation put together!

For example, when my grandmother was born, there were no such things as aeroplanes. For the few who travelled abroad, it meant going by ship. Just recently, however, I flew half way round the world to Malaysia and passed the time by using the console in my seat to listen to a range of music channels, to play a variety of computer games, and to watch the latest videos.

We are all in a constant state of change.

Literature on the subject seems to suggest that there are two basic forms of change – incremental change and transformational change.

Incremental change often happens slowly, or in small stages. Little steps lead eventually to big changes. Let's take an example from the retail sector in the last five years. A shop I know had always sold music cassette tapes. Gradually, they started selling CDs and videos as well. Now, they are introducing DVDs, and since they sell so few audiocassettes these days, these are being withdrawn. Soon, no doubt, they will stop selling videos as well.

Transformational change on the other hand usually happens fairly quickly. The build-up to it can – and should – take quite a while, and the subsequent implementation can take place over an extended period. But the change itself is so radical that it is introduced relatively quickly. One example that occurs to me happened at a university. The new vice-chancellor wanted to streamline the administrative systems and arrangements. He commissioned some outside consultants to advise the senior management team. Within a very short period of time, through a process known as 'rewiring', the administrative staff were moved from the familiar teams that were previously formed under programme leaders and associated with particular academic programmes. These professional administrators were summarily – and compulsorily – 'reallocated' into new departmental and cross-functional groupings on either an undergraduate or postgraduate basis. Needless to say, the administrators, academics and students alike all found the new systems very difficult to accommodate.

Walton (1999) suggests that, in addition to these forms of change, he could also identify others such as *transactional change* and *transitional change*. Moreover, he outlines a number of changes that have emerged in human resources development (HRD) practice and theory in the last 15 years or so:

■ the connection to corporate strategy
■ clarifying who benefits from training
■ individuals taking responsibility for their own learning
■ the broadening of the HRD constituency
■ the extension into team learning
■ the incorporation of organisational development
■ the incorporation of career development
■ the emphasis on internal consultancy
■ the focus on organisational learning
■ the link to knowledge management and intellectual capital.

This appears to contradict the view that training is only concerned with delivering new programmes! Companies wishing to carry out an audit on their training systems should consider a number of questions to ensure that they are relating training to business results:

- Is your training linked to your strategic decisions and business goals?
- Is it supported by strong leadership?
- Does it reflect the needs and values of your company's customers?
- Does it communicate your company's values?
- Does it help you address customer retention, acquisition, lower costs, less waste, higher speed and greater innovation?
- Does it build on the core principles of learning?
- Is it immediately relevant to your business?
- Can you clearly map an individual's path toward mastery?
- Does the environment empower employees to leverage what they learn?
- Does it lead to measurable results?

Learning must therefore be integrated within an overall organisational strategy. Before this can be undertaken effectively, the learning practitioner must be fully aware of organisational strategy.

Unfortunately, terms connected with the strategic analysis of organisations are often misapplied. Figure 2 shows one approach to understanding the interrelationships between such expressions of strategy.

The different elements of this strategic planning process (adapted from Brierley 1989) can be outlined as:

1. **PURPOSE**
   Changes rarely
   Why do you do what you do?

2. **MISSION**
   Key objective for the foreseeable future
   How will you implement your purpose?

3. **VISION**
   Long-term planning for the next five years
   What do you want to accomplish, and by when?

4. **DIRECTIONS**
   Five or six major themes
   Which activities will you focus upon?

5. **GOALS**
   Short-term SMART targets
   Where are you aiming?

6. **PRIORITIES**
   Allocating people, time, money, materials and facilities
   In *what* will you invest your (scarce) resources?

7. PLANS

Organising, problem-solving and decision-making
How will you, actually, achieve your expectations?

8. ACTIONS

Tangible, observable and measurable activities
Which behaviours are most likely to fulfil the plan?

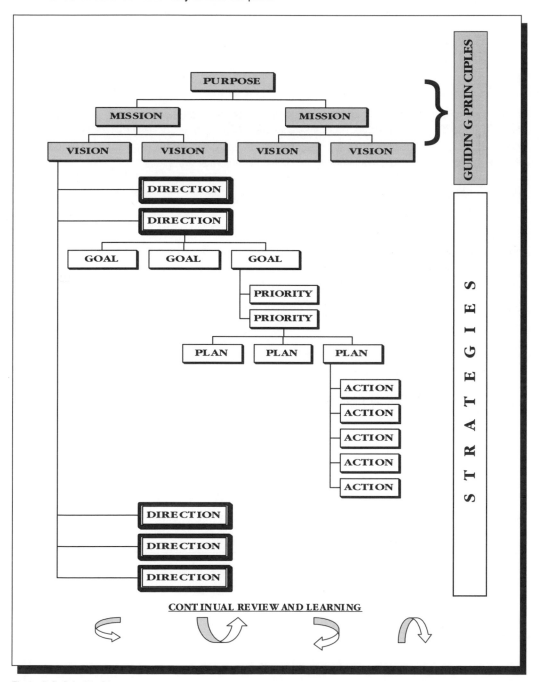

Figure 2 *Defining the future*

CONTINUAL REVIEW AND LEARNING

The entire strategic planning process must be based on continuous cycles of reflection, feedback and improvement. This will lead to learning at the organisational, departmental and individual levels.

AN ANALYSIS OF MODELS OF SHRD

Such a formalised approach to understanding the nature of organisational strategy aids us in our search for a role for training and development. We can see that it is only through continuous iterative cycles of improvement, review and learning that the organisation can aspire towards implementing its strategic plans. But, as McCracken and Wallace (2000) illustrate, this necessitates a move from training and development to strategic human resource development (SHRD), by adopting a strong proactive shaping role and a strong learning culture (see Figure 3).

We are able to distinguish from this model not only the marked differences between training, HRD and SHRD, but also the paradigms that reflect different types of focus, levels of HRD maturity and strength of learning culture. It is argued that, for SHRD to become a reality, the organisation needs to empower the HRD function to adopt a proactive approach in relation to corporate strategy.

In contrast with this model, Figure 4 on page 12 shows that of Stewart and McGoldrick (1996).

By critically utilising a number of separate parameters, we can formulate an assessment of these two different models of strategic HRD.

Deliberate or emergent?

There is some debate as to whether strategy is deliberate or emergent. Stewart and McGoldrick's model suggests that strategy is deliberate and is the result of analysis, which leads to the development of organisational plans. McCracken and Wallace on the other hand argue that strategy emerges from at times unrelated and *ad hoc* decisions as a result of compromise and competing interests. Resource-based strategy, on the other hand, focuses on internal competencies in order to gain competitive advantage. Here, HRD becomes a more prominent feature of all HRM activities.

Burgoyne's typology (Stewart 1999) of organisational maturity

In Stewart and McGoldrick's model, HRD is driven by the corporate strategy. It is reactive and can be placed at level four of Burgoyne's typology. However, in McCracken and Wallace's model, HRD also informs and shapes corporate strategy, and can therefore be placed at the highest point of sophistication and maturity at level six of the typology.

External focus for strategy (Johnson and Scholes 1997)

Stewart and McGoldrick's model makes no reference to the external environment, indicating that HRD would be slow to respond to outside transformational imperatives. McCracken and Wallace conversely make specific reference to environmental scanning. Such a model appears to be more dynamic in relation to change.

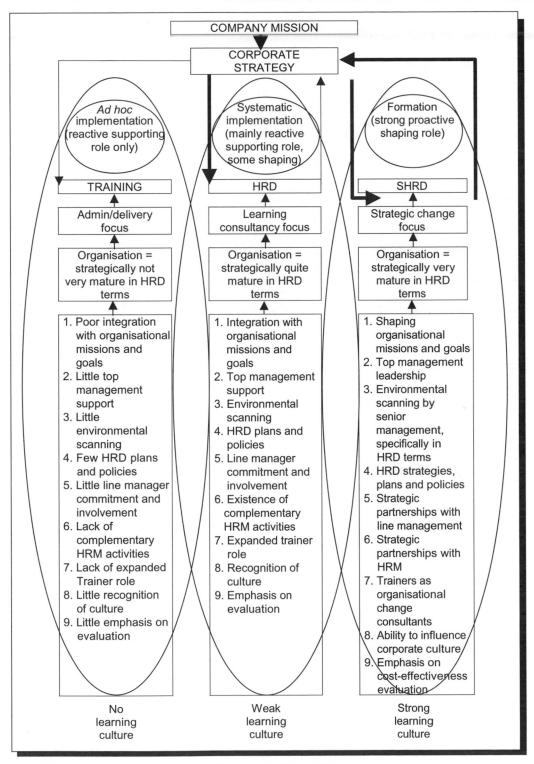

Figure 3 *Strategic human resource development – McCracken and Wallace (2000)*

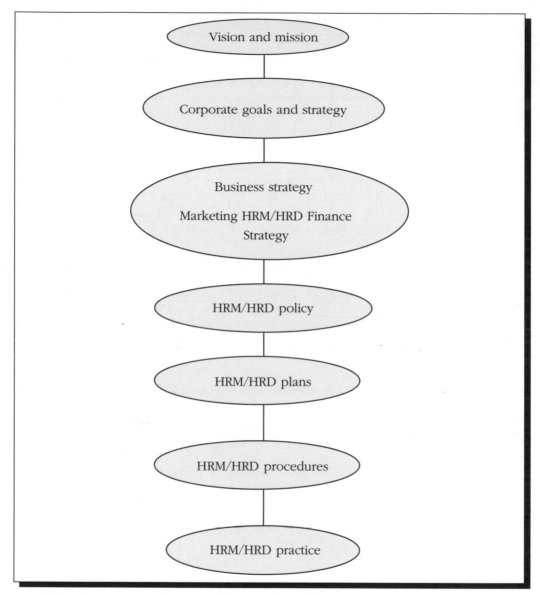

Figure 4 *Strategic human resource development – Stewart and McGoldrick (1996)*

Vertical and horizontal integration (Guest 2002)

Both models make explicit the vertical integration with wider organisational goals and strategies, but only McCracken and Wallace's model takes the further step towards horizontal integration with other HRM initiatives. Nevertheless, both Storey (2001) and Harrison (2002) question whether horizontal integration can in fact exist in practice.

Pettigrew's typology (1982) of trainer roles

With Stewart and McGoldrick's model, it can be assumed that the trainer would adopt the role of 'manager' – planning and co-ordinating the training processes and allocating training resources – according to Pettigrew's typology. Garavan (1991) proposes Pettigrew's 'innovator' or 'consultant' roles, whereas McCracken and Wallace's model goes further in advocating that the trainer adopts the 'change agent' role, where the focus is squarely upon organisational problem-solving through learning and development. This appears to be supported by Walton (1999) who observes that the trainer must be able to communicate effectively at the highest levels of the organisation.

Ownership
While Stewart and McGoldrick advocate that HRD practitioners take ownership of the organisation's learning and development, McCracken and Wallace make specific reference to the need for a strategic partnership with line managers. As a result, key stakeholders share in the ownership and implementation of HRD. In this way, the learning and development function becomes embedded in the organisational culture as a whole rather than being possessed by the training department.

Lewin's model (1951) of organisational change
McCracken and Wallace clearly see a role for learning and development in the process of organisational change in order to prevent cultural drift into former patterns and practices, whereas Stewart and McGoldrick make no mention of the importance of HRD in influencing corporate culture.

Evaluation and feedback
Overlooking the need for evaluation or feedback, Stewart and McGoldrick imply that training and development is seen as a cost or a luxury rather than as an investment in the long-term prospects of the organisation. McCracken and Wallace, though, refer explicitly to the need for an evaluation of cost-effectiveness. This should focus not only on pay-back investment to achieve short-term tangible results, but also on pay-forward investment to accomplish longer-term intangible results, as proposed by Lee (1996). The rational, linear nature of Stewart and McGoldrick's model allows no feedback into corporate strategy. The forming and shaping function of HRD, as illustrated by McCracken and Wallace, provides the necessary opportunities for continuous improvement and development. They argue against Garavan (1991), who posits a reactive or responsive view of HRD, insofar as it contributes to organisational objectives and is aware of the organisational mission. Their analysis is nearer that of Torraco and Swanson (1995) in that they see HRD as having a role that is pivotal, proactive and strategic.

The unitary or pluralistic approach
Both models assume a unilateral approach to organisational mission and vision, and that everyone in the organisation is working towards its achievement. Both models also appear to ignore the reality that all organisations comprise a range of individuals working towards a variety of goals, which may be tangential to those of their employer.

Generic or specific considerations
Stewart and McGoldrick present a generic model that could easily be applied to any one of a number of organisational functions, such as marketing, finance or purchasing, while McCracken and Wallace's representation is exclusively HRD-oriented.

Conclusion
It may appear that in effect Stewart and McGoldrick's model is not actually strategic but more operational in approach. It could be argued that their primary characteristics are in reality difficult to achieve. Garavan's nine-factor approach is even more challenging, and McCracken and Wallace's approach develops yet further complexity. A criticism of all these models is their lack of detail in terms of practical implementation or application. I would therefore recommend instead Walton's (1999) model, where there is an explicit commitment to learning in the organisation's mission and core values. It is supported by corresponding systems, policies, resources, partners, sponsors and stewards. Such collective and collaborative learning produces innovation, creativity, strategic awareness and enhanced job performance. Inevitably, this will lead to improved customer satisfaction. Walton insists that learning and development must form a foundational, and holistic, business process rather than being an accidental or tangential postscript.

So, as we have seen, all these approaches demonstrate well the need for the training and development of employees to be undertaken, not just on an organisation-wide basis, but also for SHRD to be central to the organisation's accomplishment of its strategic plan. As it addresses its plans in a cycle of continuous improvement, so SHRD will also change and adapt. At a team or departmental level, according to de Jong and his colleagues (1999), there are three major HRD tasks for first-level managers:

1. *Analytical role.* First-level managers should be expected to discuss periodically the performance and developmental needs of their subordinates. First-level managers themselves should be periodically screened with respect to their performance and their developmental needs, both in the way of production and in the way of people management.
2. *Supportive role.* Just as first-level managers should be expected to show interest in their subordinates' developmental activities on a daily basis, first-level managers themselves should experience a continuous interest and support by their superiors in their attempts to improve their skills.
3. *Trainer role.* Just as first-level managers should provide training and coaching to their subordinates, they themselves should receive instruction and guidance in order to develop in their management role.

Darling and her team of researchers (1999) concur with this association between training and the manager's responsibility for performance improvement. They find that:

Competitive edge is increasingly recognised as being achieved through people. In turn, training is becoming regarded as central to effective performance and its role intertwined with other operational issues. Discernible trends include:

■ a growing interest in frameworks which link quality, effectiveness and people

■ the promotion of positive attitudes towards lifelong learning and continuing professional development

■ the growing interest in organisational learning

■ an increase in staying-on rates in education

■ an increase in the proportion of people undertaking training-related activities.

To illustrate further these links between training and performance improvement, in Figure 5 we can see how McCracken and Wallace (2000) view SHRD as an open system. This 'open systems' model of SHRD portrays the essential elements that interrelate in an organic manner to effect organisational culture and change. Trainers are seen, not just as providers of training programmes, but as internal change consultants available to the whole organisation. They must develop strong partnerships both with colleagues in HR and also with line managers.

Among other commentators on the intrinsically interwoven nature of these organisational drivers, Gilley (2001) asserts that development and change are both central, linked, and key to the effectiveness of the organisation:

Whether change occurs in a large organisation or system, a small division or department within an organisation, or an individual employee, the primary purpose of change is to improve the organisation and make it more effective. This is the primary objective of HRD regardless of one's professional practice orientation. We believe that by adopting a three-in-one approach, such that organisational learning, performance, and change are blended into a comprehensive but integrated approach, HRD practitioners will be more effective in facilitating and promoting organisational effectiveness.

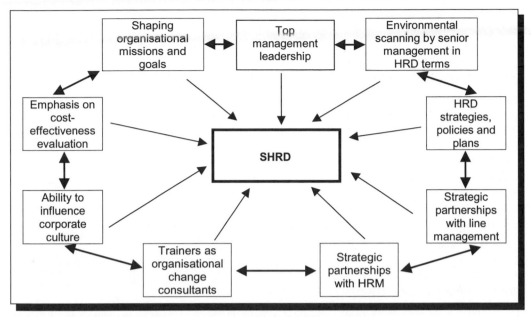

Figure 5 *Open systems model of SHRD*

How has training been involved in the change process? Dean (2001) alleges that there has been an accumulation of tools and methods for effecting change processes in organisations over the last 50 years:

- 1940s – sensitivity training for the interaction of the person and the environment
- 1950s – conflict resolution and teambuilding
- 1960s – intergroup development and open systems planning
- 1970s – socio-technical systems analysis and quality of work life
- 1980s – organisation transformation, total quality and large-scale change
- 1990s – re-engineering, large group intervention, transcultural planning, and transnational community building.

More specifically, from her recent review of the literature, West (2002) has found that learning organisations are particularly skilled at a range of activities that enable them in the change process and so to develop and integrate their learning. These include their capacity for:

- systematic problem-solving
- experimentation and learning from mistakes
- drawing upon memory and past experience
- learning with others
- effective communication
- thinking systematically and participatively in a wider context.

However, Honey and seven other leading British thinkers on learning specifically addressed such themes when they developed their 'declaration on learning' (1998). They declared that organisations had failed to capitalise on the learning ability of people:

Organisational leaders need to harness relevant knowledge and experience so that the organisation as a whole, and the people who comprise it, can learn more effectively. The same principle applies at community, national, and international levels. Every person, team, and organisation both survives and progresses through the ability to internalise and act upon this fundamental truth.

To summarise then, how can such a situation be addressed? From her review of both the theory and practice of learning and change, Harrison (2002) reflects that there seem to be four major imperatives for learning and development to achieve its strategic potential:

1. The learning and development process must be coherent and business-focused – practices and initiatives that interact with HR systems and policies to support and achieve organisational goals and values.
2. The learning and development strategy should be 'loose-coupled' – robust but not rigid, in order to remain relevant, up-to-date and sustainable.
3. The learning and development process should be flexible and value-adding – responsive to a variety of needs, at different levels and in different locations.
4. The learning and development practitioners should form business partnerships – both internal and external.

Skills imbalances and training

Having looked at the links between learning and organisations, we can now turn our attention to the changing nature of work itself. Some people have commented that in HR, for example, many of us don't actually have jobs any more; we're too busy doing tasks, or undertaking projects. Darling and her colleagues (1999) summarise this changing context in which all organisations work:

- changing work patterns
- increasing outsourcing of activities not considered to be 'core'
- the decline in manufacturing and growth in service industries
- increasing deregulation, privatisation and accountability
- increasing social and environmental expectations
- increasing globalisation and competition
- the impact of IT on strategy, roles, skills, recruitment, as well as on the way learning is delivered.

Any one of these would constitute a major training need for any organisation! Kelleher (1996) finds that even during the 1980s, the problem of such skills shortages was significant in all sectors of the economy:

Difficulties arose from a shortage of skilled professional people, engineers, nurses, construction workers, craft workers, print workers, computer personnel, secretarial staff, sales staff and those in finance and retailing.

Despite the rhetoric and avowed intentions of successive British governments since then, I wonder how much has actually been accomplished in meeting these shortages. Moreover, when we consider that, in most western economies, the very nature of work itself is changing, the situation would appear to be getting worse. Having moved away from manufacturing to service as the basis for production, many western nations are now facing the new difficulties surrounding the learning needs of knowledge workers. As Wilson (1999) points out, in many countries:

there would appear to be a developing skills gap between the labour demand arising from information-based technology and the requirements of knowledge-based industries, and the supply of suitable people within organizations and from educational institutions.

How can we encourage greater employee involvement? Leadbetter (2001) proposes a role of creativity and ownership – or authorship – for workers of the future:

'Authorship' means creating something that embodies your voice, your distinctive view of the world and the set of experiences that you bring to work. To see work as a process of authorship is to see it as a form of self-expression, not a task imposed on you from the outside. When people are authors of their work, they feel they shape it, own it. The craft that authors apply to their work gives them a sense of satisfaction and achievement. Work involving authorship cannot be managed well through detailed attention to process and yardsticks. Providing people with a sense that they are authors of their own work means managing by outcome and deadline rather than by process.

Therefore, if they are to address such a skills gap, trainers themselves need to reflect on the changing nature of their roles.

Trainer roles

Stewart and Tansley (2002) propose a future role for trainers:

A key role of the training function in the future will be in the support of knowledge management initiatives and social capital construction. Training specialists need to be involved in disseminating the message throughout the organisation that attempts to manage organisational knowledge must be founded on an understanding of how people learn, how they implement what they learn, and how they share their knowledge.

They continue:

The building of social capital, a widening client base and the support of knowledge management all imply a shift from the role of *training provider* to one of *learning facilitator*. This in turn suggests the need for the adoption of new teaching methodologies in fulfilling the new role of the training function ... In other words, *how* training and development are delivered becomes more important than *what* is delivered ... Training processes rather than content, then, are more significant in developing the ability to learn, and should therefore be the primary focus.

So, what are some of the important functions of effective training? Lynton and Pareek (2000b) outline three such functions, which are less well recognised than that of conducting training sessions: providing guidance and support through, for example, mentoring; helping to design and implement organisational change strategies, through, say, coaching in the workplace; and the leadership, managerial and administrative aspects of preparing an entire training programme.

In a more restricted sense, Burack *et al.* (1997) look at how the role of management development (MD) is also changing as organisations increasingly merge their strategic goals with human resources planning goals, in order to involve staffing and development. They assert that this new pattern of MD focuses on enhancing an organisation's effectiveness while maintaining competitive advantage. They consider the influence that MD has on performance improvement, examining the features of MD approaches adopted by the more successful organisations. The authors propose the application of core competences and the relationship between these and strategic MD. These writers introduce a general core competency model that reflects the integration of business strategy and human resources practices through the progressive building of competences and their alignment to specific jobs.

Such an approach has been developed still further by Noel and Dennehy (1991) who present us with six steps for the introduction of human resource development in an organisation:

1. the development of a focused strategic approach
2. involvement of top management
3. the 'refocusing' of course content
4. the development of 'impactful' learning methods (eg action learning)
5. focused participation of the employees who can provide significant difference
6. the provision of a learning atmosphere.

They believe that adherence to these steps will help the HRD professional become 'a significant force in the strategic transformation'. This could be very important for most organisations, including those in the public and voluntary sectors.

Other commentators have examined the theoretical issues surrounding the role of human resource development in organisational strategic planning. Torraco and Swanson (1995) point out that HRD not only plays a strategic role by assuring the competence of employees to meet the performance demands of the organisation, but also serves the additional function of helping to shape business strategy. They suggest that HRD has been a key enabling force in strategies based on product innovation, quality and cost leadership, customised service, or global relocation based on workforce skills. They also argue for the strategy-supporting and strategy-shaping roles of HRD, considering the use of HRD to support business objectives. They examine the relationship between HRD, expertise and strategy, and HRD as a shaper of strategy. In addition, they look at the need for the adoption of a strategic HRD perspective. Torraco and Swanson highlight the distinctive features of the strategic roles of HRD, which are evident in the business practices of successful organisations, and illustrate these roles with examples from some of today's most innovative companies.

THE ORGANISATIONAL CONTEXT AND BUSINESS ENVIRONMENT – IN PRACTICE

The business environment for training

One way of exploring such changes could be through an examination of an organisation's cultural web over a period of time (see Figure 6 for Johnson and Scholes' (1999) model). Each of the elements of the cultural web can be broken down further in order to obtain a fuller understanding of the organisation's culture:

- *Rituals and routines*. These are the formal and informal ways in which things take place within an organisation and the processes by which the different parts of the organisation interact. These aspects can be encapsulated in the phrase 'the way we do things around here'. For example, in an organisation like a university much emphasis is placed on formal committees and their minutes, as well as rituals like degree ceremonies.

- *Stories*. These are told about the major events and personalities, past and present, and become embedded in organisational 'folklore'. Through constant repetition, stories reflect those aspects of an organisation that people within it see as being particularly important. For example, in a local football club, the stories of heroes passed from one generation to another may be of the great centre-forwards who typified a style of game where entertainment was seen as more important than results.

- *Symbols*. These can indicate who and what is seen to be important within the organisation. Things like the design of offices, the award of company cars and the use of titles can all point to the way in which the organisation views itself. For example, in one hierarchical multinational oil company, a

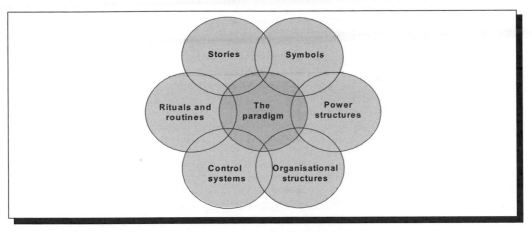

Figure 6: *The cultural web*

newly appointed manager was given an office with two doors, though his position warranted only one. It took the carpenters less than 24 hours to block off the 'surplus' door!

■ *Control systems.* The measurement and reward systems are likely to reflect those aspects of organisational activity that it is thought important to monitor or encourage, even if strategy documents or the chairman's statements may stress other issues. The extent of these systems can also indicate how much management within the organisation is centralised or devolved. For example, within most UK universities, academics are expected to engage in teaching, administration and research, but as promotion is largely based on the quantity of an individual's research publications, many feel the 'real' priority lies in this one area.

■ *Power structures.* These will indicate who are the most important groups within the organisation, the people who make the decisions. The importance of these groups and individuals might not be immediately apparent from the formal organisational structure, so there needs to be an awareness of informal networks. Such power might come from seniority or particular expertise. For example, within the UK electricity generation industry, engineers traditionally had a more prominent role than in other organisations and the priorities of the companies involved reflected this emphasis on engineering. Since privatisation, priorities that are more commercial seem to be reflected in the changing backgrounds of key decision-makers.

■ *Organisational structure.* This is likely to reflect the way in which the organisation works, as well as its power structures and important relationships. The levels of hierarchy, the decision-making bodies and what is discussed within them, as well as the information flowing within the structure, will all point towards the priorities of the organisation. For example, an advertising agency may well have a flat structure with teams formed to deal with specific projects in order to encourage innovation, and to focus on the client's needs.

Together these elements reflect and provide an insight into the overall paradigm that drives the day-to-day actions of organisational life. Furthermore, the cultural web highlights the way in which the corporate culture is reflected in both formal and informal elements of the organisation. Lying at the centre, the paradigm also tends to preserve and reinforce the key of the cultural web and this has important implications for managing strategic change.

It is particularly useful to apply the cultural web to an organisation before, during and after a major organisational change in order to map the ways in which the change is affecting different aspects of the organisation.

Does Marks & Spencer have a future?

Marks & Spencer's big store in London's Kensington High Street has recently had a refit. Instead of the usual drab Marks & Spencer interior, it is now Californian shopping mall meets modernist chrome and creamy marble floors. Roomy walkways and designer displays have replaced dreary row after row of clothes racks. By the end of the year Marks & Spencer will have 26 such stores around Britain – the first visible sign that the company is making a serious effort to pull out of the nose-dive it has been in for the past two or three years.

Things had become so bad that Marks & Spencer, until recently a national icon, was in danger of becoming a national joke. It does not help that its first ever TV advertisements – featuring plump naked women on mountains – met with an embarrassed titter. Moreover, a leading TV consumer programme savaged Marks & Spencer for overcharging and poor quality in its range of garments for the fuller figure.

As the attacks grow in intensity, so do the doubts about Marks & Spencer's ability to protect its core value: a reputation for better quality that justified a price premium – at least in basic items such as underwear. It is a long time since any self-respecting teenager went willingly into a Marks & Spencer store to buy clothes. Now even parents have learned to say no. Shoppers in their 30s and 40s used to dress like their parents. Now many of them want to dress like their kids.

Marks & Spencer's makeover comes not a moment too soon. Compared with the jazzy store lay-outs of rivals such as Gap or H & M, Marks & Spencer shops look like a hangover from a bygone era. The makeover aims to bring it into the present. The 26 stores being overhauled account for around a fifth of Marks & Spencer's turnover. According to one former director, the retailer makes most of its profit from around 40 stores. So, it makes sense to play to the company's strengths.

But Marks & Spencer will still be left with a long tail of some 270 relatively dowdy stores. Before the company rolls out its new look nationwide, it will have to work out how many of the stores are even worth hanging on to. Marks & Spencer has always had difficulties with such issues. When its profits were growing strongly, it was inclined to add floor space, such as the 19 stores it took over from Littlewoods a few years ago – just before profits peaked. It rarely closes down any of its high-street shops. Worse still, the company had no satisfactory system for evaluating which of its stores, most of which it owns outright, were making money: the company did not, until recently, charge notional rents to its stores.

The rot began appearing in 1998, when Marks & Spencer announced a 23 per cent fall in half-year results and warned of further bad news. Since then profits have more than halved and the share price has declined from a peak of £6.65 to less than £2.

Heads have rolled. Sir Richard Greenbury, the firm's autocratic boss, was forced to step down, first as chief executive, then as chairman. His successor as chief executive, Peter Salsbury (another lifelong Marks & Spencer man), laid out bold plans to overhaul the company's supply chain, buying more stuff abroad, and spruced up the tattiest stores. In September 2000, he was one of three executives fired by Mr Vandevelde, after a further slump in sales.

Behind this decline lie two basic faults. The first is the rigid, top-down, 'head office knows best' culture that built Marks & Spencer's proud record of success. This was fine so long as customers kept coming and the competition lagged behind, but it also made it difficult to question the Marks

& Spencer way of doing things. It is only now scrapping outmoded rules that meant staff spent too much time on rituals such as checking stock or counting cash in the tills, just because somebody at its head office in London's Baker Street had decreed years ago that such tasks were essential.

Added to this is in-bred top management. People tended to join Marks & Spencer straight from college and work their way slowly up the ranks. Few senior appointments were made from outside the company. This meant that the company rested on its laurels, harking back to 'innovations' such as machine-washable pullovers and chilled food.

The organisation missed out on the retailing revolution that began in the mid-1980s, when the likes of Gap and Next shook up the industry with attractive displays and marketing gimmicks. Their supply chains were overhauled to provide what customers were actually buying – a surprisingly radical idea at the time.

Marks & Spencer, by contrast, continued with an outdated business model. It clung to its 'buy British' policy and it based its buying decisions too rigidly on its own buyers' guesses about what ranges of clothes would sell, rather than reacting quickly to results from the tills. Meanwhile, its competitors were putting together global purchasing networks that were not only more responsive, but were not locked into high costs linked to the strength of sterling.

In clothing, moreover, the retailer faces problems that cannot be solved simply by improving its fashion judgements. The verdict points out that overall demand for clothing has at best stabilised and may be set to decline. This is because changing demographics mean that an ever-higher share of spending is being done by the affluent over-45s. They are less inclined than youngsters to spend a high proportion of their disposable income on clothes.

The results of Marks & Spencer's rigid management approach were not confined to clothes. The company got an enormous boost 30 years ago when it spotted a gap in the food market, and started selling fancy convenience foods. Its success in this area capitalised on the fact that, compared with clothes, food generates high revenues per square metre of floor space. While food takes up 15 per cent of the floor space in Marks & Spencer's stores, it accounts for around 40 per cent of sales. But the company gradually lost its advantage as mainstream food chains copied its formula. Marks & Spencer's share of the British market is under 3 per cent and falling, compared with around 20 per cent for its biggest supermarket rival, Tesco.

Marks & Spencer has been unable to respond to this competitive challenge. In fact, rather than leading the way, it has been copying rivals' features by introducing in-house bakeries, delicatessens and meat counters. Food sales have been sluggish, and operating margins have fallen as a result of the extra space and staff needed for these services.

Perhaps the most egregious example of the company's insularity was the way it held out for more than 20 years against the use of credit cards, launching its own store card instead. Only fairly recently did Marks & Spencer bow to the inevitable and began accepting credit cards. To do this it had to give away around 3 per cent of its revenues from card transactions to the card companies, but failed to generate a big enough increase in sales to offset this. Worst of all, it had to slash the interest rate on its own card, undermining the core of its own finance business.

Adapted from an article in *The Economist* 28 October 2000

PAUSE FOR THOUGHT

Review the Marks & Spencer case study on pages 20–21, and undertake a cultural web analysis of that organisation at the time that the problems started to emerge in 1998.

Rituals and routines

Stories

Symbols

Control systems

Power structures

Organisational structures

The paradigm

Skills imbalances and training

Many countries adopt a variety of fiscal approaches to fund their vocational training systems. In part, some are similar to the 'grant/levy' approach used by the former industrial training boards in Britain. There have been a number of approaches taken by successive British governments over the years in an attempt to meet the chronic needs created by persistent skills shortages, as Kelleher (1996) indicates:

- market-dominated training policies that reinforce the problem, namely the reluctance of employers to train their employees
- voluntarism, and on the whole weak state intervention
- state intervention for only about 15 years in the 1960s and 1970s through the industrial training boards, which became highly bureaucratic, narrowly focused, tended to favour larger organisations and emphasised off-the-job training
- corporatist strategies, weakened by rising unemployment
- laissez-faire attitudes to those actually in work.

Consequently, organisations are having to adopt new policies for themselves, in order to address the problems caused by chronic skills shortages. These include innovative approaches to horizontal and vertical task reorientation, autonomous work teams, multi-skilling, and job rotation. The NHS is a case in point. It takes many years to educate, train, and develop a competent and qualified health professional. When the Government took the shortsighted decision to cut back on funding the training of some of these professionals, the subsequent skills shortages could not so easily be reversed. Some health trusts were forced to adopt short-term solutions such as contracting staff from other countries – possibly causing yet further problems for the health economies in those developing nations. Other solutions have included the job enrichment and job enhancement of support workers in order to release others to priority tasks. For example, there has been a massive training programme to enable nurses to take on the prescribing of certain medicines. We have also seen the upskilling of health assistants to undertake routine screening programmes and developmental checks, previously undertaken by more qualified staff.

> In the UK, short-termism still dominates the financial base of most organisations and the structure of industry generally, and there is a persistent over-reliance by employers on market forces to provide their skill supply. (Harrison 2002)

However, at a national and international level, there are complex arguments concerning the demand and supply of skills. Vocational education and training can so often, and so easily, become focused almost entirely on resolving the problems of the young, unqualified unemployed. Consequently, those who are actually in work can often feel disregarded in any of the latest government training initiatives. It will be interesting to see what effect the European Social Charter will have, since it states quite clearly that every worker must be able to have access to vocational training throughout their working life.

Let's turn to the implications of this for training practitioners.

Trainer roles

Sawdon (1999) traces three broad development paths for trainers in the future:

- from training to consulting
- from training to learning
- from individual change to organisational change

and arrives at four approaches to training and consultancy:

- trainer
- training consultant
- learning consultant
- organisational change consultant.

My own situation is a case in point. When deciding to become a self-employed practitioner, I thought long and hard about how best to describe myself, and where to position my business. In the end, I chose to be known as a 'learning consultant' (see: http://www.searchconsultant.co.uk/assoc/dsimmonds.htm.).

PAUSE FOR THOUGHT

How do you see the future role for trainers and developers?

Compare your answers with the research findings by Darling and her colleagues (1999). In practice, people describe the roles they carry out in training in one of three broad categories (see Table 1).

Training roles, and their description, have changed over time. Summarising much of the literature on trainer roles over the past three decades, Walton (1999) provides a most helpful synopsis of the scope and development of trainer roles in this country and America since the 1970s, and offers a useful comparison of traditional and emergent functions (see Table 2 on page 24).

On the other hand, Harrison (2002) proposes that her typology of learning and development roles must be aligned with national occupational standards (see Table 3 on page 25).

While, on the face of it, such a typology has much to commend it, Harrison does in my opinion further confound our view of the reality that exists for a large number of training practitioners in many organisations.

Table 1 *Trainer roles – perspectives*

Philosophical	Strategic	Operational
■ Moderniser ■ Stabiliser of chaos ■ Creator/supporter of an innovative culture ■ Leader/supporter of the vision/champion ■ Surfacer of myths and assumptions ■ Banner carrier (in conjunction with HR) ■ Gateway to learning – supporter of lifelong learning – illuminator ■ Prophet	■ Facilitator at organisational level ■ Integrator ■ Internal adviser – organisational development ■ Organisational *'confidante'* ■ Interpreter of people implications of changes in the business ■ Change agent (learning is by definition change) ■ Influencer ■ Manager of expectations	■ Facilitator at personal and team level ■ Direct trainer ■ Internal adviser – personal development ■ Coach/mentor ■ Modeller ■ Manager of learning ■ Operational manager, team leader

The similarities between the standards levels for different roles serve to confuse rather than clarify. She also appears to reinforce former notions of status and hierarchy that may no longer be appropriate or relevant. Furthermore, the titles, roles and functions of learning professionals convey different impressions in a variety of organisations, and are changing fast.

However, Lecky-Thompson (1997) points out that the personnel and training practices of firms operating in the City of London could be improved, arguing that these practices have been neglected despite their importance to the success of the companies involved. He looks at the reason why personnel and training

Table 2 *Trainer roles – developments*

OLD		EMERGENT	
Functional roles	*Interpretive roles*	*Functional roles*	*Interpretive roles*
■ Direct trainer ■ Training administrator ■ Technical instructor ■ Needs analyst ■ Programme designer ■ Transfer agent	■ Passive provider ■ Provider ■ Caretaker ■ Evangelist ■ Innovator ■ Educator ■ Change agent	■ Learning and development manager ■ Contract/partnership manager ■ Facilitator at corporate university ■ Internal consultant ■ Performance consultant ■ Organisational development consultant ■ Knowledge manager/intellectual asset controller	■ Co-learner ■ Change facilitator ■ Learning architect ■ Orchestrator of learning processes ■ Intrapreneur ■ Facilitator of strategic processes

Table 3 *Trainer roles – focuses*

Role	National occupational standards level at which it is commonly practised	Major focus of role
Strategic change agent	4, 5	Promotion and facilitation of strategically focused learning and development process, particularly at divisional and corporate level
Consultant	3, 4, 5	Business partnership, to ensure learning and development advice, planning provision and assessment at any organisational level to achieve added value
Manager	4, 5	Management of the learning and development function across the organisation, whether through learning and development specialists, line manager, or internal/external partnerships
Trainer/learning facilitator	3, 4	Design, delivery/facilitation and evaluation of training events, learning processes and work-place learning
Administrator	3	Support of learning and development operations a all organisation levels

issues may have been ignored. He finds some hope in the increasing interest in human resources as a strategic issue, but still finds evidence of problems in the relationship between human resources and line managers. He lists the actions that need to be taken, recommending that chief executives in these financial institutions need to show more support for the human resource function.

There is a further, most important, role for trainers in establishing the link between human resource development and business strategy. Walton (1999) stresses that:

HRD is a set of processes for developing people at work which should be linked to business strategy and integrated with other major business processes such as supplier management or purchasing. The processes involved in HRD are ... training and development ... performance management ... resourcing ...

He emphasises the importance of an organisational climate where it is recognised that:

- Active learning starts at the top.
- Senior managers embrace an open, active approach rather than portraying HRD as an expensive 'treatment'.
- Business and HRD managers are operating in partnership.

He goes on to suggest three steps, which he believes will contribute towards such an organisational climate:

1. Human resource development professionals decide jointly with senior management 'what we need to be good at'.
2. Refocus the training function – streamline it and encourage joint working with business managers, to ensure that trainers address business issues.
3. Increase the pace of learning – use innovative approaches to reduce the inertia usually associated with lengthy programmes of off-site courses.

One of the roles in which trainers can have a major impact is in helping their employers to begin the journey towards becoming a learning organisation. Hoffman and Withers (1995) tabulate their comparison of traditional training with the learning organisation (Table 4).

Table 4 *From training to learning*

Traditional training	Learning organisation
Teaching content	Learning processes
Classroom-focused	Workplace-focused
Teacher-centred	Learner-centred
'Belongs to' training department	'Belongs to' each person
Activity-centred	Outcomes-based
Training specialist	Learning consultants

Applying such an analysis will enable many organisations to embrace organisational learning strategies, rather than having to rely on traditional approaches to training and development. As we focus more on the impact and consequences of our roles in organisations, we will see the importance of adopting a contingency approach. Situations and contexts call for adaptability and flexibility above all. Training professionals need to take the lead here.

So how can trainers encourage their organisations to meet the development needs of their employees? The *psychological contract* has become a useful construct to use when considering employees' training and development needs. Trainers have often embraced this approach. However, even here, there have been recent changes, as we can see in Table 5 (adapted from McGoldrick *et al* 2002).

Looking at the application of theories of the *psychological contract* and the learning organisation to the voluntary and charitable sector, Walton (1999) evaluates the status of English Nature as a learning organisation by investigating the progress it has made so far against certain criteria. This is shown in Table 6.

Table 5 *Psychological contract*

Characteristic	Past form	Emergent form
Focus	Security, continuity, loyalty	Exchange, future, employability
Format	Structured, predictable, stable	Contingent, situational
Underlying basis	Tradition, fairness, justice, socio-economic class	Market forces, saleable abilities and skills, added value
Employer's responsibilities	Continuity, job security, training, career prospects	Perceived equity, reward for added value
Employee's responsibilities	Loyalty, attendance, satisfactory performance, compliance	Entrepreneurship, innovation, enacting changes for improvement
Contractual relations	Formalised, mostly via collective bargaining	Individual's responsibility to barter for their skills internally or externally
Career management	Organisational responsibility, in-spiralling careers planned and facilitated through HR	Individual's responsibility, out-spiralling careers by personal reskilling and retraining

Table 6 *Towards a learning organisation*

Feature	Progress so far
Learning approach to strategy	Strategy is reviewed and refined but it is not always seen as easy to change direction.
Participative policy-making	Everyone has an opportunity to influence policy; there are tensions between bottom-up and top-down management.
Open information systems	Information is not always readily accessible: a project aims to improve information flow and use.
Formative accounting and control	Government accounting procedures require some control, although the finance team does help other teams to control their own resources.
Internal exchange	Variable. The internal customer ethos is still not fully accepted. Some teams have made considerable progress. Networking is crude.
Flexibility of rewards	Government rules restrict options. Performance-related pay, small special bonuses and flexible working are possible.
Enabling structures	Individuals do move and flexibility is encouraged, but boundaries are seen as fixed in the short to medium term.
Boundary workers act as environmental scanners	Local teams and national partner teams have access to considerable information but to date have not always taken opportunities to influence their environmental scanners.
Inter-company learning	Although there is liaison with nature conservation groups, in both Britain and abroad, meetings with organisations not involved in nature issues are rare.
Learning climate	There is history of knowledge-based learning and expectations are high. Process reviews for continual improvement are less common.
Self-development opportunities for all	There are many opportunities to learn and develop, but time and money often limit such activity to key areas of the job.

So, we have seen the links between learning, strategy and change, together with the developing roles of HRD in effecting continuous cycles of performance improvement throughout an organisation.

PAUSE FOR THOUGHT

Assess an organisation known to you in terms of the progress it has made towards becoming a learning organisation:

Feature	Progress so far
Learning approach to strategy	
Participative policy-making	
Open information systems	
Formative accounting and control	
Internal exchange	
Flexibility of rewards	
Enabling structures	
Boundary workers act as environmental scanners	
Inter-company learning	
Learning climate	
Self-development opportunities for all	

SUMMARY

We have seen how change can be viewed as learning and individual development. The amount and rate of change in work and life roles will continue to have a profound effect on the nature and function of adult development. Training – and trainers – will have a pivotal and foundational role to play in those organisations that seek to embrace an agenda of innovation and creativity.

QUESTIONS

1. What are the links between learning, development and corporate strategy?
2. How can training and development affect national skills shortages?
3. Critically evaluate two models of strategic human resource development.

The identification of training needs

We need to learn to set our course by the stars, not by the lights of every passing ship.

Omar Bradley

LEARNING OUTCOMES

- Explain how to determine and gain agreement on those organisational and individual needs for which training is the best solution.

- Outline competency frameworks in current or planned use in organisations, and their implications for training needs identification.

- Analyse the choice, use and monitoring of different training needs analysis approaches and techniques.

CHAPTER OUTLINE

- Different approaches for identifying and analysing job-related and individual needs for which training is a solution; how to provide support and advice for non-training solutions.

- Links between performance improvement and the identification of training needs; selecting and using appropriate analytical approaches and techniques.

- Common models and frameworks for aligning training events with business needs and

  - their strengths and weaknesses

  - the skills and processes they involve.

INTRODUCTION

In the first chapter, training and development was firmly located in the centre of the organisational change management process. We can now begin to progress through the classic systematic training cycle. In this second chapter, we begin the process by taking a close look at the different – and sometimes conflicting – needs of various stakeholders in the training function. Then, the importance and use of competence frameworks is explored in HR in general, and in HRD in particular. Finally, we investigate a range of approaches to the identification and analysis of training and learning needs.

THE IDENTIFICATION OF TRAINING NEEDS – IN THEORY

Gaining agreement on training solutions

For us to discuss training solutions implies that there must first be organisational performance problems. The **problem-centred approach** to training and development in general, and to learning needs analysis in particular, has held sway among many training professionals for at least half a century.

In essence, the problem-centred approach requires a form of investigation that appears to be based on a paradigm of scientific Taylorism, or even clinical diagnosis. There are several key elements to this type of investigation:

- It requires someone to reveal that a problem actually exists.
- It needs at least two people to own that the problem needs dealing with.
- It is historical in orientation.
- It demands a high degree of objectivity and reflectivity.
- It calls for considerable observational, linguistic and cognitive abilities.
- It asks for a cessation to the normal workflow.
- It presents a linear, inorganic, masculine, step-by-step outlook of the nature of work.
- It has its roots in manufacturing industries.
- It uses examples that require manual dexterity or physical skills.
- It compounds the employee's lack of self-confidence or competence.
- It supports a blame culture and a fear of failure.
- It denies the benefits to be gained from making mistakes.
- It reduces opportunities for experimentation, creativity and innovation.
- It reinforces a hierarchical, individualistic or militaristic approach to management.
- It gives training professionals unwarranted, unsought, and unjustified power and prestige.
- It strengthens a culture of dependency.
- It suggests a systematic or mechanistic method.
- It implies a simplistic, or one-size-fits-all, position.
- It encourages a view of task analysis based on disaggregation, deconstructionism or atomisation.

However, and most important of all, the problem-centred approach too often substantiates a view of training that is based on a *reactive, responsive, unthinking* attitude. This could be part of the reason why training has so frequently been ignored, denied, or considered irrelevant. Hence, there is difficulty in gaining agreement to training solutions! Employees and their managers are well practised in giving 101 reasons why a training solution would not work!

The time has come for a paradigm shift. A completely new worldview of training and learning is required.

The speed, nature and scope of the changes around us have been coupled with a radical reorientation of the function, organisation and character of work. Consequently, the easy, stereotypical and prescriptive solutions of yesterday will not fit tomorrow's situation. Instead of seeing training as a 'cure' or a 'fix' to a difficult situation, practitioners need to harness instead the benefits of continuous learning. If managers are anticipating change in the working environment, then trainers need to equip their people to be prepared for it in advance.

Many of the systematic methods used in the past to identify the root causes of problems can be equally well employed to anticipate future situations, and apply good training practice in a pre-emptive mode. Such analytical techniques might include, for example (Mullins 2002):

- SWOT
- PESTLE

- Brainstorming
- Force-field
- Fishbone (Ishikawa or cause-and-effect)
- Pareto (or 80/20).

In addition, one particular instrument that has proved particularly useful in determining present and future skills gaps at the working-group level is known as a *skills matrix*, or *versatility chart*. Team leaders and managers find this extremely effective since it provides, at a glance, and on one side of A4, a considerable amount of information. It has a number of immediate benefits (an example is given in Table 7):

- It helps in organising the group for planned absences, such as for holidays and retirements.
- It assists the leader in making decisions about workloads during unplanned absences such as sickness or maternity leave.
- It provides the means for an appropriate multi-skilling programme for the team.
- And, most of all, it enables the whole team to take responsibility for their individual and corporate development.

Table 7 *Versatility chart*

Team members	Competencies				
	1 **Adverts (a)**	**2** **Internal memos (b)**	**3** **Displays (b)**	**4** **Promotions**	**5** **Seasonal (c)**
Avril	C		C		
Bob	C	C			C
Colin	C		T	C	
David	C			C	D
Esther	C				
Farouk	C	D	D	D	
Graham	C			T	
Helen	C	T			

C = Fully *competent*; performs this regularly
D = Can cover for colleagues if necessary (eg sickness, holidays etc) but needs *development*
T = Identified as an area for *training* as part of the performance appraisal

(a) From this example, 'Adverts' appears to be a key task for all the team.

(b) If the team leader feels that two people should be regularly performing each task, you can easily identify where the gaps and vulnerabilities exist, who needs training, and who is overburdened. In this example, perhaps Helen could be trained to perform 'Internal memos' and Colin could be trained to do 'Displays'.

(c) If top management suddenly decides that, say, 'Seasonal' is a key task, and wants four people to carry it out, the versatility chart allows you to train and move people around very easily.

Versatility charts from several departments can also be collated centrally to form part of a wider organisational skills audit.

Typically, however, one of the major techniques adopted by HRD professionals to identify and analyse training and learning needs is that of *job analysis*. Palmer (1999) reports more than 40 different such approaches. Whatever the number available, suffice it to say that, unfortunately, for most HR practitioners, such procedures are neither widely known nor generally used.

Training and development professionals will only be effective to the extent that they seek to help others meet their own needs. That will be true for individuals, business units, and organisations. HRD professionals must strive to rid their language and vocabulary of its precious terms and phrases if they want to gain the trust and confidence of those in positions of power and influence. They need to use *their* language, and *their* reports, and be present at *their* meetings, and help *them* achieve *their* targets. For that is the power of learning. The *raison d'être* is always to enable others achieve their potential in an environment of constant change.

Stewart (1999) reports the need for training professionals to be able to use a variety of strategies to deal with failure. Fortunately, however, he goes on to illustrate a more optimistic approach, when he suggests a range of tactics for trainers to adopt:

- Identify key players, that is, those with power and influence. These are likely to be chief executives and other senior managers.
- Ensure the HRD function and contribution is compatible with what is important to key players.
- Involve key players and other managers in all HRD activities and all stages in the process.
- Produce evidence of success from HRD activities in terms which make sense and are important to key players and other managers.
- Be aware of changing priorities in the organisation and be prepared to adapt and change HRD products and services.

We now continue, by looking at training needs analysis in an organisational context. Wilson (1999) proposes a three-stage process for prioritising training needs:

1. Include training needs predetermined at policy level.
2. Divide remaining needs into essential and desirable.
3. Cost the essential needs and prioritise via Pareto. (80/20)

By adopting such an approach, HRD professionals will be able to secure agreement on training solutions.

How can training professionals enable the necessary *collaboration* for establishing training needs at this macro-level? To answer this question, Lynton and Pareek (2000b) submit a very helpful tabulation (Table 8).

Clearly, such a traditional approach would appeal more to a bureaucratic or hierarchical culture or business. Nevertheless, I believe it has something to offer many other organisations as well. We can see, for example, how such an approach reveals the need for involvement and collaboration between all stakeholders and at different levels.

How important are competency frameworks to the identification and analysis of training and learning needs?

Table 8 *Collaborative training framework*

	The system	In order to	By means of	Limits
1.	(a) States training course	Clarify issues for organisation; decide	Brochure/course announcement	One-way; no modification through organisation's response
	(b) Requires applications to come through organisation; organisation to pay fees/salary	Increase organisation's commitment to training goals	Brochure/course announcement	One-way; no modification through organisation's response
2.	Discussion with senior officers	Signal interest in collaboration and respect for senior staff	Meetings and seminars	Relation to needs indirect and uncertain
3.	(a) Required detailed job analysis	Focus organisation on operational needs	Course announcement	Organisation's ability and inclination
	(b) Requires organisation's plans for change	Focus organisation on complete program of change	Course announcement	Organisation's ability and inclination
4.	(a) Collaborates with existing organisation	Ensure matching training goals and motivation for change	Extended face-to-face contact	Organisation's ability and inclination plus resources
	(b) Collaborates to establish new services	Involve related organisations	Extended field-work	Organisation's ability and inclination plus resources

Competency frameworks

Much has been written about competency frameworks. Ever since Richard Boyatzis published his seminal text on the competent manager in the early 1980s, the idea of competence has been developed in this country and abroad. However, the whole conception of competence in America and Australia is quite different to that which has been developed in this country.

In America, competence is synonymous with excellence, achievement, recognition and having performed well, whereas in this country it is about minimalism, or 'good enough'. Moreover, in the language of those who develop the frameworks, certainly for the NVQ model, people were not even allowed to say that a worker was incompetent; because of political correctness, we have to say they are 'not yet competent'. Since the early 1980s, then, other countries have adopted or modified one or other of these approaches to reflect local employment and cultural norms. For Britain, the declared intention by the Government was to establish a framework of work-based qualifications to which all employees and school-leavers could aim. In reality, however, those in power had been aware for some time that the national standards of skills fell far short of our continental neighbours. Therefore, when the Single European Market was proposed to take effect from the early 1990s, Parliament enacted a whole series of measures to enhance the skills and protect the jobs of our own workers. This included the introduction of NVQs.

In spite of the wealth of well-researched job analysis techniques available, it was decided instead to impose on the whole country a national competency framework for all jobs by using the relatively unknown and untested method of functional analysis. At the time, one of the major consultancy firms involved in the process was Godfrey Durham and Associates, one of whose principal consultants was, I believe, Shirley Fletcher. There has been considerable and protracted criticism by trainers and learners alike of the new framework. Stewart (1999) highlights significant pieces of research that were undertaken by, among others, Smithers, Capey, Beaumont, Senker and Dearing. All these analysts found evidence for considerable weaknesses and problems associated with the national framework for vocational education and training. Moreover, the system of qualifications in the UK compares unfavourably with those in other EU countries. Despite such criticism, the fundamental nature of the national qualifications framework has since been amended very little.

The competency framework for trainers is a case in point. I became involved in the so-called 'consultative processes' for these in 1990 and again about 10 years later. On both occasions, professional HRD specialists expressed considerable concern with the analytical method, the overall structure and the detailed outcomes of the framework. However, it was made clear by representatives of both the consultants and the Government departments alike, that such considerations were not open for prolonged debate or fundamental alteration! What functional analysis essentially does is to break down a job into its component elements. It atomises, deconstructs, or disaggregates a role, a function or a job into its smallest components. It disassembles the tasks of a worker into their smallest constituent parts, and in excruciating detail. Moreover, the problem is that, in the end, we are left with elements that look nothing like what a worker should actually be doing.

For example, if somebody used functional analysis to try to identify the nature of a rose, they would cut it and take it away from the plant. They would lay it out on a board and chop off the leaves and dissect the stem and pick off the petals and separate the stamen, and so on, and so on. And all that you would have left would look nothing like a rose. And its beauty, its scent, and its very nature would have been lost for ever. So it is with work, so it is with tasks; that in their precise deconstruction, something of the very nature of its purpose and meaning is lost.

Moving on, skills acquisition, and therefore needs analysis, can be seen as sequential or developmental, and part of a more meaningful set of competences, as shown in Table 9 (Cheetham and Chivers 2001).

At a strategic level, Garavan and McGuire (2001) argue for the adoption of competencies for workplace learning in order to aid the process of analysing needs and meeting organisational objectives:

> Increasingly organisations seek, through the implementation of sophisticated human resource development and workplace learning strategies, to develop competencies to enable employees to respond quickly and flexibly to business needs. The need for greater flexibility has resulted in a more widespread use of competency approaches as a basis for workplace learning provision ... The use of competency frameworks as the focus of workplace learning serves the dual purpose of facilitating the identification of learning needs and ensuring that learning provision addresses business needs ... national competency standards are now considered invaluable in establishing a foundation for the implementation of workplace level training and development initiatives ... However, ... training initiatives are having little impact in addressing the training needs of the small business sector. Specifically ... the actual provision of training in small firms fails significantly to keep pace with the perceived needs of owner/managers and their workforce.

Table 9 *Skills acquisition*

Level	Characteristics
1. Novice	Rigid adherence to taught rules or plans Little situational perception No discretionary judgement
2. Advanced beginner	Guidelines for action based on attributes or aspects Situational perception still limited All attributes and aspects are treated separately and given equal importance
3. Competent	Coping with overcrowding Sees actions at least partially in terms of longer-term goals Conscious, deliberate planning Standardised and routinised procedures
4. Proficient	Sees situations holistically, rather than in terms of aspects Sees what is most important in situation Perceives deviations from the normal pattern Decision-making less laboured Uses maxims for guidance whose meanings vary according to the situation
5. Expert	No longer relies on rules, guidelines or maxims Intuitive grasp of situations based on deep, tacit understanding Analytical approaches used only in novel situation Vision of what is possible

Garavan and McGuire (2001) go on to point out still further major flaws of many competence-based approaches:

There is a clear assumption that those who perform effectively are considered to have a superior set of competencies. There is a strong bias to consider notions of competency in a context-free way. This tendency manifests itself in prescriptive comments about how possession of specific competencies can lead to high performance, irrespective of the organisational context within which they are utilised. This literature tends to postulate a notion of competency as atomistic, mechanistic, bureaucratic and one that reinforces a notion of competency as a strait-jacket.

Nevertheless, there are ways practitioners can approach the task of organisational and training needs analysis in a more professional manner. Darling *et al* (1999) have tabulated various organisational learning needs and appropriate responses (Table 10 on page 36).

A number of commentators have each advocated certain approaches to the task of training needs analysis. However, none appears to be devoid of particular weaknesses. Garavan and McGuire (2001), in their useful summary of the literature on competency identification methods, outline the relative effectiveness of each (Table 11 on page 36–37).
They conclude that:

Many pragmatic criticisms exist. Chief among them is the lack of a coherent definition. The approaches broadly divide along US and UK lines. The US approach identifies itself with an input, worker-oriented model, whereas the UK model focuses more on an output, work-oriented model. Some commentators call for a more multidimensional approach.

Table 10 *Responses to organisational learning needs*

Need	Response
Managing change	Developing flexible responses to new situations, increasing the capability and quality of people, encouraging enthusiasm and energy Managing the impact of structural changes
Improving effectiveness	Continuous improvement Developing a learning culture Need to give graduates people skills to help them to become 'rounded people' Raising the profile of the business Improve customer relations Developing innovation Forward-planning, target-setting IT skills for managing virtual teams
Recruiting and keeping the right staff	Finding new managers Coaching/mentoring skills for managers Reduce staff turnover, selection of effective managers/consultants, especially at senior levels Valuing staff more, supporting them Improving communications within the business Teambuilding – shift to multidisciplinary teams
Globalisation	Developing a global mindset, including the acquisition of languages

Table 11 *Competency identification*

Method	Researchers	Process	Effectiveness
Direct observation	Boam and Sparrow (1992) Mirabile (1997)	Employees are asked to perform a number of critical tasks Observers record the tasks being performed which in turn form the basis of competencies	Relatively cheap to implement and not time-consuming Provides a clear picture of the observable elements Not effective observing mental processes Subject to observer error
Critical incident technique	New (1996) Thomson and Mabey (1994)	Involves clarifying the differences between average and superior performers Interviews with the job-holder, supervisor or other relevant person Participants asked to describe what behaviours were displayed, who was involved and the outcome	Ability to capture unusual behaviours Involves key individuals in the job Tends to focus on job functions and overlook personal attributes May take some time to generate an outcome

Job competency assessment method	Spencer and Spencer (1993) McClelland (1973)	A team is formed to identify the skills and knowledge required Team conducts interviews to identify attributes of outstanding performers Expert panels validate the model to determine its effectiveness	Data can be collected in an effective manner Useful to identify job functions of individual jobs Tends to focus on job functions and overlook personal attributes May take some time to generate an outcome
Expert panels	Spencer and Spencer (1993) Cockerill and Hunt (1995) Boam and Sparrow (1992)	Selection of a panel of in-house experts and others who have superior knowledge Panel observes employees performing tasks and identifies a list of competencies which they consider relevant to job Prioritising of the list to identify those that require priority development	May give the process legitimacy and credibility within the organisation May have difficulty pulling together a panel of appropriate experts Suitable to larger organisations A tendency to miss out on certain competencies

Different approaches to training needs analysis

There are a number of approaches to job training analysis, according to Stewart (1999):

- *Comprehensive analysis.* As the name implies, this approach consists of a full and exhaustive analysis of all aspects of a job. It will produce a detailed specification of all tasks and associated performance requirements, together with KSA (knowledge skills and attitudes) specifications for each task and activity
- *Key task analysis.* Again, the nature of the approach is reflected in the name. The intention here is to first determine which tasks are critical to successful performance, and second to analyse only those and ignore others. This approach tends to be appropriate for more complex jobs with high degrees of discretion.
- *Problem-centred analysis.* A further descriptive title. The approach here is to focus exclusively on particular and specific areas of the job which jobholders themselves and/or their managers find problematic. Thus, the analysis is limited and tightly focused, and is likely to involve job holders themselves identifying and specifying problems.

Such macro-approaches can then be applied at different organisational levels. It is important, however, to take account of various characteristics for discrete levels of learning potential (Table 12 on page 38, McGoldrick *et al* 2002):

On the other hand, a micro-approach that I have found particularly helpful over the years in helping trainers and personnel managers to identify and analyse their own training needs, is the model put forward by Craig (1994). He clearly distinguishes between different elements of the job, namely its constituent functions, tasks, skills and abilities. Many people working in HR today are so intent on meeting the operational requirements of their work that they find it increasingly difficult to isolate any specific learning needs. Craig posits that, when attempting to analyse training needs, instead of looking at the overall nature of a job or even its essential components, we should focus instead on the *abilities* required for each skill. Such abilities are generic in scope and transferable in nature. Therefore, separate abilities can be combined in different formations of a variety of skills in order to accomplish different tasks. By focusing on these essential

Table 12 *Organisational TNA*

Level	Characteristics
Individual	People take an active role in identifying and undertaking self-development activities that lead to continuous learning and improvement in knowledge, skills, aptitude and performance
Group	Good communication, trust and understanding of shared meanings within groups in order to identify and solve problems and to experiment with measures for change and improvement
Departmental	Encouragement for self-development, experimentation and creativity within an environment that tolerates mistakes. Toleration of ambiguity and uncertainty and a good understanding of their contribution to the effective performance of the 'whole' organisation
Organisational	The organisation is unique in terms of its ability to promote and sustain the learning processes that are required for all stakeholders so that change is an ongoing process for both the individual and the organisation in terms of its ability to promote further learning and change
Intra-organisational	Excellent communication between departments with celebration of 'difference and variety'. Avoidance of 'compartmentalisation' with cross-fertilisation of ideas, HRD and work approaches within the organisation
Inter-organisational	Deliberate and continuous attempts to transfer learning and information between organisations by experimentation and sharing best practices through collaborative ventures and exchange of ideas, personnel and approaches to work organisation
Extra-organisational	Continuous attempts to understand, anticipate and create environmental change and translate it to the advantage of the organisation and all its stakeholders by undertaking and/or exploring contemporary practical and analytical research, learning from this and promoting any required changes or adjustments to work organisation.

abilities, we can then more easily identify specific learning needs. Moreover, we are likely to be able to influence the learner's competence in performing a whole range of tasks, some as yet unknown.

In the example of the job of a *production manager* in Figure 7, you can see how an ability called *'word-fluency'* has been highlighted. If the jobholder has an identified need with this ability, then relevant learning strategies can be planned and designed as appropriate. For example, she could use a workbook from the learning resource centre on *'Report-writing at work'*, followed by leading a seminar with her peers on the learning points she has gained from the experience. She might conclude by writing a short summary sheet for distribution and discussion with all the people in her team. By developing her ability in *'word-fluency'*, she would increase her performance on three separate key skills of her job, namely: 'listening and questioning', 'recording', and' negotiating'. These in turn would benefit her in accomplishing two of the three tasks required when fulfilling the function of 'planning a schedule', namely, 'gathering information', and 'allocating resources'.

Alternatively, Figure 8 (on page 40) shows Gilley *et al* (2001) adopting very much a process-driven view to needs analysis, presenting us with their approach as a means of performance improvement. If we espouse such an approach, we can see the causal links between, firstly, an analysis of the gap between actual and desired performance, and, secondly, the outcomes of that analysis and appropriate learning interventions.

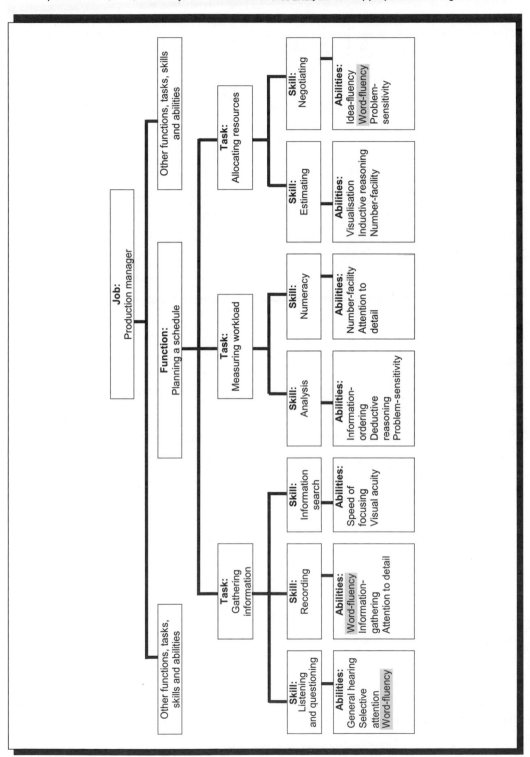

Figure 7 *Identifying abilities for TNA*

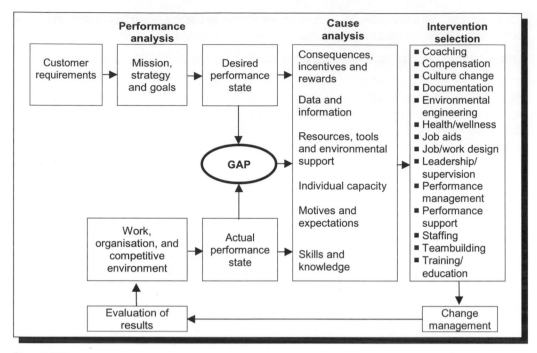

Figure 8 *TNA as process*

By contrast, as O'Donnell and Garavan (1997) are keen to point out, there are several problems associated with such a methodology for traditional training needs analysis:

■ Non-training solutions are often ignored or not fully considered.

■ Skills analysis and training are not linked with the organisation's goals and strategies.

■ Skills analysis is not linked to present and future changes in work organisation and job redesign.

■ The approach is management-oriented and does not necessarily involve consultation with employees and union representatives.

They offer the common-sense advice that traditional methods of training needs analysis can be adapted to provide skills-audit techniques by adding analysis of organisation strategy, changes in work practice and job redesign, and integrating these with usual training needs analysis procedures.

THE IDENTIFICATION OF TRAINING NEEDS – IN PRACTICE

Gaining agreement on training solutions

O'Dwyer and Ryan (2000) highlight the issue of training needs analysis in micro-enterprises:

> The perception of need by owners/managers is a critical factor in the decision by owners/managers to participate in management education programmes. It is clear that small business owners/managers vary considerably in their perception of a need for formal management education.

Training needs come in many different shapes and sizes. However, there must be agreement that there is a need important enough for at least two people to want to do something about it. It must include the learner, together with somebody who is going to help them meet that need. Typically, that would be a supervisor, a manager or a trainer. It may be a peer, a colleague, a subordinate or somebody else in the department, perhaps, who can help them. Sometimes, however, needs arise which the learner themselves can meet, either on their own, or with support and resource from others.

This is one of the most significant differences between learning and training. Most learning is carried out on an incidental or accidental basis. It is informal, and usually occurs on the job. But let us assume that an employee is faced with a problem, a difficulty, a change, a new situation, an unfamiliar process, a new system that's introduced, or a new way of working, a new machine or a new tool, a piece of software or a programme, a new customer or product, a new service line or market. For her this is new and different. It is beyond her current ability, knowledge, skill or attitude. She cannot easily transfer her existing understanding or competence in a non-specific, generalised way. She cannot easily see how her current awareness can be applied to this new situation, because if she could, then she would probably already have done so.

When the learner is faced with a set of circumstances that is beyond and above her ability levels, she transfers the subconscious or unconscious need into a conscious reality. Then a problem exists. She says: 'I can't', or 'How can I?'. She might say 'I won't' or 'It's not part of my job.' Alternatively, she could say, to somebody she knows and trusts, 'Please would you help me?' or 'How could I go about this? What would you have done? How did you do this in the past?' On the other hand, she could say to her manager, 'I've got a training need.' Nevertheless, for that need to be analysed, it needs first to be identified, and then clarified.

This analysis should happen regularly as part of the normal daily or weekly performance management approach. At the very least, it needs to be part of an organisation's appraisal or performance management system. The best leaders are those who 'manage by walking around', and spend a few minutes regularly with each member of the team. They are quick to spot needs that training could meet. There are many other needs training cannot meet, and yet which can be met on an organisational basis. These would include, for example, changing workflow patterns, promotion, outsourcing, bringing in experts, releasing new resources, or finding different suppliers. However, there are certain needs, which are specific to an individual or a group of individuals where training and learning can be used. This then becomes the responsibility of the line manager.

For example, a number of years ago I was asked to go into an organisation called the Drug Control Centre, which was part of Kings College London. This was a very small organisation with only about 25 people, all of whom were extremely highly qualified and sophisticated in their knowledge, most of whom had doctorates in biochemistry and other allied fields.

The Centre was established to investigate alleged breaches of regulations by, principally, athletes and others in the taking of banned substances. So if an athlete had a regular, or sudden, check on their accomplishment, they would produce a urine sample and that would be despatched to the Centre for analysis. Increasingly the Drug Control Centre was also being used to test other employees, like underground train drivers. Therefore, this small organisation asked me to come and undertake some training for them. The Head of the Centre asked me to carry out some courses to help their communications improve. Of course, I could have met their request and carried out what they wanted. However, I felt that there was more to it than that and I asked the head of the Centre, 'Why do you want me to do these courses?' He said 'Because I've asked you.' I pursued the question, 'Well, why?' He said, 'Because I'm paying.' Therefore, I took a more analytical approach which I knew would appeal to his scientific mind and I said 'Well let's investigate the causes of the problem.'

And with that, he agreed to me interviewing every single member of staff for about an hour each. I started with him, and then spoke privately to every member of staff, including somebody who was brought in from their maternity leave, and someone else who was only about six months away from retirement. Moreover, as I spoke with each of them, asking them about the work, asking them about the organisation, their role, their function, problems, why things were the way they were, a certain pattern seemed to emerge.

There was a set of needs within the organisation that I knew could be met through training, but there was another set of needs which I knew could best be met through organisational change.

Having spoken with all these people I drafted a report, which I shared with the Head of the Centre and then asked to be able to communicate this with the rest of the staff and he said 'Well why, we don't do that?', which I think highlighted the need for communications improvement! However, some of the difficulties were centred on workflow patterns. The vast majority of the urine samples would arrive on a Tuesday morning and needed to be analysed and the results returned as quickly as possible. In addition, physical changes to the rooms and the laboratories could ease some of the difficulties. Another way of improving the situation, as far as I saw it, and which I recommended, was for a particular worker to be promoted. He clearly had team leadership qualities, and seemed to be held back and frustrated in his position. He had the respect and the following of those around him, and a lot of skill and technical qualities and abilities as well. In addition, I also questioned, naively, certain processes and systems and whether and how they could take place more effectively. And yes, I did also agree to undertake some teambuilding workshops, together with some communication improvement seminars. Based on the evaluation I undertook, these were successful. I believe that from this, the Centre was able to enter into a new contract with their main client organisation.

Horwitz (1999) draws attention to the importance of training needs analysis in situations where line managers have the responsibility for HRD:

> The apparent reduction in size of central HRD departments, through decentralisation or outsourcing, suggests that HRD is being shifted to line managers, who may then hire specialised expertise from outside to assist with particular HRD priorities. Identifying training needs arising from strategic goals, new technology and work process redesign then becomes critical at the operational level for which a line manager is responsible. ... Some organisations have reversed the process of decentralised HRD. Johnson & Johnson, for example, had training experts in each of its business units. Through re-engineering they created a centre of training expertise, staffed by 12 HRD specialists who contract their services to the business units.

Therefore, training needs analysis is about gaining agreement on training solutions. It's not about the training department assuming that they know all about the training needs of the employees and the managers. It is paramount that the people are involved in the identification and analysis of needs. Often this is done on a formal basis through appraisals, but if an appraisal or performance management approach is only carried out annually, then by definition it is out of date. Moreover, any training based on that approach would be 18 months out of date, at least. Far better for the appraisal to be done twice, three or even four times a year. At British Telecom, it is carried out on a four- to six-week rolling basis – only taking five or ten minutes at a time – but the manager or supervisor is able quickly to pick up performance needs among the team.

Coleman and Kleiner (1999) provide a useful reminder of the importance of determining the training needs of the newest recruit from the time when they are being oriented to the organisation through an induction programme:

It is important to remember the following four simple statements:

1. If the time is not made available to do the orientation correctly, the employee's productivity may initially suffer.
2. If it is not accomplished within an open and honest teambuilding environment, the employee's attitude and perception of the company will suffer.
3. If it is not done with both the needs of the company and the needs of the employee equally in mind, the company's bottom line will suffer.
4. If the bottom line suffers too greatly, then there will no longer be a company.

PAUSE FOR THOUGHT

Take time now to complete a versatility chart for your team: **C** = Fully *competent*; performs this regularly; **D** = Can cover for colleagues if necessary (eg sickness, holidays etc) but needs *development*; **T** = Identified as an area for *training* as part of the performance appraisal.

Team members	Competences				
	1	2	3	4	5

Competency frameworks
Competency frameworks are being adopted in a number of organisations, particularly in large or public sector establishments.

Training needs analysis and competences in the Prison Service

The Prison Service is an executive agency of the Home Office, with an annual budget of £1.3 billion and 36,000 directly employed staff. There are 135 prison establishments in England and Wales, holding 65,000 prisoners. The role of the service is captured in its statement of purpose:

Her Majesty's Prison Service serves the public by keeping in custody those committed by the courts. Our duty is to look after them with humanity and help them lead law-abiding and useful lives in custody and after release.

The Prison Service is in a period of enormous change. It is expanding rapidly as it faces unprecedented growth in the prison population at the same time as being required to become more effective, both in custodial and rehabilitative work, and more efficient through a demanding cost-reduction programme. An average prison will, for example, have a budget of £20 million and will employ upwards of 500 staff. (contd)

The major impact of developments has been on the governor of each prison. Running prisons is becoming an increasingly complex and demanding managerial task. The progressive devolution of responsibility for delivery of services, and the management of resources (money, staff, buildings and plant) to deliver those services, has increased significantly the role of the governor as general manager, in addition to traditional duties.

In the light of these changes, a number of high-profile prisoner escapes, together with the White Paper, 'Development and Training for Civil Servants' and a desire to adopt a strategic approach, the Prisons Board commissioned reviews of what competences governors require and what training and development framework would provide those competences.

The Prison Service, like other executive agencies, developed a core competency framework (CCF) in 1996. The CCF was intended to inform the recruitment, selection and development processes of staff. Unlike the Home Office, the Prison Service CCF does not have competences identified for each managerial level but is a framework of 12 competences applicable to all staff in the service. Each of the 12 competences has three overarching sentences attached to describe it, and a number of performance indicators.

Using the CCF, a 360-degree (line manager–peer–subordinate–self) profiling of the governor's job was undertaken in order to create a model, or benchmark, against which governors could be assessed for promotion, selection and appraisal, and to identify training and development needs. In addition to the behavioural competences, a training needs analysis was undertaken to identify the present and future training and development needs of governors. This involved questionnaires to all governors and a number of semi-structured interviews.

What emerged from the training needs analysis was that governors required both formal and informal development opportunities. Formal elements included training in general management, prison operational management, incident command and public sector management. The demand was for classroom-based work, together with distance-learning material, thematic seminars, project work and secondments. The informal elements consisted of coaching/mentoring, action learning sets, broader development opportunities and personal study.

The Prison Service has, as a result, made a major investment in the training and development of governors. Contracts have been signed with external providers for a Certificate and Diploma in Management Studies, and for a Master's degree in Applied Criminology and Management. A coaching/mentoring scheme has been introduced and thematic seminars have taken place. A Senior Command course has been developed for senior staff, which they attend prior to becoming a governor. The Civil Service College is providing the public sector/civil service modules.

A project is underway to assess the organisational impact of this major investment in training and development for governors. At an individual level, the end-of-training questionnaires indicate that the objectives set have been met, and follow-up questionnaires suggest that people perceive themselves to be more effective having undertaken the activity. Evaluating the impact on the organisation continues to be problematic. Directly attributing the improvement in the Prison Service's key performance indicators (such as number of escapes, time out of cell) to the investment in training and development is too simplistic to be defensible. However, the investment in training and development has helped to create a perception that the Prison Service values its senior staff and that in itself is of benefit.

Another problem with identifying and analysing training needs is that in the past the model used was called *gap analysis*. Typically, the experienced worker or the trainer would be deemed to be at a specific level with a certain ability with knowledge, skills and attitudes at the peak of perfection. The learner, meanwhile, would be 'not as good as' the trainer or the experienced worker, the supervisor or manager.

Leaving aside for now the argument about disempowerment or disenfranchisement, and putting on one side the whole view of training as demeaning or bullying, there is, nevertheless, a fault in the assumption between what many people viewed as 'the current level of ability' of a person and the assumed 'gap' between that and what they should accomplish. There is a premise that somebody outside of the learner is able to determine what the learner should be doing, or achieving. This is based on a worldview of guilt, obligation, duty and fear.

By definition, the standard the learner has achieved is not good enough. Aligned to this whole view of incompetence, guilt, self-blame and low self-esteem, is the fact that it is compounded often by the view that even if a learner were helped to improve, or to increase their knowledge, skills and attitudes, then somehow they would never, ever, quite get to the top, because somebody (the trainer?) would always be changing the expectations.

Consequently, this approach is very limited in both scope and application. There are considerable restraints inherent within competency frameworks. They merely measure what a worker may have been able to do in the past. However, there is no generalisable, transferable, or generic application for the employee's future development. Moreover, there is an all-pervasive sense that there is an in-built competitiveness in such frameworks. There is a desire to perform to the standard that an assessor deems appropriate. One of the major faults of competency frameworks is the concept that a worker is not yet competent.

Competency frameworks are historical by nature; they can only ever enable the certification of the worker in the current, or usually previous, job. They are not developmental. Such frameworks appear to be inappropriate to the organisation's strategic training plan! In addition, one of the difficulties of achieving competence in the NVQ model is that some workers have no opportunities to demonstrate competence within the constraints of their current role. Many NVQ candidates have encountered great difficulties in meeting the competency requirements, since their current role does not include particular elements of work, even though, clearly, those prescribing the qualification think it should! They can therefore provide no evidence in these areas.

There is also a wide variety of different methods of constructing competency frameworks. There are a number of different job analysis techniques based on observation, critical incident analysis, the Delphi technique and others. However, the government of the day chose not to exploit these, but instead to adopt an untried, little-researched approach called *functional analysis*. It needs to be remembered that this was espoused at a time when post-modernism and deconstructionism were prevalent in the philosophy supported by many influential thinkers in government and universities alike.

The other factor, which I believe has not been well addressed in competency frameworks, because it is very difficult to deal with and often gets distorted, is that work is, by definition, undertaken in relation to others. Work is relational. It has a social element. Work exists between people. A competency framework may be appropriate at NVQ levels 1 and 2, for many essential tasks, which are either mundane or repetitive. But at level 3, there is much that is omitted from the relational or sociological context in which the tasks are being undertaken.

Fortunately, several organisations have developed their own competency frameworks, based on respected job analysis techniques, and much good work has been accomplished. For example, generic or core competences have been developed for one particular organisation, and for all the people in it, so that each employee has a core component to their job, which is aligned with the organisational strategy and purpose. Every member of staff needs to accomplish those core competences at different levels and applied in different ways. Following, there will be optional, technical or peripheral competences, which are specific for only one particular job or task. For some organisations, these are then incorporated into appraisals or a performance management system. For others they may be aligned to a reward management strategy. These core and optional competencies are then published for all employees. For the HR professional, these are available on a database, and can easily be applied to every element of the HR value chain.

The benefits of competency frameworks are that they can be used throughout the personnel and training function with great effect, from recruitment and selection, to induction, to training and development, to succession planning, to outsourcing, redeployment, redundancy and retirement. Through the whole value chain, a rigorous and robust competency framework will assist both the professional and the line manager in their decision-making about each employee throughout their lifecycle in the organisation. This results in a more objective approach. Practitioners will have easy access to criteria which have already been agreed, and against which they can select and assess. A good competence system will help:

- when it comes to shortlisting and interviewing
- during assessment and development centres
- when identifying and analysing training needs
- when approaching people for promotion
- when developing a rewards strategy
- when choosing who to make redundant.

At those times, trainers can actually address the needs of both the individual and the organisation in an overt, transparent and honest manner. Assessment can be undertaken objectively because the criteria have already been clarified. Certainly, when identifying and analysing training needs, the individual worker or learner can be involved in the process. They can be encouraged to ascertain areas where they need to develop for the future, because of their awareness of future competency requirements. If they are anticipating that their career will not remain with that organisation, then they will be developing skills, knowledge, abilities and attitudes that are generic to other organisations. Consequently, the whole of the skill level of the external labour market will be enhanced.

We can apply the notion of competence to a wide range of different situations.

For example, take a look at Figure 9 (Cowling *et al* 1999). Five clusters of competencies have been identified relevant to evidence-based health care. From this example, we can see that the training needs of individuals are dependent upon the degree of autonomy and empowerment they personally hold, rather than that held by the particular professional staff group to which they belong.

Such an approach is extremely valuable to all those working in HR, and particularly those in HRD, since it affords an easy diagnosis of learning needs.

PAUSE FOR THOUGHT

Review what you have learnt about competence frameworks.
How could this be applied to the future responsibilities of HRD practitioners?

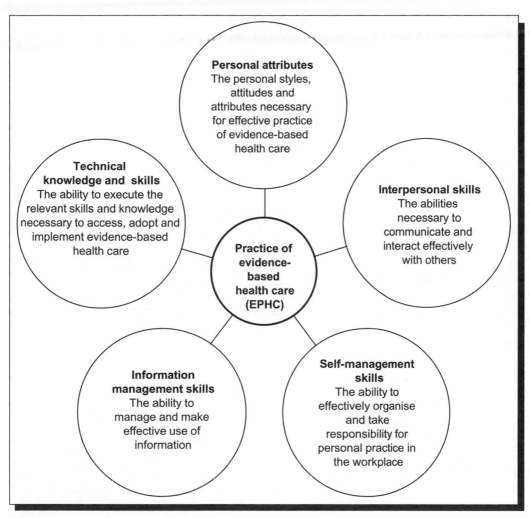

Figure 9 *Competencies for evidence-based health care*

Different approaches to training needs analysis

We have seen a wide variety of different approaches to training needs analysis. In the literature, many writers go to great lengths to show the different methods of gathering data, whether directly or indirectly. Training needs analysis can be based on data gained through interviews and focus groups, through observation of the learner, their manager, their workgroup or stakeholders. Alternatively, training needs analysis can be indirect, by looking at records and documents, such as accident statistics, sickness and absenteeism rates, or complaint levels. However, such data-gathering only gives part of the picture. At best, it is inferential. That is to say, it is an estimate of what might be some of the reasons behind some of the causes of some of the problems. Again, it is historical, backward-looking and reactive. Far better, surely, for there to be an identification of future needs. We need to take into account where the learner would like to develop tomorrow, next month and next year. Organisations must consider how competencies can be accomplished in the future, rather than merely focusing on the reasons why they may not been achieved in the past.

Most training needs analysis in the past has been problem-focused. The assumption has been that if there is a problem, there must be a solution. That kind of thinking is dangerous because it assumes that the trainer knows what the problem is, and the way to solve it.

Instead, HRD practitioners must adopt a more proactive approach by, for example, implementing personal development plans (Higson and Wilson 1995). In order to develop employees, certain information needs to be identified:

- What skills do they have now?
- What roles and tasks do they currently fulfil?
- What is the next logical progression?
- What roles and tasks will be different?
- What training will they need?
- What is the timeframe for the training?

Training needs analysis can be just as easily applied to an individual, a job, a business unit, an organisation or a profession.

For example, in Russia, problem-centred analysis is used with those working in medical research (Vartanian 1997). Community-oriented therapeutic and preventive programmes must respond to community health needs. Medical science and technology must also reflect healthcare needs and consequently community health needs. Ultimately, community health depends on achievement in biomedical sciences with public health and medical science becoming integrated into one coherent whole. This independent integration stimulates action and at the same time contributes to the effectiveness of activities undertaken at all levels. Such logical integration also determines a manpower development process, which helps to solve fundamental and applied medical problems. Training or educational programmes should therefore derive from the needs in each of these areas and they must be problem-oriented. Of considerable importance is the individual training and development of specialists and scientists, for it is the individuals who make up the research teams, centres and institutes who get things done. That is why continuing education has become a priority and effective educational technology is the best strategy to develop research manpower potential. Here, however, problems of psychology, personality peculiarities, and psychodynamics have their place and role in the course of research manpower training, which is prevalent in its nature and has a wide spectrum of variations ranging from intellectual abilities and capacities to motivation. At present in Russia, there are training programmes for obtaining a degree in medical sciences and this is the endpoint in specialist training.

Training needs analysis can also pertain at an organisational level in the assessment of different perspectives. So, by way of summary of this area, look at the example in Table 13 where training needs analysis is used to manage diversity. We can see that there emerges not only the accompanying attitudes, but also the training and non-training implications (Moore 1999).

Of relevance here to the analysis of diversity training needs is the conclusion by McCarthy and Garavan (1999) on the requirement for self-awareness and, in particular, the awareness of any discrepancy between how we see ourselves and how others see us. They assert that an awareness and appreciation of development needs is a factor that influences employee participation in training and development activities.

Table 13 *TNA of 'diversity'*

Perspective on diversity	Accompanying attitudes to diversity	Training implications	Organisational implications
Diversity blindness	Neutral: 'Diversity is not an issue'	Ignoring diversity training needs in the design and development of organisational training initiatives	Extra, unrecognised demands on diverse members. No organisational arena for discussing or highlighting opportunities and problems associated with diversity
Diversity hostility	Negative: 'Diversity is bad'	Active suppression of diversity. Promotion of 'sameness' in training interventions Attempts to 'homogenise' the workforce	Explicit and implicit discrimination. Horizontal and vertical segregation
Diversity naiveté	Positive: 'Diversity is good'	One-sided 'romantic' training interventions focusing on 'celebrating or welcoming diversity' May heighten awareness in the diversity issues awareness, but is unlikely to help tackle the potential problems associated with diversity	Can damage and polarise groups that do not subscribe to the espoused position on diversity Can lead to unrealistic expectations from diverse groups
Diversity integration	Realistic and functional: 'Diversity does not automatically lead to positive or negative outcomes, but needs to be managed and integrated'	Active training for diverse groups and development of skills in the management of diversity. Managing the opportunities and problems of diversity. Creating important preconditions for effective communication within heterogeneous groups	Networks, mentoring and structural integration of 'minority groups in organisations' Supportive organisational interventions such as flexible working conditions, childcare arrangements, ergonomic adjustments for disabled employees

PAUSE FOR THOUGHT

To help you analyse learning needs, it is essential that you establish the requirements of your job.

To undertake a training needs analysis, it is important first of all to help the individual clarify the purpose of their job and the key results areas. Talk to somebody you know.

In just one sentence, write down in the central box the overall purpose of the job.

Then, using the Pareto principle (80/20) to prioritise what you actually do, identify the six most important *key results areas* of your work, and write them in the spaces provided.

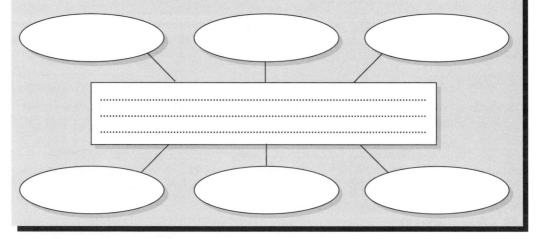

SUMMARY

When undertaking the identification and analysis of training and learning needs at individual, job or organisational levels (Boydell and Leary 1996), it is important to include all stakeholders in an iterative process of job and task analysis. This should include gathering data that informs the analytical method. Competency frameworks can be used to great effect, since they enlighten the decision-making process throughout the HR value chain. Through effective analysis, organisations and their employees can gradually move from the customary demand-led method in their design of training programmes, to a much more effective needs-led approach.

QUESTIONS

1. How could you apply a competency framework to learning and development in your own organisation?
2. What are the major differences between identifying and analysing training and learning needs?
3. Why should training and learning needs be analysed at different levels?

The planning of training solutions

CHAPTER

3

 I have never in my life learned anything from any man who agreed with me.
Dudley Field Malone

LEARNING OUTCOMES

- Work with stakeholders to plan training solutions to agreed training needs.

- Identify the costs and benefits of options to meet needs, and to assess the likely added value of each.

- Source and utilize internal and external expertise and other resources for training.

- Reach agreement on plans that will respond to needs in accessible and effective ways, and to an appropriate timescale.

CHAPTER OUTLINE

- Issues involved in working with stakeholders to generate options to meet training needs and

  - development of shared and realistic perceptions among stakeholders about training solutions

  - handling the tensions involved in stakeholder relationships, including those relating to ethical training practice and equal access to training opportunities.

- Methods of identifying the costs and benefits of different options to meet training needs, and assessing

  - how to secure and utilise necessary resources and other support from outside and within the organisation

  - criteria to ensure that chosen training solutions are feasible and accessible for all types of potential learners.

- How to plan training events that respond to organisational and individual needs and contexts; drawing up and agreeing plans that will

  - meet learning needs arising from changes in business strategy

  - meet needs on departmental, team and individual bases

  - meet the needs of diversified learner types and cohorts

  - fit an appropriate timescale.

INTRODUCTION

The next phase in the systematic approach to training and development is the planning with stakeholders of appropriate interventions to meet identified and analysed training and learning needs. In this chapter, therefore, we take a closer look at how training professionals can collaborate with others to plan effective training solutions. We will see how an organisation's training and learning policies, priorities, plans, procedures and practices can each be affected by an appropriate selection from the possible choices of HRD outcomes.

THE PLANNING OF TRAINING SOLUTIONS – IN THEORY
Working with stakeholders

As O'Donnell and Garavan (1997) make clear, the training goals of different stakeholders can vary considerably:

- Top managers desire to see attitudes and cultural values change, particularly in the areas of disposition to change, teamwork and innovativeness.
- Line managers believe that HRD should be skills-based and centred on the current job.
- HRD specialists see their role primarily in terms of supporting the achievement of organisational goals, mainly in the service, advisory and consultancy areas.

Additionally, Mayo (2000) tabulates the value that could be added by an HRD function, contributing to the benefit of each group of stakeholders appropriate to the particular organisation (see Table 14).

He goes on to say that:

> Delivering performance is more than just having individuals with the necessary capability. It is suggested the following factors combine together to produce a climate of people growth, and each needs separate attention:
>
> - *individual capability.* Knowledge/skill/experience/network; ability to achieve results, potential for growth; and what they bring into work from other parts of their life
>
> - *individual motivation.* Aspirations, ambitions and drive; work motivations; productivity
>
> - *leadership.* The clarity of vision of top managers and their ability to communicate it and behave in a way that is consistent with it
>
> - *organisational climate.* The culture of the organisation, especially in its freedom to innovate, openness, flexibility and respect for the individual
>
> - *workgroup effectiveness.* Supportiveness, mutual respect, sharing in common goals and values.

All these factors are interrelated, and form part of one system (see Figure 10). However, deficiencies in any one of them can affect the overall goal of continual progress in the value of a person. This can seem to be an almost Olympian ideal! The HRD tasks of managers often conflict with their operational responsibilities (de Jong *et al* 1999). There may also be a conflict between the manager's opposing roles. A solution is for trainers to develop partnership relationships:

Table 14 Stakeholders and value

Stakeholder	Adding current value	Creating future value
Shareholders	Generating revenues and controlling/reducing costs Process efficiency and organisational effectiveness	Acquiring/developing the capability needed to meet tomorrow's goals Managing alliances and mergers to maximise intellectual capital
Customers	Customer satisfaction/loyalty – relationship management	New products/services Innovation
Employees	Motivation/commitment/ competence enhancement Recruitment Team effectiveness	Developing new competencies/potential Knowledge transfer Culture change management
Community	Support for local needs	Development of young people

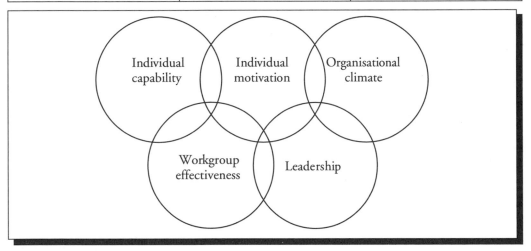

Figure 10 *People growth factors*

Higher managers must show a sincere interest in the HRD responsibilities of first-level managers by acting as a model themselves, and by explicitly rewarding investment in human resources ... First-level managers have to be thoroughly prepared for and coached in their HRD responsibility ... HRD specialists ... have to be recognised as HRD advisers instead of HRD providers. This asks for a 'partnership' between managers and HRD specialists. HRD specialists should offer regular support to managers, helping them to analyse performance problems, chart training needs, develop team-directed and individual HRD plans, and develop their own coaching skills.

How can training professionals develop just such a partnership between stakeholders, as applied to a structured train-the-trainer initiative? In Table 15 (on page 54), we see Philips and Jacobs' (2000) suggestion for a particularly effective method. Conversely, this approach to stakeholder involvement has also been displayed as a systems model (Lynton and Pareek 2000a). We can see in Figure 11 (on page 55) how strategic linkages drive the system from both within and outside the HR function. Key to the whole system is the centrality of performance

Table 15 *Stakeholder partnership for train-the-trainer initiative*

Stakeholders	Before	During	After
Managers	Participate in assessing training needs Support training staff in establishing performance standards Co-facilitate meetings and briefings to demonstrate support Require attendance at scheduled briefings Approve training time for target audience Approve control group arrangement for pilot offering Participate in establishing evaluation plan	Demonstrate commitment to training by attending training sessions Co-facilitate meetings and briefings to demonstrate support Communicate the importance and relevance of training to organisational goals	Participation in reviewing evaluation plan Reinforce follow-up and application of action plans Recognise individuals for successful completion of programme qualification Assist in removing barriers Support training staff in continuous improvement efforts with train-the-trainer programme design and delivery Provide incentives Co-facilitate 30-day follow-up session
Supervisors	Participate in needs assessment focus groups Attend sessions prior to structured OJT implementation Reinforce trainee participation	Remove barriers to trainees' attendance Attend sessions as available Ask trainees about training progress	Reinforce follow-up and application of action plans Assist in removing barriers Monitor performance
Training and development	Conduct performance analysis Communicate structured OJT process implementation requirements Establish learning and performance objectives Design curriculum to meet desired objectives Incorporate benchmarked strategies into course design Prepare training materials and job aids Deliver briefings Design evaluation plan Perform training administration duties Establish incentives	Communicate the importance of training Assess trainees for reaction, learning and skill/knowledge transfer Facilitate pre- and post-assessment process Introduce action plan Facilitate skill-building to support trainees' successful completion of the qualification Deliver training	Implement evaluation plan for structured OJT process programme Conduct qualification and action-planning sessions with individual trainees Enter qualifications in database Facilitate 30-day follow-up session and questionnaire process Report results Work with management to continuously improve quality of service and product
Trainees	Participate in needs assessment focus groups Assist training staff in job/task	Complete pre- and post-assessment Attend full programme Demonstrate active participation in skill practices	Demonstrate proficiency with structured OJT skill sets with 100% accuracy Apply training on the job Implement action plans Identify barriers Complete 30-day questionnaire

management and its connections with training and development. While such a systems approach may appear attractive, it nevertheless lacks the authenticity of the everyday reality facing most HR professionals. Neat and tidy boxes of deterministic structures, together with mechanised flows of information and resources, are for many of us a utopian ideal. Instead, personnel and training practitioners are too often caught up in a seemingly endless round of hiring and firing, inductions and assessments, payroll calculations and 'happy sheets'.

Perhaps one way to confront this operational imperative is to focus instead on external stakeholders, and in particular the needs of our customers:

> The representation of the needs of customers within the training evaluation framework of an organisation is an important consideration. Meeting customer needs on time every time is a route to achieving and sustaining competitive advantage and training is a tool that organisations can use to accomplish this. Unfortunately, while many organisations recognise the need for training, not all of them link training with establishing and maintaining a competitive advantage. Even fewer try to assess the effectiveness of training programmes in the light of facilitating the achievement of competitive advantage. (Burden and Proctor 2000)

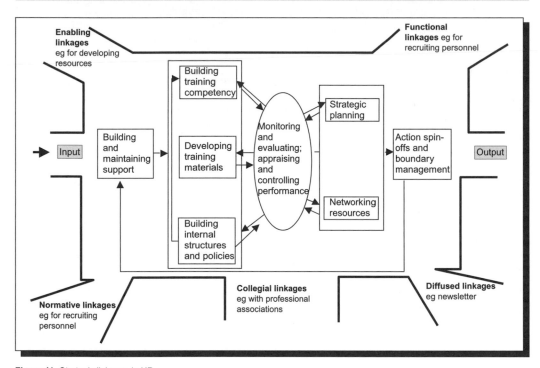

Figure 11 *Strategic linkages in HR*

Identifying costs and benefits of training options

Stewart (1999) offers a *systems view* of how financial techniques can impact on the classic training cycle (Figure 12 on page 56). It will be important for training professionals to approach their opposite numbers in the finance department to obtain their assistance in these four distinct areas. By including such experts at an early stage in the planning process, it will be far easier to obtain agreement from other stakeholders.

On the other hand, Fitz-enz (2000) prefers a more *process-driven* approach to determining value analysis, outlined in Figure 13 on page 56.

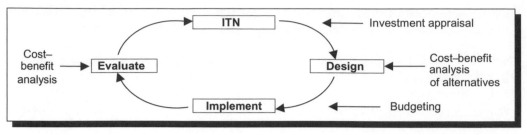

Figure 12 *Financial techniques and the training cycle*

Situation analysis
1. What is the business problem: service, quality, or productivity (SQP)?
2. What is the current performance level: SQP indices?
3. How is current performance affecting competitive advantage?
4. What are the critical work processes in this situation?

Intervention
1. What is the source of the problem?
   Equipment ☐   Material ☐   People ☐   Process ☐

2. If the problem is with people or process, what is the best solution?
   Benchmark ☐   Re-engineer ☐   Provide incentives ☐   Counsel ☐   Train ☐

3. Agree on a solution, plan and act.
   Describe: _____
   _____

Impact
1. Did performance change?   Positively ☐   Negatively ☐
2. How much change occurred?
                    Cost: _____
                    Time: _____
                    Quantity: _____
                    Error: _____
                    Human reaction: _____
3. What caused the change?
                    Your action: _____
                    Extraneous factors: _____

Value
1. What are the *internal* effects on service, quality or productivity?
2. What are the *external* effects on competitive advantage?
                    Sales: _____
                    Margins: _____
                    Customers: _____
                    Time to market: _____

Figure 13 *Value analysis*

Utilisation of resources

Let us now look at how well the organisation's often-scarce resources are used. The management of the costs of the training and development department is often characterised as including both tangible and intangible resources (Harrison 2002):

- main tangible resources
    - personnel
    - physical resources
    - finance
- main intangible resources
    - time
    - the past image and reputation of learning and development
    - employees' competence, learning capability, potential commitment
    - external learning networks
    - natural learning opportunities.

Despite her assertions to the contrary, this would appear to fuel the argument of those who see resourcing training and development activities as a cost rather than as an investment. Often, the costs of training are grouped under four categories:

- people costs
- equipment costs
- administration costs
- materials costs.

However, if practitioners are to avoid becoming entangled in a complex cost-justification argument, they need to focus instead on 'return-on-investment' analysis. As Garavan and McGuire (2001) warn:

> The advocacy of utilitarian-instrumentalist notions of competencies are associated with learning initiatives designed to contribute to bottom-line performance, so this means that line managers' efforts will concentrate on revenue-producing learning at the expense of ensuring that employees are developed.

Naturally enough, this leads us to look at how we can reach agreement on training plans.

Reaching agreement on training plans

'WISE and OPEN' is a very helpful mnemonic (Woods and Cortada 2002) that can be used when reaching agreement on training plans:

W	Workable (rooted in the complex realities of the workplace)
I	Intelligent (thoughtful and alert to a wide range of ideas and factors)
S	Situated (in a network of relationships in the organisational context)
E	Experimental (ready to take risks, try out new ways and formulate new aims)
O	Open (responsive to a wide range of ideas and influences)
P	Participative (emphasising inclusivity and shared learning)
E	Experiential (seeing learning as rooted in reflection on experience
N	New knowledge (creating new knowledge rather than managing what is known).

Woods and Cortada (2000) go further to provide us with the seven steps in the process that are necessary for gaining approval for training projects:

1. Identify your target.
2. Meet with that person.
3. Survey the stakeholders.
4. Conduct a design session.
5. Document the meeting.
6. Get approvals.
7. Do the work and follow up on it.

However, other commentators feel that, when gaining the agreement of an approval team, technical expertise is important, but so too is the commitment and ownership of those who will be ultimately affected by the training programme:

Design teams select their approval teams near the beginning of the module-writing activity. Team members show who is best qualified to serve on the approval team. Members should be experts in the tasks – and this may vary by task. For example, in one corporation a design team who wrote a training module on how to operate a piece of high-technology test equipment chose as their approval team appropriate representatives from the vendor who sold the equipment. In another instance, design teams at an insurance company frequently asked company legal experts to serve on the approval teams to verify the accuracy of certain sections of the training modules. To save time, they eventually invited the experts to sit in on the actual module-writing sessions so that their input was obtained up front. At a parts manufacturer, engineers served as approval teams for critical tasks in which the technicians lacked expertise. For other tasks, the design teams served as approval teams for one another.

As you can see from these examples, approval team members may come from anywhere. In most cases, however, they are employees who do the same job, sometimes on another shift or in another location. Approval team participation is an excellent way to ensure contribution and buy-in from employees who ultimately will be affected by the results. (Walter 2002)

THE PLANNING OF TRAINING SOLUTIONS – IN PRACTICE
Working with stakeholders

The Neville Russell case study below shows just how important it is for training practitioners to explore opportunities for working with a range of stakeholders in order to reach agreement on training plans.

Neville Russell Chartered Accountants

Walton (1999) offers a great insight into the application of fundamental values and ethics to a staff charter within a firm of professional accountants. His wonderful example shows how the needs of employers and employees can be met through a realistic application of the psychological contract.

Neville Russell Chartered Accountancy was founded in 1890. The company offers a number of accountancy services, such as tax, audit and insolvency. In 1996 there were 20 practices and offices spread throughout the UK, employing approximately 800 people. The company's mission statement (which they call Going the Extra Mile) comprises three elements with a distinctive HRD flavour:

■ by exceeding our clients' expectations through the content, quality and integrity of our service delivered in a personal and professional manner;
■ by developing the potential of our people through individual recognition, tailored training and constructive appraisal, leading to personal fulfillment, proper reward and enjoyment;

■ by being a successful firm hallmarked through its national and international outlook, high ethical and technical standards, profitability, growth and corporate pride.

The firm has developed a reciprocal staff charter, or psychological contract, which all HRD professionals would do well to critically analyse and which all organisations should investigate the possibility of developing:

Neville Russell's commitment	Your commitment
We will:	In return we expect you to:
■ Share our plans for the firm with you	■ Ensure that the firm's mission and values are reflected in your work
■ Let you know regularly how your office and the firm are performing financially	■ Treat colleagues and clients with consideration and respect
■ Treat you with consideration and respect	■ Take pride in all aspects of your work
■ Be honest and open with you, and give you regular feedback on your performance	■ Be honest and open with us
■ Consult and communicate with you on matters that affect you and your work	■ Ensure you gain the most out of the training and development opportunities provided
■ Encourage you to use your initiative and develop new ideas	■ Take ownership of your work and ensure that you meet required performance standards
■ Treat you fairly, based on your performance, skills and attitude	■ Maintain others' confidence in your honesty and integrity
■ Help you identify your personal development and training needs	■ Ensure that you treat sensitive information confidentially
■ Provide means to meeting those needs, which also meet the firm's business needs	■ Develop innovative ways of improving the way we do things
■ Provide you with a safe and healthy work environment	■ Communicate in a friendly manner with colleagues and clients, avoiding unnecessary conflict
■ Keep future employees informed during the recruitment process	■ Develop appropriate skills in order to carry out your job effectively
■ Provide you with details of your responsibilities and expected performance standards	■ Be well presented and professional at all times
■ Provide you with pay and benefits to reward your contribution to the firm	■ Take care of your environment and any equipment which the firm provides for you
■ Make sure you have the appropriate accommodation and equipment necessary to carry out your job	■ Help to make your office a place where people enjoy working
■ Make sure that each office is an enjoyable and fun place to work	

Equally, in the context of developing strategic alliances in the higher education sector, Bryans (2000) highlights the need for universities to cultivate working partnerships within industry and commerce:

■ When partnering public sector organisations, universities should be aware of their role in changing the focus from the human capital approach (efficient) to the socio-capital approach (effective). This is facilitating public sector organisations to look outwards and focus on their broad purpose. In this way, more appropriate solutions to the problems of society can be created by these more effective organisations. **59**

- The role of the university to facilitate inter-professional dialogue between individuals in the partner organisations can help the current government aim of 'joined up' policy and produce creative solutions to multidisciplinary problems in the public sector.

- Universities have to learn the new types of roles they can play in today's society. For example, their role as a community resource is under-recognised and under-utilised.

- In playing a role in public sector partnerships, universities have to acknowledge that they have as much to learn from the partner organisations and that learning and development are not one-way.

- As trust and shared interest grows and mutual benefits are realised, there is a likelihood that the partners may move along the spectrum towards a mutually driven approach to development.

- In the final analysis, it is people who make and sustain partnerships. Individuals must feel a benefit to themselves as well as to the organisation. Personal frustration and demotivation can destroy partnerships; for example, when individuals feel that they are not allowed to transfer learning back to organisations. Sometimes key individuals or tiers of the management hierarchy exclude themselves (or are excluded) from the learning experience and/or the partnership. A block to development can easily result from a middle management layer that will not co-operate or a senior management tier that does not buy in to the philosophy.

- Partnerships are not easy to sustain but should be expected to evolve, change, develop and dissolve.

However, Lawless *et al* (2000) do not believe that managers in small and medium-sized enterprises, for example, are significantly different from other managers undergoing education on schemes, like the Open University Business Studies certificate, diploma, and MBA, in that such managers are:

- pressed for time
- primarily interested in learning that is immediately applicable
- primarily interested in learning that is focused on performance rather than analysis or planning; and
- have difficulty in funding education/training (unless sponsored by a large corporation).

Instead, Barclay (1996) finds from his research that the partnership that is most likely to succeed is that between the learner and their manager. He advocates that the learning log is a useful mechanism to be used in this relationship. However, he urges caution:

While the learning log may be a useful mechanism to help individuals and managers to discuss development, the learning log in itself is unlikely to improve a problematic relationship.

He goes on to outline from his study some other sources of partnership support:

While the immediate manager was seen as a key figure for the individual's development, many participants also valued, and obtained help from other colleagues, peers or mentors. This highlights the importance of viewing learning as a social process. Much learning theory tends to present learning as a personal, individual activity. While it is true that learning, i.e., developments in knowledge and understanding, go on inside the mind, this is often underpinned by processes that are social in nature. As well as improving the learning process itself, this support was often beneficial to the relationship of the learner and the manager.

Demonstrating that the readiness of an enterprise and its workforces to participate in varying work experiences is the crucial basis for securing the various kinds of outcomes desired, according to Billett's research (2000). He believes that this readiness is founded both on organisational factors (eg security of employment, openness, trust, existence of expertise) and the individual's (both mentors' and mentees') willingness to engage in the process of constructing new knowledge.

But, there appear not to be transnational barriers here in this area. In investigating the training of librarians in Ghana, for example, Effah (1998) identified two broad areas of responsibility for training. First, the employee has a responsibility for his or her own training and development. The responsibilities of the academic librarian include:

- an honest self-assessment of training needs
- taking initiative to pursue training and to improve performance
- taking active part in managing career interests
- reading professional journals to update oneself
- looking for appropriate courses/seminars
- applying for sponsorship (including self-sponsorship) where necessary.

Second, the responsibility for training and development for a subordinate lies with the line manager who, in the university setting, may be defined as the head of department. They are responsible for describing what is expected for effective performance, identifying areas where improved skills will enhance performance, and providing access to the best ways of developing these skills.

PAUSE FOR THOUGHT

Review Neville Russell's psychological contract with its employees.

Then complete a similar one for an organisation known to you.

The organisation's commitment to its employees	The employee's commitment to the organisation

Identifying costs and benefits of training options

How can HRD activities be costed? Using a simple matrix from Wilson (1999) as shown in Table 16, we can easily apportion training costs against the phases of the systematic training cycle.

This approach appears to take account of most of the major costs facing training planners, including fixed and variable costs, and direct and indirect costs. Increasingly, training departments need to break even against budgeted expenditure. Alternatively, the training manager is required to make a profit or make a contribution to overheads. Whatever the goal, such a straightforward method will assist in gaining both credibility and agreement.

This in turn will lead to more effective utilisation of resources.

Table 16 *Apportioning training costs*

	Development	Planning	Publicity and recruitment	Delivery	Evaluation	Follow-up
Internal accommodation						
External accommodation						
Equipment						
Materials						
Consumables						
Reception						
External staff fees						
External staff expenses						
Internal staff time						
Participants' time						
Participants' expenses						
Catering						
Total						

Utilisation of resources

As an example of how a training solution can be resource-efficient while still remaining learning-effective, Philips and Jacobs (2002) found that, for one particular organisation at least, there was no need for compromise:

> SubmitOrder chose its Learning Management System based on the functionality of the software, the vendor's application of e-learning methodology in its creative services offering, and the vendor's reputation for follow-through after the implementation.

Inevitably, this leads to the need for agreement on training plans.

Reaching agreement on training plans

An example of how to reach agreement can be seen in the personal development plan, or PDP (Higson and Wilson 1995):

1. *Part one* consists of the *job* ie the roles and tasks for a given position. To complete the PDP at this stage the employee assesses their performance against all the tasks with their manager. Gaps in skill and/or knowledge will be marked on the PDP.
2. *Part two* consists of the *learning plan*. The manager and learner transfer only three of the learning needs in priority order to the learning plan. The learning plan also defines how the trainee will learn, and by when. This could include:

   - coaching from the manager
   - sitting with an 'expert'
   - visiting another office
   - job swap
   - reading
   - training course
   - distance-learning package.

3. *Part three* consists of the *learning log*. This is a simple document which the employee completes each week to demonstrate what has been learnt.

Is there a difference for training practitioners in small and medium-sized enterprises (SMEs)? Freel (1999) points out the need for trainers to be particularly sensitive to the needs of owners and managers in small and medium-sized enterprises when they are seeking to gain agreement to training plans. Such people tend to have one of two approaches, each of which requires a flexible approach to the delivery of courses:

- *Just in time*. It is generally accepted that small businesses are reactive, rather than proactive, and invariably fail to plan, particularly the small firms. This results in a crisis-driven approach to learning, where an immediate need has to be satisfied, rather than a foreseen need being planned for and met in a structured fashion. This approach spills over into SMEs' attitudes towards management learning. Small firms do not, in general, have a lifelong learning culture nor do they see a need for sustained improvement in organisational management.
- *Just enough*. The flexible, responsive manner in which SMEs operate means that managers do not feel able to spend long periods away from their work, but prefer short chunks of training – 'just enough'.

Gaining agreement is often best achieved when training and learning are embedded in the organisational culture. Using an *organisational training policy* can be a most beneficial method for gaining the agreement of others to training plans. Here is a template for such a policy, which can be adapted by any organisation:

- commitment of the organisation / board / senior management to the training and development of all staff
- responding to the needs of the organisation/becoming a learning organisation
- named senior manager responsible for implementing the training policy and for reviewing its effectiveness
- roles of those contributing to the training function and training department
- responsibilities of individual staff members and line managers for training
- acceptable and realistic training strategies eg
    - further/higher education
    - induction
    - initial/advanced coaching
    - formal qualifications/membership of professional institutes
    - technology-based training
    - off-job training
    - on-job training
    - external training
    - open, distance, and flexible learning
- equal opportunities/access
- training and development priorities
- funding/budgeting/resources for training
- process for identifying and analysing individual and organisational training needs
- individual performance reviews/appraisals linked to training
- career development plans/succession plans
- individual development plans
- systematic training/evaluation.

Consider and state also:

- how and whether the policy will be communicated to all staff
- how the policy will be implemented
- how the policy will be reviewed and developed
- what level of consultation and participation there will be

and have the policy agreed, signed and dated by the chief executive.

Are there any further needs that the training practitioner should take account of, in addition to those just mentioned? In a most exciting article, Rolls (1999) explores what she sees as the imperative for the transforming organisation to acknowledge the soul needs of its employees. This then becomes a true partnership for learning:

> The work environment that corporations provide needs to be meaning-rich in order to acknowledge the values of an increasingly soul-conscious workforce – and not just out of altruism. What motivates employees has changed from receiving a pay cheque to an opportunity for fulfillment. Identifying and fostering the soul in business is likely to result in some big wins for corporations … All organisations

are in transformation. Transformation is about changing relationships. Transforming cultures is about changing relationships – with the customer, with the employee, with the manager, with work, with each other. Rethinking work to allow for the emergence of the soul may well provide an impetus to transformation.

Businesses can unwittingly starve the soul and taste the consequences, or celebrate it and profit from it. Where the soul is neglected, it doesn't just go away. It can appear symptomatically in emptiness, meaninglessness, vague depression, lack of connection to the company and its purpose, a lacklustre just-enough performance, absenteeism, poor morale, drug abuse, and lack of fulfillment.

She feels there can be a true harmony of interests for the individual and the organisation, as expressed in Table 17 below.

Too often in the past, managers have sent members of staff away on training courses for all the wrong reasons:

- It was their turn.
- It seemed like a good idea at the time.
- There was money in the budget.
- Their appraisal was particularly bad.
- Their appraisal was particularly good.
- Somebody else was on holiday/away sick.

Consequently, managers' views of the value of training were fairly poor and they often deemed it irrelevant. When employees then returned to work, perhaps remotivated and eager to implement their new learning, a stereotypical retort may have been:

'Well, I'm glad you had a good time, and that the lunch was good, but you can forget all that stuff now, because you're back at work. We've had to do all your work while you've been away, and now we've got this rush job to finish by Friday.'

Far better for the learner, the manager and the trainer to agree to a learning plan *before* the learning event. Then the learning objectives can be itemised, appropriate learning strategies can be selected, and the learning outcomes can be implemented in an organised manner. The best way to reach agreement on training is for the learner, the manager and the trainer to hold a three-way conversation once the learning need has been identified. This discussion can be focused and recorded by using the learning plan, a sample of which is given in Figure 14.

Table 17 *Transformation and the bottom line*

Needs of business to remain competitive	Employees' soul needs
Learning	Learning and exploration
Change-agile	Experimentation
Creativity and innovation	Creativity and innovation
Partnering	Relationship

Continuous training	Discovery
Teaming	Connection
Dialogue	Expression
Participation	Engagement
Risk-taking	Space to make mistakes
Proactive	Empowerment
Peer assessment	Reaching out and friendship
Mentoring	Closeness
Vision	Meaning
Large context	Complexity and depth
Alternating roles	Experience
Invention	Possibilities
Imagination	Reflection
Communication	Communication
Integration	Wholeness
Broadening of boundaries	Expansiveness
Employee growth	Growth
Communal sense of self	Attachment
Community	Neighbourhood
Stewardship	Family

Learner's name: ....

Manager: ....

Department: ....

Trainer/mentor/coach: ....

1. Which specific learning need has been identified?

2. What other learning needs does this relate to, for either yourself or others you work with?

3. What is your learning objective?

4. What is your preferred learning style?

5. By when would you like the learning to be completed?

6. What constraints can you identify that could limit the effectiveness of your learning?

7. What will you do after the training in order to implement your learning, and so improve your work?

Signatures: ....

Employee: .... Date: ....

Manager: .... Date: ....

Trainer: .... Date: ....

Figure 14 *The learning plan*

Training Policy

Vanessa James has recently been promoted to group HRD adviser in the EWA Group of companies. The Group consists primarily of employee welfare companies, providing services for HR managers and their organisations. Increasingly, counselling, advocacy, employee benefits, welfare, arbitration and conciliation services have been outsourced by organisations and EWA have found that, in the last couple of years or so, business has been booming.

Vanessa previously worked in one of the subsidiary companies for five years as the training manager. Among other things, she now has responsibility for reviewing and producing recommendations on the potential for NVQs across the whole Group, especially in relation to non-managerial and professional employees. In addition, she provides advice and support to companies across the whole Group, including PEL, a company specialising in employee counselling.

Ruth Evans is chief executive of PEL, and is currently engaged in the design and rollout of a new bereavement counselling service. As with all the companies in the Group, PEL is subject to financial and performance targets, which are expanding year on year. Results over the past five years have been more than satisfactory, and shareholders have been particularly impressed by the consistent pattern of growth. The last full year's performance showed profits of £100,000 on sales close to £1M. These figures reflect PEL's history as a professional and highly regarded company, but Ruth is keen not to take anything for granted. However, the 100 or so employees in the company have come to expect PEL to take the lead in professional developments, and to enjoy a reputation of high standing among their counselling peers.

Ruth has been in her post for just a little over 12 months, and while recognising the employees' achievements, regards their attitude as complacent. She understands well the demands of both the EWA board for continuing success, as well as those of client organisations for improvements in quality, service, provision and costs. This will not be an easy task. One of her main problems has been to balance and integrate counsellors with a range of styles and from a variety of psychological perspectives. There have been instances of cliques and factions squabbling between themselves. On one occasion, a number refused to attend any more staff development workshops until 'that awful man Freud was banned from the room'.

Employee development in PEL forms part of the role of the personnel manager, Caroline Pitchman, who reports directly to Ruth. The services she provides are advisory and supportive to line managers and team leaders, and include employee relations advice, recruitment and selection, and training.

Ruth is determined to use HR to overcome the problems of fragmentation, and has fully briefed Vanessa on her plans for the future of PEL. She wants to bring in more modern methods of management, and is committed to introduce both a continuous improvement cycle know as 'kaizen', and also autonomous work teams. The former will demand greater levels of involvement and integration, whereas the latter will require increasing levels of autonomy.

Vanessa has already spoken to a number of professional and administrative employees at PEL and has found that, because of the increasing demands on their time, they tend to adopt a pragmatic approach to any difficulties. Rarely do they consider wider or more strategic issues.

PAUSE FOR THOUGHT

Have a look at the case study above.

a) Draft a training and development policy for PEL.
b) How should Vanessa and Ruth go about implementing such a policy?

You could compare your response with this example:

CAFOD staff training and development policy

Introduction

CAFOD has always treated the training and development of staff as a priority. The quality and effectiveness of our work is directly related to our levels of skill, knowledge and expertise. We are committed to working strategically and effectively and our approach to the training and development of staff reflects this. With the establishment of a personnel and administrative services (PAS) department, we have consolidated our policy and practice in this area and refined our procedures in certain respects. The paragraphs below set out a consolidated training and development policy for CAFOD.

Aims

■ To develop staff potential to meet the present and future needs of the organisation.

■ To ensure that all staff have access and opportunities to develop the skills and acquire the knowledge needed for them to carry out their work effectively.

- To facilitate and support self-managed and self-directed learning with staff taking personal responsibility for their learning.

- 'Action learning' – the creation of groups committed to bringing about significant change and improvement to the way we work and our effectiveness.

- To build a 'learning organisation' at CAFOD by facilitating the learning, growth and continuing development of all our staff.

Training needs

Individual and organisational training and development needs will be identified primarily through annual staff reviews and CAFOD's corporate plan. The key factors that will determine training needs are:

- CAFOD objectives, which will affect the way in which an individual performs his/her work

- new developments within an individual's job that that person will need support to carry out

- areas of current job that could be improved on or developed further

- other things which the individual may want to develop outside his/her role, but which CAFOD may see value in supporting.

Priorities and general principles

Divisions/departments will prioritise according to their own needs so that resources can be allocated to the most important areas. Senior managers will seek to be systematic and fair when approving/rejecting requests for expenditure on training and development activities. The head of PAS will maintain an overview to ensure consistency between divisions/departments.

With limits on financial resources, CAFOD is unlikely to be able to meet all identified needs. The general principle is that CAFOD will give financial support to staff undertaking certain study courses when it is clear that attendance at the course is of benefit to CAFOD, either directly or indirectly. The more a course is tied in with helping the staff member to function better at work, the more likely it is that assistance will be provided.

Courses can be short-term (such as a WP course) or long-term (such as day release for one or two years). They can also involve time off work during ordinary hours, or be entirely out of office hours. All of these things have to be considered.

The assistance provided can be payment of fees only, or it can involve time off plus fees, and possibly books, etc.

Staff are encouraged to undertake evening courses that are likely to benefit them in their work. To this end, fees may be paid in whole or in part; and if time off is required for exams this may be allowed in certain cases. Staff must always obtain prior approval from CAFOD before entering into any contract that assumes whole or part payment by CAFOD.

Where staff wish to undertake short external courses of one or two days' duration, they should initially seek the approval of their head of section who will then make a recommendation to their senior manager. Where staff wish to become involved in a longer or more expensive course, this needs careful discussion with both the head of section and senior manager. Long-term commitment to a major training and development programme that involves substantial cost needs discussion with, and the agreement of, the head of PAS and the director. In all cases where assistance is given it is understood that the staff member intends to stay with CAFOD for at least a further year after the course is finished. A signed undertaking to this effect is required. CAFOD reserves the right to claim back the cost of the course if a member of staff decides to leave without fulfilling this obligation.

CAFOD will also support staff who undertake studies which, while not essential to the satisfactory performance of the person's duties in their current job, will broaden and deepen their skills and knowledge and enhance both their own and CAFOD's effectiveness. In any one year staff may claim 50 per cent of such course fees up to a maximum of £100.

Procedure

Annual reviews will remain the catalyst for identifying broadly what, if any, training and development opportunities the individual may be seeking, and skills and knowledge that CAFOD may want him/her to acquire.

Individual development planning (IDP) is the process by which detailed consideration will be given to how training and development needs will be met. An IDP will be drawn up which will focus on specific training and development need and the most appropriate methods by which these needs can be met, and to allow for evaluation and review.

Methods

Methods of meeting training needs will be varied depending on the preferred learning style of the individual and the type of course. Options include trainer-centred approaches (eg structured presentations by trainers, attendance on external courses/programmes); group-centred approaches (eg action learning sets, project teams); and individual approaches (eg open and flexible learning, computer-based training, coaching, guided reading, self-managed learning).

The individual member of staff is expected to play an active role in researching learning methods that meets his/her requirements. Both line managers and the head of PAS are available to assist with this.

Internal and external providers

Individual divisions/departments will provide in-house training and development courses within their areas of specialism. Courses, both internal and external, will be initiated through the request of heads of divisions/departments or heads of section and by divisions/departments promoting workshops. In addition, divisions/departments will often lead lunchtime talks and staff briefings. The PAS Department will hold a (non-exhaustive) central file on available external courses and will promote CAFOD-wide training and development courses.

Budgets

Heads of division/department will, in conjunction with the director, establish an annual training budget for their division/department. This figure should reflect the proposed level of training envisaged at the start of the financial year for the staff of that division/department and for any CAFOD-wide programmes, which that division/department proposes to offer. In addition, the PAS Department will establish a small central budget to provide other CAFOD-wide programmes (eg induction, management development, health and safety, group learning offered to staff, equal opportunities).

Responsibilities

Line managers

Line managers are responsible for ensuring that their staff have annual reviews, IDPs and the opportunity to acquire the necessary knowledge, skills, and abilities that will enable them to perform their current work to the highest levels of quality and effectiveness. Line managers are also responsible for evaluating training with the staff member.

Heads of division/department

Heads of division/department will, on the formation of CAFOD's corporate plan, identify and prioritise future knowledge and skills which will be required by CAFOD staff to pursue long-term strategic and division/departmental objectives and for ensuring that these needs are met.

All training courses will have to be agreed with the relevant head of division/department.

Staff

Staff are expected to take the initiative in planning their future learning and development and to contribute their ideas and suggestions. While this is particularly important at the time of staff annual reviews and IDPs, individual and organisational learning is a continuous process, which should flow naturally and progressively. Consequently, staff development discussions may also take place at other times.

All staff who undertake planned training will normally be required to complete an IDP to be reviewed at the time of evaluation.

All permanent staff (and those on fixed-term contracts of one or more years) will be treated equally, with the same general criteria, to determine the provision of training and financial support.

Paid temporary staff on short-term contracts are recruited on the assumption that they possess the knowledge and skills necessary for them to carry out their work effectively. They may, exceptionally, receive training, which is essential to their work.

Volunteer temporary staff may attend in-house training courses and other training required for their work.

All staff will receive induction and relevant health and safety training.

Personnel

Personnel staff will be available to provide advice and guidance to members of staff in producing and implementing their IDPs, and to the management team. Staff development discussions with Personnel can be requested by individuals at any time, although any resultant plans for training and development action will be subject to the agreement of the appropriate head of section and/or head of division/department.

The head of PAS will follow up, at appropriate times, with staff who have attended training programmes to assess their effectiveness and the benefits gained.

Personnel will co-ordinate staff induction.

Evaluation

The investment in training and development at CAFOD will be subject to regular evaluation both in terms of the quality of the training that takes place, and the quality and value of the learning that results. Participants on training and development courses will be required to complete a review to allow for pre- and post-course evaluation. Learning outcomes should lead to the improved performance of CAFOD.

SUMMARY

For training and learning to be effective, there needs to be agreement among the stakeholders from the moment the learning need has been identified. Naturally, if learning is embedded in the organisational culture, this will be easier than if training is still seen as an unnecessary and expensive distraction to fulfilling operational targets. The psychological contract and the learning plan are good ways of involving the learner in the process of helping them take responsibility of their own learning. For evaluation of training to be successful, realistic costings of training design variables needs to take place at an early stage. Consequently, the often-scarce resources available for training and development can be utilised more effectively.

QUESTIONS

1. How effective is the learning and development policy of your own organisation?
2. A small software company is thinking of applying for the Investors in People award. The managing director, a friend of yours, has been told that they need to have a training plan. What advice would you give her on the steps she needs to take to develop a training plan?
3. How relevant and effective is the systematic approach to learning and development in your own organisation?

The design of training events

> Since the brain is indisputably a multi-path, multimodal apparatus, the notion of mandatory sequences or even of any fixed sequences is unsupportable. Each of us learns in a personal, highly individual, mainly random way ... That being the case any group instruction that has been tightly, logically planned will have been wrongly planned for most of the group, and will inevitably inhibit, prevent or distort learning. **L. A. Hart**

LEARNING OUTCOMES

- Achieve collaborative design of training, including agreement on measures to determine the success of training events (including short- and long-term programmes).

- Explain the implications for training design of organisational factors and learner characteristics.

- List criteria to guide the use of learning and training methods in different kinds of training event.

- Choose and assess training materials.

- Design support processes and systems for learners.

CHAPTER OUTLINE

- The principles of learning in which training design, delivery, transfer and evaluation should be embedded.

- How to identify and work with partners in the design process; how to handle conflict with the aim of achieving continuous collaboration.

- Formal and informal learning processes and methods that can be incorporated into training activity, including

    - their fit with the learners' characteristics and with workplace culture

    - the value they can produce, given their financial and non-financial cost

    - how to integrate chosen methods into training design.

- How to choose, design, pilot and assess training materials; how to incorporate them into training events.

- How to incorporate learner support systems and processes into the design of training events.

INTRODUCTION

We have arrived at one of the most important chapters in the book! And yet, designing training and learning often takes place in a darkened room, with a cold towel round your head! So, the purpose of this chapter is to remove some of the hidden mysteries that have surrounded the subject in many people's minds. By breaking the subject down into manageable sections, and by using an effective framework, you will be able to turn your new-found knowledge and skills to good effect. I would go further; by employing the techniques outlined in this chapter efficiently and effectively, you should be able to design any learning event for any learners in any organisation at any stage in your career!

THE DESIGN OF TRAINING EVENTS – IN THEORY
The principles of learning

In their significant review of the theory and practice of training, which I wholeheartedly recommend, Cheetham and Chivers (2001) outline – among many other themes – some of the major theories of how professionals learn:

- *Behaviourism.* Simple behaviourist theory is now widely regarded as overly reductionist, but aspects of it undoubtedly work, and most people would agree their behaviour is affected by the various forms of reward (or punishment) that result from their actions ... Echoes of behaviourism can still be found in the importance educators attach to feedback and reinforcement, and within various instructional techniques used in professional development.

- *Behaviourism applied.* Behaviourism has also successfully influenced the design of programmed learning, teaching machines, computer-based training and interactive video ... In all of these areas training is offered in small steps, responses are required from trainees at various points, and feedback is given.

- *Cognitive approaches.* In contrast to behaviourism, with its concentration on inputs and outputs, cognitive approaches are more concerned with what goes on between two stages, in other words, the mental processes that accompany such activities as learning, reasoning or problem-solving. These kinds of cerebral activity are likely to involve processes such as memorising, concept formation, and the use of symbols and language. Cognitive approaches look at the way people absorb information from their environment, sort it mentally and apply it in everyday activities.

- *Gestalt theories.* This school views consciousness as involving organised structures, patterns and configurations, and learning as a holistic process that cannot meaningfully be broken down into constituent parts, even for the purpose of analysis. The German word *Gestalt* simply means shape or pattern, but can also refer to 'an integrated whole' ... Gestalt theorists advocate that learning techniques should themselves be holistic, rather than fragmented, and should recognise the importance of developing appropriate mental patterns and structures.

- *Mixed approaches.* 'Social learning'... sees learning as a continuous, dynamic and reciprocal interaction between individuals affecting, in particular, their attributes, values and behaviours. It also recognises the importance of the learning environment.

- *Constructivism and discovery learning.* This holds that the construction of knowledge is very much an individual process and that different learners find their own way of making sense of the world ... They form and test their own hypotheses, based on what they see and hear around them. The view has been used to support 'discovery learning' methods, but this approach has been criticised for expecting too much of the learner and risking critical gaps in what is learned.

While such approaches are fascinating, they have caused problems for many years for professional HRD practitioners. So, many trainers were extremely grateful to Knowles (1998) when he first published his views on adult learning, for they had found difficulty for a long time with, on the one hand, the animal-based research theories of Skinner, Thorndike and Pavlov, and on the other hand with the ancient pedagogical approaches still holding sway throughout much of the British higher education system. Knowles' theory of *andragogy*, or adult learning, built on earlier efforts by Lewin, and offers an alternative view of learning at work that more closely matched the reality most trainers encounter on a daily basis. Knowles' principles of andragogy may be simplified as follows:

■ Mature adults are self-directed and autonomous in their approach to learning.

■ They learn best through experiential methods.

■ They are aware of their own specific learning needs generated by life or work.

■ They have a need to apply newly acquired knowledge or skills to their immediate circumstances.

■ Learning should be seen as a partnership between trainers and learners, and learners' own experiences should be used as a resource

Despite generalised acceptance of his theory, there have been some criticisms. Jarvis (1984) feels that andragogy has acquired the status of an

Established doctrine ... without being grounded in sufficient research to justify its dominant position.

Moreover, Brookfield (1986) points out that although learner autonomy and self-directedness are at the core of andragogy, these may not be generalised traits. From his observation, he argues that:

Many adults pursue lifestyles in which self-directed behaviours are noticeably absent.

Furthermore, Cheetham and Chivers (2001) declare that:

Various pieces of research suggest, for example, that these traits may be affected by both class differences ... and cultural differences. Knowles' assertion that adult learners are aware of their own learning needs is also open to challenge, at least as a general proposition. Some adults may be aware of some of the gaps in their knowledge and competence, but it is doubtful whether anyone is fully aware of his/her own shortcomings. It might be argued that professionals in particular ought at least to have a general awareness of their own learning needs, and indeed ought to be self-directed learners. But saying that they *ought* does not guarantee that they *will*. It seems likely that such traits would be variable, even amongst professionals.

Recognising the limits of one's own competence (and therefore learning needs) would certainly seem to be an essential trait for a professional. Self-development skills would also seem to be important. But both may have to be learned, rather than occurring naturally ... Despite some shortcomings, andragogy does offer a set of principles, which many trainers seem to have found useful. Andragogy has also made an important contribution to the design of professional development programmes in the past and no doubt will continue to do so.

Instead, Cheetham and Chivers (2001) offer a novel perspective on adult learning, which they call *symbolic interactionism*:

■ Adults are more concerned with whether they are changing in the direction of an idealised self-concept than whether they are meeting objectives set by others.

■ Adults with higher self-esteem learn better than those with lower self-esteem.

- The self is affected by each new role undertaken by the learner.
- Adults learn best when they perceive themselves as learners.

To begin to understand any theory of adult learning, we must first explore Kolb's famous theory (1981) of experiential learning:

- Learning is best conceived as a process, rather than in terms of outcomes.
- Learning is a continuous process grounded in experience.
- The process of learning requires the resolution of conflicts between dialectically opposed modes of adaptation to the world.
- Learning is a holistic process of adaptation to the world.
- Learning involves transactions between the person and the environment.
- Learning is the process of creating knowledge.

From this original work on experiential learning, he developed four learning modes: concrete experience; reflective observation; abstract conceptualisation; and active experimentation, which are expressed in Figure 15.

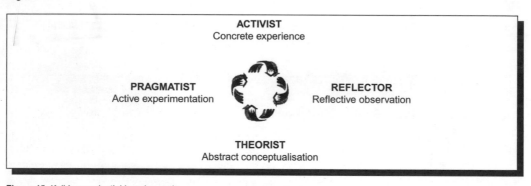

Figure 15 *Kolb's experiential learning cycle*

These in turn led to four learning approaches (as in Figure 16):

- converger – a person who combines abstract conceptualisation with active experimentation
- diverger – one who combines concrete experience and reflective observation
- assimilator – one who combines abstract conceptualisation and reflective observation
- accommodator – one who combines concrete experience and active experimentation.

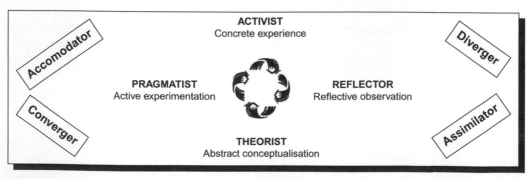

Figure 16 *Four approaches to learning*

These approaches later became adapted by Honey and Mumford (1986) to become their four preferences of learning style, which are shown in Figure 17.

ACTIVIST
Concrete experience

PRAGMATIST   **REFLECTOR**
Active experimentation   Reflective observation

THEORIST
Abstract conceptualisation

Figure 17 *Honey and Mumford's learning preferences*

- activist – a person who learns through constant and enthusiastic activity
- reflector – a person who stands back, observes and thinks a lot before getting actively involved
- theorist – a person who likes to rationalise and synthesise information into logical patterns
- pragmatist – a person who likes to try out ideas and turn theories into practice.

And we can also see associations with the four main ways of learning: imitation; thinking; being told; and trial and error, as illustrated in Figure 18.

IMITATION
Concrete experience

TRIAL AND ERROR   *THINKING*
Active experimentation   Reflective observation

BEING TOLD
Abstract conceptualisation

Figure 18 *Four ways of learning*

Having made these important links, we are now in a position to note some echoes of the concerns some commentators have expressed about andragogy. Self-directedness is not necessarily a requirement of experiential learning. Similarly, experiential learning does not necessarily require learners to be consciously aware of their own specific learning needs. Indeed, it is often not until some time after the initial learning experience that learners are able to recognise the things they have learnt. Others have challenged this approach, saying that learning through experience takes the form of a neat cycle. Conversely, learning seems to many trainers to be more multi-dimensional and multi-faceted. Learning is much more fragmented and often more chaotic than a circle suggests.

Selecting different training and learning methods

We could construct a tentative taxonomy of learning methods for, say, information professionals:

- practice and repetition
- reflection
- observation and copying
- feedback
- transfer
- stretching activities
- perspective changing/switching
- mentor/coach interaction
- unconscious absorption
- use of psychological devices/mental tricks
- articulation
- collaboration.

Having the opportunity to put something into practice immediately (not at some time in the future) is felt by most learners to be of great importance. Other researchers have even gone so far as to add one-to-one coaching after a formal training programme in order to enable participants to implement their learning. This leads us to consider the nature of learning in action:

- Learning is gained from action in real situations.
- Learning and understanding come from reflection.
- Learning is often greater in the company of others who are also learning.
- People's own work situations usually offer the best material for learning.
- Management must be committed to the process and its benefits.

In particular, we can identify certain functions of a particularly effective method, namely the *action learning set:*

- Everyone in the set receives mutual support and encouragement.
- Every group member can ask questions and make suggestions.
- Each set member can ask for help from others.
- Each group member is responsible for the discipline of the set.
- The set should regularly review both the process and the progress.
- Common ownership of individual problems is developed.
- Issues of power are not allowed, but peer pressure challenges the individual to perform.
- People are encouraged to contribute a wide range of experience.
- Problems are tackled from different perspectives.
- Set meetings are used as a test-bed for new ideas.

And this will raise specific issues for an action learning set *facilitator.*

- Address emotions in the here and now.

- Prioritise and negotiate the use of time.
- Employ a variety of planning techniques.
- Discuss and agree the ground rules.
- Facilitate the tone – an appropriate setting, free from interruptions.
- Begin with where people are at the moment – problems and successes.
- Question – confront issues, not people; challenge assumptions.
- Concentrate on process issues.
- Review regularly to ascertain the learning gain.
- Examine relevance and appropriateness of contributions.
- Plan for action – avoid discussion for its own sake.
- Record and review actions and decisions regularly.

What could help us in the selection of different training and learning methods? Cole (1993) offers a helpful analysis, which is reproduced in Table 18 on page 80.

A further example of categorisation comes from Wilson (1999):

- attending short courses, seminars, workshops, conferences
- being coached by a more experienced colleague
- forming a learning agreement
- establishing a mentorship relationship
- participating in a learning/support group
- teamworking
- undertaking a special project, assignment or consultancy
- taking on a new area of responsibility
- changing work practices or systems
- a variety of on-the-job methods such as focused staff meetings, reading, discussion, reflection, observation and maintenance of a learning log
- undertaking a research contract
- seeking and receiving feedback
- engaging in action research
- action learning sets
- qualification courses – educational eg MBA, masters degrees, or vocational programmes
- outdoor management development (OMD)
- development portfolios
- a secondment or exchange
- critical incident techniques
- SWOT analysis – strengths weaknesses, opportunities, threats
- specialist development consultants
- providing cover, deputising, shadowing.

Finally, Wilson (1999) underlines various steps that are important when selecting learning methods:

Table 18 *Training and learning methods*

On-the-job training methods	Advantages	Disadvantages
On-the-job instruction	Relevant; develops trainee–supervisor links	Noise, bustle and pressure of workplace
Coaching	Job-related; develops boss–subordinate relationship	Subject to work pressures; may be done piecemeal
Counselling	Employee needs help and boss provides it	Counselling skills have to be developed
Delegation by boss	Increases scope of job; provides greater motivation	Employees may make mistakes or fail to achieve task
Secondment	Increases experience of employee; creates new interest	Employee may not succeed in new position
Guided projects/action learning	Increases knowledge and skills in work situation, but under guidance	Finding suitable guides and mentors
Off-the-job training methods	**Advantages**	**Disadvantages**
(a) *In-company*		
Lectures/talks	Useful for factual information	One-way emphasis; little participation
Group discussions	Useful for generating ideas and solutions	Requires adequate leadership
Role-playing exercises	Useful for developing social skills	Requires careful organising; giving tactful feedback is not easy
Skills development exercises eg manual operations, communication skills etc.	A safe way to practise key skills	Careful organisation required
(b) *External*		
College courses (long)	Leads to qualification; comprehensive coverage of theory; wide range of teaching methods	Length of training time; not enough practical work
College courses (short)	Supplement in-company training; independent of internal politics	May not meet client's needs precisely enough
Consultants/other training organisations	Clients' needs given high priority; fills gaps in company provision; good range of teaching methods	Can be expensive; may rely heavily on 'packages'

Marchington and Wilkinson (1996), on the other hand, prefer to categorise training and learning methods according to two dimensions, namely pedagogical/andragogical, and individually or group-based, as shown in Figure 19.

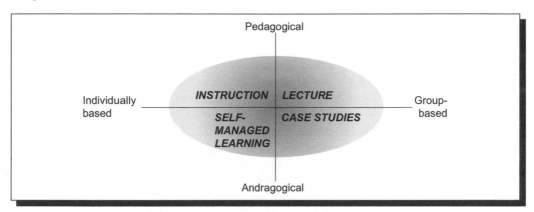

Figure 19 *Plotting learning methods*

1. Consider carefully all the information from the assessment of training needs.
2. Examine in detail the aims and objectives – break them down into their constituent parts.
3. Decide on specific content – and themes.
4. Consider any constraints and opportunities and make the learning in keeping with the group.
5. Consider creating a good learning atmosphere – the physical and psychological setting.
6. Choose, modify or create learning methods.
7. Organise and check the sequence of all the methods.
8. Consider all the things that might go wrong or not work and plan for contingencies.
9. Consider methods that help the programme review, and support the transfer of learning.
10. Evaluate everything – make notes on your computer about training methods improvements while they are fresh in your mind.
11. Feedback all this information into future course designs.

PAUSE FOR THOUGHT

It would be possible to plot a large number of different learning methods against the axes illustrated in Figure 19. On a separate piece of paper, draw these two axes right now and try to map the following management development interventions (Woodall and Winstanley 1998):

On-the-job methods	Off-the-job methods	Techniques used in off-the-job management development
■ Action learning	■ Management education	■ Lectures/presentations
■ Coaching	■ Qualifications	■ Case studies
■ Mentoring	■ Short courses	■ Syndicate/discussion groups
■ Sponsorship	■ Seminars	■ Distance/open learning
■ Role-modelling	■ In-company management	■ Work-related projects
■ Job enrichment	training	■ Games and simulations
■ Job rotation	■ Workshops	■ Role-plays
■ Secondment	■ Seminars	■ Individual/group
■ Special projects	■ 'Academies'	presentations
■ Task forces	■ External providers	■ External speakers
■ Deputising	■ Specialist packages	
■ Networking	■ Outdoor development	
■ Visioning		

Selecting different training and learning media and materials

Helpfully, Woodall and Winstanley (1998) describe the learning processes involved in a variety of learning methods. This will help the learning practitioner in the task of selecting appropriate media and materials:

Table 19 *Learning processes*

Method	Learning process

Learning from another person
    Coaching
    Mentoring and sponsorship
    Role models
	Feedback, reflection, challenge
	Support, advice, feedback, opportunity, challenge
	Observation, reflection, imitation

Learning from tasks
    Special projects
    Job rotation
    Shadowing
    Secondment
    Acting-up delegation
	Problem-solving, taking responsibility, taking risks and making decisions, managing without mastering
	Exposure to other cultures and points of view
	Observation of tasks, new techniques, skills
	Exposure to other cultures and points of view
	Trial of new tasks and skills, challenge

Learning with others
    Task forces/working parties
    Action learning
    Networking
	Strategic understanding, building awareness and confidence
	Problem-solving, interaction, influencing
	Interaction and building awareness

So, the choice of media must be determined firstly by the learning outcomes and secondly by the learners' entry behaviour. Once these two essential variables have been ascertained, then the selection of learning media becomes much easier.

At this point it is worth reflecting on some of the advantages and disadvantages of learning materials, from the learner's viewpoint. For example, Table 20 shows an analysis of open and distance learning (ODL) (Wilson 1999).

Table 20 *Example analysis of a training method – open and distance learning*

Potential advantages	Potential disadvantages
Access to learning materials and programmes may be easier.	There may be less guidance on the level, relevance and appropriateness of learning materials and programmes.
Learning may be achieved on a flexible basis in terms of time.	Lack of time-tabled classes may lead to learning being neglected.
Learning can be carried out at a pace to suit the learner.	Lack of a clear timetable may lead to learning taking place too slowly, and ultimately petering out.
Learning may be achiever on a flexible basis in terms of place.	No suitable place for learning may be identifiable.
Learning can be carried out in one's own time.	No designated time is allowed (eg by employers for work-related learning).

Learning programmes may be tailored to individual's needs.	Employer's needs may be inadequately covered without this being recognised by learners.
Cognitive learning at one's own pace may be very effective.	Learning in the effectiveness and skills domains may be difficult to achieve.
ODL encourages autonomy in learning.	Lack of tutor support may lead to loss of motivation and failure to overcome learning blocks.
The absence of 'lessons' can make ODL less 'intimidatory'.	Lack of 'lessons' may lead to lack of discipline in study.
There is less chance of interpersonal conflict with tutors.	Informal mentoring relationships are unlikely to develop.
Lack of face-to-face involvement with tutors and learners may be helpful to introverts.	Lack of opportunity for comradeship, and peer learning may be demotivating.
Learning programmes and materials may be better structured and of high quality in terms of content and presentation.	Programmes and materials may be expensive, not tailored, out-of-date or even of poor quality. They may be over-dependent on one form of presentation.
Learning via new technologies can be exciting and motivating.	New technologies may involved high equipment or software costs, and can be daunting to learners.
Virtual reality systems can helpfully stimulate environments for learning which are difficult to achieve otherwise.	Such systems may be used as cheaper and poorer substitutes for experiential learning in real environments.
Assessment methods may be better thought out and more clearly explained.	Learners may still have difficulty determining what is required in assessments and less opportunity to negotiate these.

PAUSE FOR THOUGHT

Choose another type of learning medium. Carry out a similar analysis to that shown in Table 19.

Medium: ....

Advantages	Disadvantages

Supporting learning processes

In Figure 20, Barclay (1996) highlights two specific points in the learning cycle when help with learning is particularly important.

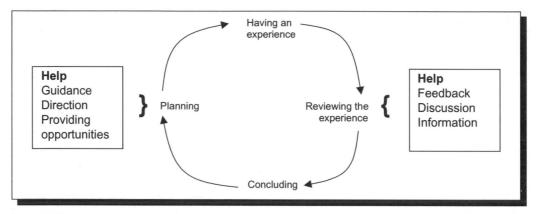

Figure 20 *Supporting learning processes*

THE DESIGN OF TRAINING EVENTS – IN PRACTICE

Achieving collaborative training designs

Successful learning design can fundamentally change an employee's effectiveness at work. For example, Cheetham and Chivers (2001) tell us:

> A number of interviewees spoke of early difficulties that were overcome by subsequent high levels of exposure to the very thing they found difficult. Several examples were offered. A physiotherapist, who had initially found it hard to control her emotions when dealing with severely sick or handicapped patients, found she had overcome this problem after a period working at a hospice where everyone was terminally ill.
>
> A hospital doctor who had initially found making clinical decisions difficult had a period supervising critically ill patients in an intensive care unit. After this, in her own words, 'no-one seemed ill anymore.'
>
> A civil servant had worked for a time in the personnel function and had volunteered to be a 'guinea pig' interviewee for the training of promotion panel members. As a result of being the interviewee in dozens of mock panels, she claimed she had completely lost her fear of interviews and similar situations.

Achieving collaborative training designs involves deliberate interrogation of stakeholders. By connecting with those people who are most likely to be affected by the outcomes, trainers are more likely to be able to achieve their aims. We must, therefore, engage others in a process of questioning dialogue.

In order to be able to design a learning event effectively, there are seven questions that need to be asked. And if these questions are asked appropriately and sensitively, of the right people, in the right way, at the right time, and if the trainer or manager succeeds in achieving a good range of responses, then I believe that this structure will facilitate the design of any learning event for any learner, in any organisation, at any time.

Firstly, you need to ask Who?

Who is the training for? In addition, who is going to undertake it? Who is the learner, or who are the learners? How many of them are there, and what are their characteristics? You need to be able to identify learner entry behaviour and this will include a wide variety of different issues including their previous experience, their experience in the job, and their experience in the organisation. It will also include their experience of similar tasks outside, and their experience of training and education.

Additionally, you need to find out something about their current level of knowledge, skills and attitudes, and how these have been developed. You may need to know something about their seniority, or how long they have been with the organisation. You would certainly need to discover something about their motivation. Are they being sent? Have they self-nominated? How does this learning event fit in with their personal development plans or succession plans? Will they be rewarded for their learning? In addition, you need to find something out about their learning styles. Different people have preferences to learn in different ways, and certainly, specific skills and certain knowledge are best learnt in different ways. Moreover, if there is more than one learner with this need, will they be learning in groups, and if so, how many will there be in a group?

What about the competences of the trainer(s)? What are their current levels of relevant knowledge, skills and attitudes? If the line manager or supervisor is involved, do they have the training skills as well as the technical knowledge? If an external consultant is being asked to undertake the delivery, does she understand the necessary organisational context?

Secondly, you need to ask Why?

Having thought about the learner, you must then determine the learning objective. What is the purpose? What is the outcome? What is the goal and aim? In what way do you want the employee to be able to improve? A good learning objective needs to be *behavioural* in approach. That is to say, because we are focusing on *performance* improvement, the statement of an objective must have at its core a verb. It is something that the worker will *do* as a result of the learning and training; better still, it is something that they can demonstrate, and which can be observed and measured. In addition, there will be two qualifications – firstly, the *conditions* under which that performance is accomplished, and secondly, the *standard* that is expected. So, taken together, performance, conditions, and standards will make an effective learning objective, stated in behavioural terms, and observable and measurable. In addition, these objectives must flow from, and be aligned with, the team and departmental plans, and with the organisational strategy.

Many trainers find writing behavioural objectives quite difficult at first. Table 21 on pages 86–88 contains a valuable aid (Clark 1999) that you might want to use.

Thirdly, you need to ask What?

What do you want the learner specifically to know, or to be able to do? That is to say, the content or syllabus – how much do you want them to increase by? In establishing the content, by definition what you are delimiting is what you *don't* want them to do on this learning occasion. You are drawing boundaries; you are setting limits. Most training designers are over-ambitious. They try to cram far too much into too short a period of time. This is often for justifiable reasons, and mostly because of short-term economics. However, for training and learning to be effective, rather than just efficient, it is often in the limiting of content that great gains can be made. So how do you prioritise, how can you limit or select what should go in to a plan, and what can be left out? Perhaps the material could be kept until another time, another course, or another learning event.

Table 21 *Writing behavioural objectives*

Cognitive domain (knowledge)	
The cognitive domain involves knowledge and the development of intellectual skills. This includes the recall or recognition of facts, procedural patterns and concepts that serve in the development of intellectual abilities and skills. There are six major categories, which are listed in order below, starting from the simplest behaviour to the most complex. The categories can be thought of as degrees of difficulties. That is, the first one must be mastered before the next one can take place.	
Knowledge: Recall of data	Examples: Recites a policy. Quotes prices from memory to a customer. Lists the safety rules Key words: defines, describes, identifies, labels, lists, matches, names, outlines, recalls, recognises, reproduces, selects, states.
Comprehension: Understanding the meaning, translation, interpolation, and interpretation of instructions and problems. Stating a problem in one's own words	Examples: Rewrites the principles of test writing. Explains in one's own words the steps for performing a complex task. Translates an equation into a computer spreadsheet Key words: comprehends, converts, defends, distinguishes, estimates, explains, extends, generalises, gives examples, infers, interprets, paraphrases, predicts, rewrites, summarises, and translates.
Application: Using a concept in a new situation or unprompted use of an abstraction. Applying what was learned in the classroom to novel situations in the workplace	Examples: Uses a manual to calculate an employee's vacation time. Applies laws of statistics to evaluate the reliability of a written test Key words: applies, changes, computes, constructs, demonstrates, discovers, manipulates, modifies, operates, predicts, prepares, produces, relates, shows, solves, uses.
Analysis: Separating material or concepts into component parts so that its organisational structure may be understood. Distinguishing between facts and inferences	Examples: Troubleshoot a piece of equipment by using logical deduction. Recognises fallacies in reasoning. Gathers information from a department and selects the required tasks for training Key words: analyses, breaks down, compares, contrasts, uses diagrams, deconstructs, differentiates, distinguishes, identifies, illustrates, infers, outlines, relates, selects, separates.
Synthesis: Building a structure or pattern from diverse elements. Putting parts together to form a whole, with emphasis on creating a new meaning or structure	Examples: Writes a company operations or process manual. Designs a machine to perform a specific task. Integrates training from several sources to solve a problem. Revises a process to improve the outcome Key words: categorises, combines, compiles, composes, creates, devises, designs, explains, generates, modifies, organises, plans, rearranges, reconstructs, relates, reorganises, revises, rewrites, summarises, tells, writes.
Evaluation: Making judgements about the value of ideas or materials	Examples: Selects the most effective solution. Hires the most qualified candidate. Explains and justify a new budget Key words: appraises, compares, concludes, contrasts, criticises, critiques, defends, describes, discriminates, evaluates, explains, interprets, justifies, relates, summarises, supports

(contd)

Table 21 *continued*

Psychomotor domain (skills)	
The psychomotor domain includes physical movement, co-ordination, and the use of the motor-skill areas. Development of these skills requires practice and is measured in terms of speed, precision, distance, procedures, or techniques in execution. The seven major categories are listed in order of increasing complexity and innovation.	
Perception: The ability to use sensory cues to guide motor activity. This ranges from sensory stimulation, through cue selection, to translation	Examples: Detects non-verbal communication cues. Estimate where a ball will land after it is thrown and then moving to the correct location to catch the ball. Adjusts heat of stove to correct temperature by smell and taste of food. Adjusts the height of the forks on a forklift by comparing where the forks are in relation to the pallet Key words: chooses, describes, detects, differentiates, distinguishes, identifies, isolates, relates, selects.
Set: Readiness to act. It includes mental, physical and emotional sets. These three sets are dispositions that predetermined a person's response to different situations (sometimes called mindsets)	Examples: Knows and acts on a sequence of steps in a manufacturing process. Recognises own abilities and limitations. Shows desire to learn a new process. Key words: begins, displays, explains, moves, proceeds, reacts, shows, states, volunteers
Guided response: The early stages in learning a complex skill that includes imitation and trail and error. Adequacy of performance is achieved by practising	Examples: Performs a mathematical equation as demonstrated. Follows instructions to build a model. Responds to hand-signals of instructor while learning to operate a forklift Key words: copes, traces, follows, react, reproduce, responds
Mechanism: This is the intermediate stage in learning a complex skill. Learned responses have become habitual and the movements can be performed with some confidence and proficiency	Examples: Uses a personal computer. Repairs a leaking tap. Drives a car Key words: assembles, calibrates, constructs, dismantles, displays, fastens, fixes, grinds, heats, manipulates, measures, mends, mixes, organises, sketches.
Complex overt response: The skilful performance of motor acts that involve complex movement patterns. Proficiency is indicated by a quick, accurate and highly coordinated performance, requiring a minimum of energy. This category includes performing without hesitation, and automatic performance. For example, players often utter sounds of satisfaction or expletives as soon as they hit a tennis ball or kick a football, because they can tell by the feel of the act what the result will produce	Examples: Manoeuvres a car into a tight parallel-parking spot. Operates a computer quickly and accurately. Displays tone and feeling while playing the piano Key words: assembles, builds, calibrates, constructs, dismantles, displays, fastens, fixes, grinds, heats, manipulates, measures, mends, mixes, organises, sketches. NOTE: the key words are the same as under Mechanism, but will have adverbs or adjectives that indicate that the performance is quicker, better, more accurate, etc.
Adaptation: Skills are well developed and the individual can modify movement patterns to fit special requirements	Examples: Responds effectively to unexpected experiences. Modifies instruction to meet the needs of the learners. Perform a task with a machine that it was not originally intended to do Key words: adapts, alters, changes, rearranges, reorganises, revises, varies.
Origination: Creating new movement patterns to fit a particular situation or specific problem. Learning outcomes emphasise creativity based upon highly developed skills	Examples: Constructs a new theory. Develops a new and comprehensive training programming. Creates a new gymnastic routine Key words: arranges, builds, combines, composes, constructs, creates, designs, initiate, makes, originates.

Table 21 *continued*

Affective domain (attitudes)	
This domain includes the manner in which we deal with things emotionally, such as feelings, values, appreciation, enthusiasm, motivation, and attitudes.	
Receiving phenomena: Awareness, willingness to hear, selected attention	Examples: Listens to others with respect. Listens for and remember the names of newly introduced people Key words: asks, chooses, describes, follows, gives, holds, identifies, locates, names, points to, selects, sits, erects, relies, uses
Responding to phenomena: Active participation on the part of the learner. Attends and reacts to a particular phenomenon. Learning outcomes may emphasise compliance in responding, willingness to respond, or satisfaction in responding	Examples: Participates in class discussions. Gives a presentation. Questions new ideals, concepts, models etc in order to fully understand them. Knows the safety rules and practises them Key words: answers, assists, aids, complies, conforms, discusses, greets, helps, labels, performs, practises, presents, reads, recites, reports, selects, tells, writes.
Valuing: The worth or value a person attaches to a particular object, phenomenon, or behaviour. This ranges from simple acceptance of the more complex state of commitment. Valuing is based on the internalisation of a set of specified values, while clues to these values are expressed in the learner's overt behaviour and are often identifiable	Examples: Demonstrates belief in the democratic process. Is sensitive towards individual and cultural difference. Shows the ability to solve problems. Proposes a plan for social improvement and follows through with commitment. Informs management on matters that the learner feels strongly about Key words: completes, demonstrates, differentiates, explains, follows, forms, initiates, invites, joins, justifies, proposes, reads, reports, selects, shares, studies, works
Organisation: This means organising values into priorities by contrasting different values, resolving conflicts between them and creating a unique value system. The emphasis is on comparing, relating and synthesising values	Examples: Recognises the need for balance between freedom and responsible behaviour. Accepts responsibility for one's behaviour. Explains the role of systematic planning in solving problems. Accepts professional ethical standards. Creates a life plan in harmony with abilities, interests and beliefs. Prioritises time effectively to meet the needs of the organisation, family and self Key words: adheres, alters, arranges, combines, compares, completes, defends, explains, formulates, generalises, identifies, integrates, modifies, orders, organises, prepares, relates, synthesises
Internalising values: The learner gains a value system that controls their behaviour. The behaviour is pervasive, consistent, predictable, and most importantly, characteristic of the learner. Instructional objectives are concerned with the learner's general patterns of adjustment (personal, social, emotional)	Examples: Shows self-reliance when working independently. Co-operates in group activities. Uses an objective approach in problem-solving. Displays a professional commitment to ethical practice on a daily basis. Revises judgements and changes behaviour in light of new evidence. Values people for what they are, not how they look Key words: acts, discriminates, displays, influences, listens, modifies, performs, practices, proposes, qualifies, questions, revises, serves, solves, verifies

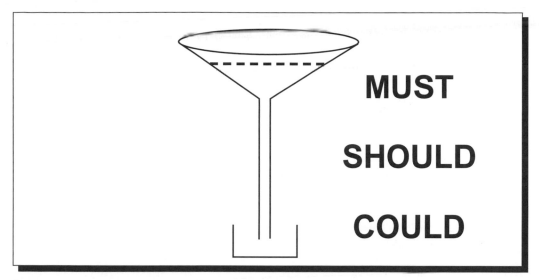

Figure 21 *Prioritising content*

I liken the method of prioritising content to a funnel, or a filtration process, like that shown in Figure 21. At the very top there are those things that 'must' be included, core competences, if you like; those essential elements that are fundamental to the achievement of the task, for the increase in knowledge, for the development of attitudes, and the enhancement of skills. And after 'must', comes 'should'. These are those things you ought to include if you have time, and if the learner has the ability and the motivation, or if the group comes together, and works together effectively. Those are things that are available to develop the learning further. Finally, 'could'. These might be the added extras, maybe through handouts, or distance, open and flexible learning, e-learning or blended learning. They may be the additional and complementary aspects of the learning that are unlikely to take place in an off-the-job setting. They might be enhanced through further coaching and mentoring back in the workplace. Perhaps the learner will take advantage of private reading, listening to tapes, or watching videos.

Therefore, it is by using this filtration method, down through the funnel, that you are better able to select what is appropriate and relevant.

PAUSE FOR THOUGHT

Knowing the three types of learning objective and what they represent, as outlined in Table 21, will aid you when selecting learning strategies. Review this classification of objectives. Now select a learning event with which you have been involved recently, and rewrite one of its objectives. Include in your objective the essential components of performance, conditions and standards. For example:

'Wordprocess a coursework assignment, from written notes, using Microsoft Word®, ready for submission, by the end of the week.'

Performance:
Conditions:
Standards:

Another way to select content is through the Pareto principle, the 80/20 syndrome. Because, in each worker's job, in each team's task, in each organisation's strategy, 80 per cent of what needs to be accomplished will be carried out in only 20 per cent of the key tasks. So, what is core, what is fundamental, what is imperative? Moreover, the employees know well enough what those key results areas are.

The fourth question is Where?

Where is the learning going to take place? Is it going to be in the workplace? On the job? At the workstation? By the machine? In the factory? In the office? Is it going to be when you are driving or flying to a meeting? Or is it going to be off the job, in a training room, a classroom, a simulator, a conference hall? Perhaps the learning will be at home, or in a hotel room. In addition, there are big differences and big gains to be had in all these different settings. Leaving aside the safety aspects of flight simulators and the need to help pilots practise using a 747 before they do it for real, or perhaps driving an underground train in a simulator first of all, there are many similarities that can be drawn between using a simulator and practising running a business. Learning often includes rehearsing how to lead teams, or trying out skills of negotiation, in an off-the-job, relatively safe, environment.

Having said that, most learning takes place on the job. Most people learn most things most of the time by trying it out. As an approach to learning, it is justifiable. The problem is, it is quite expensive, in the use of resource, time, money, facilities, materials, and equipment. It is also expensive in terms of consequential loss, or mistakes, lost customers, downtime, accidents, and wastage rates. It's expensive in terms of what the learner hopes to accomplish, and this can lead to frustration and anger, as well as loss of self-esteem and self-worth. It can be expensive in organisational terms because of the effect it has on relationships of people in the team, or other departments, and other stakeholders.

Nevertheless, learning in the workplace is often very effective if it is well structured and approached in a professional manner. Because the learner identifies a need and if that need can be met in a realistic and timely manner, then it is likely to have greater long-term benefits. But, this will only be effective if the learners themselves see a need, a problem, or a difficulty and also have access to a mentor, a coach, a manager, a supervisor, a colleague or a peer, or a trainer. And if that need can be met where they are working, they will see the relevance and importance more quickly than if it is carried out in a rarefied atmosphere of a training room, conference centre or hotel suite.

On the other hand, it is often better to take learners away from the working environment because of all the distractions, noise, interruptions, lack of space, and lack of opportunity to focus and concentrate on the learning issues. That is why quite a lot of training is actually carried out away from work, sometimes in the employees' own time. Therefore, a lot of training happens in an unusual setting. It is an artificial arrangement and therefore the trainer, coach, or instructor needs to work extremely hard at helping the learner to transfer that learning back into the work place.

There are advantages of having a training department on the premises, in the working situation, either in the department, or in the office, at region, or headquarters. Because then, the organisational culture, the framework, the product knowledge and understanding of systems and processes will be specific. Increasingly, trainers are using learning resource centres, e-learning, or the company's intranet, in order to facilitate learning that is culturally specific to the organisation. One of the major problems of work these days is that there are great demands upon most people to achieve so much more in so much less time. Therefore, the temptation is great at coffee and lunch breaks during an off-the-job course to 'pop back' to the office, and then either not to return, or to return late for the training, whereas, in a hotel or a conference centre, at least that temptation is reduced.

Consequently, a lot of training is still carried out in those environments, which have the added advantage of being separated from the distractions of the working environment. However, in those kinds of settings there are many other problems. There is much greater loss of control for the trainer in the practical arrangements of desks, chairs, overhead projectors and the use of PowerPoint®. They will have far less power over where and when the tea and coffee will be served. They will have less influence over the quality of the lunch, and when the learners will arrive, and what the accommodation and other facilities might be like. So, there is much greater scope for all the peripheral aspects of the programme to reduce the benefit of the learning itself.

Increasingly training is undertaken not in the workplace, or in a conference centre, but can be undertaken virtually anywhere. And by 'virtually', I mean not just the electronic aspects of e-learning, or on the Internet at home; but by the use of satellites and distributed learning systems; the use of mobile phones and PDAs; the use of interactive television, and CD-ROM, or DVD; or by the use of cassettes and CDs in the car. Certainly, one of the fundamental aspects of the Government's Learndirect and University for Industry is that learning needs be distributed more equitably, to take place *outside* the normal institutions and settings that people have become used to. So that, there are opportunities for people to use facilities to develop their knowledge, skills and attitudes in the home, pub, club, school hall, empty church hall or an Internet café.

Where learning takes place is very important, because again it's about empowering the learner to take responsibility for their learning at a place and a time to suit them, and in a way that appeals to their different learning styles, in bite-size chunks that they can cope with, and specific to their current learning needs. So, increasingly, it is known as *just-in-time* learning. If an employee has a difficulty or a problem in the workplace, it can be possible for them to phone, fax, or e-mail somebody to help them. It is also possible for them to use a CD-ROM on their own machine, or on a server. They could access the Internet, intranet, or extranet. Perhaps they could access a learning resource centre and read a book, use a workbook, watch a video, or have a discussion. It is possible for them to borrow a cassette tape or use video-conferencing or satellite systems to discuss the nature of the problem with others. None of this learning has taken place in a traditional training room or classroom. So, increasingly, learning is not limited by space or location.

The fifth question that needs to be asked is When?
At what time will the learning take place? What time of day? Which day of the week? Or week of the month, or month of the year? All these questions have a strange yet marked influence on our learning and our training.

The time of day is very important for learning. Without going into the whole nature of biorhythms, we can nevertheless see that some people learn better at different times of the day. You may remember that, at school, often Maths was taught in the morning and English in the afternoon. Many people prefer to learn and be trained early in the morning. Some people wake quickly, expectantly, hopefully, and a number of writers that I know do their best work immediately on waking in the morning. Others of us, ... well, we take longer to wake up, but some of our best time for learning is in the evening. Yes, we may have put in a hard day's work, but somehow the ability to develop, grow, and mature is easier in the evening. Just look at the large number of students who undertake part-time courses, often coming twice a week for two years! And yes, it has to be acknowledged, that many of them also seem to do their best assignments at two o'clock in the morning, just before the hand-in date!

So, we learn differently, at various times of the day. In addition, it is well known, that straight after lunch is often not a good time to learn. That is why trainers are so often urged not to show a video at that time; the post-prandial stupor is difficult for learning! Therefore, at that particular time of day, a good trainer will often put an activity into the design of the programme.

Another aspect of learning, since we are considering time, is the length of adult concentration spans. No doubt, we have seen many times the classic learning curve, and people talk glibly about a difficulty in a new job or in a new situation as being on 'a steep learning curve'. However, just as there is a learning curve, there is also a *forgetting* curve. Adults, generally speaking, cannot concentrate on any one piece of learning for longer than about 20 minutes, before there is a need to change the texture of the design. Therefore, after a short period of input, there is a need for discussion or questioning, for a case study or skills development exercise. Another aspect as we are considering time and learning is: how often and how many times will the training take place? That is to say, will the learning be concentrated in one large chunk, or will it be split into smaller parts, modules, sessions, seminars, and workshops.

When can people be released from work? How often are they able to get away? Is it going to be for half a day, a whole day, or longer? We know that in most organisations two or three days is the maximum that people can be released from the workplace these days. Some organisations are now experimenting with mini-sessions lasting just one or two hours. These are repeated during the day, and the learners just arrive at the training room without booking an appointment. If there is a spare space, they can join in with the session, and if not, then they can come back later.

For most organisations, gone are the days of the one- or even two-week residential course. However, there is still much to be gained from staying at a hotel or conference centre overnight, particularly in relation to the intangible, social, relational elements of the learning. This can be crucial for attitudinal development.

Considering aspects of time, it is also important to consider the day of the week, month, season or year, because different departments and functions are busier at different times, and therefore the availability of learners is reduced. It is impossible to get people from finance, for example, to be released for training courses just before the financial year-end. In addition, in the whole of the retail sector, it is very difficult for people to be released to go on training courses in November/December. Similar problems exist at other times of the year in the travel industry.

Therefore, we can see that time is very important when we are considering learning design. But an element that is often overlooked is the needs of the non-employed, that is to say, the casual, the temporary, and the job-share worker. What about people on shift work, perhaps nurses on permanent night shift in a hospital. Are they required to come on *our* courses at *our* times, starting at 9.30 in the morning? Furthermore, what about the needs of single parents? What are the implications for them? Can they suddenly be expected to change their normal work pattern to fit in with our agendas?

The amount of time given over to learning is usually less than is required. Time is money – yes! But, far too often, money determines the training or the learning. Unfortunately, many trainers start with the amount of time that is available and try to shoehorn into it all the learning that is required. It is far better to start with the learners, their needs, and their objectives, and what is to be achieved – and then to say: 'What is manageable within the time?'

The sixth crucial question is Which?
Which learning strategy? In what way will the learners be helped to develop? That is to say, within the organisational strategy, the HR policy and plans, and the training philosophy, there need to be statements made concerning the overall learning strategy for all the employees, or certain groups of employees. For example, it could be that the whole organisation, or the HR department, the accounts office or the regional store decides that everybody under the age of 21 will be given time to go on day-release to the local college, to obtain a qualification, perhaps linked to NVQs, modern apprenticeships or A-levels. Another strategy could be to do with e-learning; it could be decided, say, that every employee in the headquarters building will be given access to an intranet-based set of modules. Alternatively, a strategy that might affect a particular group of workers could be for middle and senior managers to have the right to go on a Diploma in Management Studies course or MBA programme.

PAUSE FOR THOUGHT

This real case study looks at the learning needs of two very similar groups of people, called clinical supervisors, in two different NHS trusts. The training design for these people was based on very similar identified learning needs. However, you can see that the time allotted in one example is twice that which was given over to the other group. Carry out an assessment of these training designs:

	'X' COMMUNITY HEALTH PROGRAMME	'Y' UNIVERSITY and 'Z' HOSPITAL PROGRAMME
OBJECTIVES and ASSESSMENT	■ On-course learning contract ■ Self- and peer assessment ■ End of each workshop evaluations	■ Critically analyse the role and function of the clinical supervisor ■ Appraise a variety of clinical supervision models ■ Appraise the outcomes of clinical supervision ■ Identify own strengths and weaknesses as a facilitator ■ Demonstrate effective use of supervisory skills in both the group and individual supervision settings ■ Examine the ethical, legal and cultural issues within clinical supervision ■ Identify and apply appropriate documentation procedures ■ End of each day evaluations
CONTENT	■ Overview of supervision ■ Six categories of intervention ■ Group facilitation ■ Criteria for effectiveness	■ Role of supervisor/supervisee ■ Functions of supervision ■ Group dynamics ■ Boundary negotiation/agreeing a contract ■ Ethical dilemmas ■ Transference ■ Communication patterning within supervision
LEARNING STRATEGY	■ Pre-course open learning ■ On-job application ■ Off-job workshops	■ Post-course open learning ■ Off-job workshop
LEARNING METHODS	■ Tutor inputs ■ Skills practice ■ Review, feedback and reflection ■ Groupwork ■ Action planning	■ Experiential sessions ■ Discussion ■ Group work ■ Reflection ■ End of Day 1 homework
LOCATION	■ Learner's own place ■ Off-job learning centre	■ Learner's own place ■ Off-job learning centre
TIME	■ 1.5 hours open learning ■ Two x two-days (3-week gap)	■ Two hours open learning ■ One x two-day workshop

For example, here is the assessment that I submitted to the 'X' Community Health Trust:

PROGRAMME DESIGN ASSESSMENT

1. This assessment is based solely on the written, published documents available, and the author's understanding of clinical supervision within the context of the NHS.
2. In broad terms, both programmes contain elements of good training practice, and appear to take account of several aspects of learning theory.
3. There seems to be general congruence between the explicit or implicit objectives of the programmes and the learning strategy and methods selected, although there is no indication of group size. It is recommended that such programmes should have a maximum group size of about 12, with opportunities for working in pairs, threes, fours, and sixes.
4. The author had no evidence of stated entry behaviour for the learners. It is recommended that notice should be taken of their existing knowledge, skills and attitudes; relevant experience; previous exposure to experiential learning; learning style preferences; availability; links to appraisals or personal/professional development plans; and motivation and commitment.
5. While the use of pre- or post-course open learning is commendable, there is some doubt concerning its efficacy in practice. Learners regularly do not take advantage of such provision, particularly when, as seems to be the case here, it appears to lack tutorial support, and is neither assessed nor directly referred to during the workshops.
6. The end-of-workshop and end-of-day evaluations are predictable, if disappointing. It is recommended that a complete evaluation strategy should be implemented to include internal and external validation; transfer of learning; job behaviour and performance measures; and return-on-investment calculations.
7. For the 'X' programme, the author had no evidence of stated objectives, aims or outcomes. The use of an on-course learning contract and action plans is considered good practice. The pace of the programme appears appropriate to the strategy and methods selected. There seems to be good use made of skills practice with feedback. Review and reflection are employed well. The use of self- and peer-assessment is good practice. While the provision of a gap between the two workshops is considered to be noteworthy, there may be difficulties with the availability/release of learners for Part II. In addition, the three weeks allowed is unlikely to be sufficient to give learners the opportunities necessary to apply all the learning from Part I.
   OVERALL ASSESSMENT – GOOD. This programme design is likely to meet the learning needs.
8. For the 'Y/Z' programme, the author had no evidence of assessment strategies and procedures, which is disappointing considering the excellent formulation of behavioural objectives. However, it is considered that, owing to the number, range, scope and standards of the objectives, they are unlikely to be met in the time allocated. Moreover, there seems to be too little time set apart for some of the experiential learning sessions. It is difficult to see where some of the stated content is to be found in the workshop, and how some of the content relates to the objectives.
   OVERALL ASSESSMENT – FAIR. This programme design is considered too ambitious for the time allocated, and unlikely to meet the learning needs.

Similarly, there could be a strategy for all professionals to be supported in developing their professional education and development at a college or university. Another strategy might concern the extent to which learning and training is carried out on the job, or off the job. Learning strategy also involves consideration of whether it is for individuals or groups. Increasingly, a major strategy decision that is being taken by many organisations concerns the outsourcing of the training function. Will there be a training department? Alternatively, will consultants be brought in?

And in order to decide which strategy to adopt, clearly there are major decisions that need to be taken at senior levels relating to resources and their allocation. Unfortunately, a number of organisations tend to take the very short-term and pragmatic view. But when the outcomes of training and learning can only be seen many months or even years later, beyond the scope of any one particular financial year, then the benefits are often neglected. So, which strategy to adopt will largely determine the nature, outcome and function of the learning.

And the final questions, How?/How much?

'How' refers to the learning methods that are available, and 'how much' is clearly to do with costs and benefits, standards and quality.

There are many, many different forms of learning methods. In Table 22 on page 96, a number of the most well known and well used are listed (Bournier and Flowers 1997). It has been said that most trainers know of about a dozen different learning methods, and only use half of them. There are in fact well over 70 different forms of learning method that could be used to increase the learning of employees at work. Moreover, according to the table, you will see that there are different learning methods that are applicable and appropriate for different learning outcomes.

Therefore, if we want the learners to *understand* certain concepts, facts or elements of knowledge, then perhaps a lecture or reading would be appropriate. But, if we then want to take the learners further to help them *apply* that knowledge and understanding, then a lecture or reading alone will be inappropriate and we must choose a different learning method for the *application* of the knowledge. That could include, for example, a case study, a discussion or a debate.

If you were asked to construct a list of participative learning methods, I wonder how many of the following (Woods and Cortada 2002) you would have included!

Application projects	Mentoring
Articles and books	Metaphors
Audiotapes (music and speaking)	Newsletter
Book groups	Participatory lecture
Brainstorming	Planned interruptive lecture
Case studies	Post-work
Chain-gang lecture	Prep-work
Challenge courses	Press conference lecture
Charts, graphs, posters	Programmed instruction lecture
Computer/web-based training	Props
Concept interference lecture	Real-time video tutorial lectures
Concert reading	Role plays
Confederate lecture	Self-analysis, reflection
Continuing learning	Sharing best practices
Demonstration	Simulation
Experiential lecture	Story
Expert call-in lecture	Study groups
Field trips	Synergogic lecture
Five-minute fables	Teach back
Games	Team quiz lecture
Ice-breakers	TV and videotape
Job aids	Visualisation
Lecture in a fishbowl	Voice mail, e-mail
Magic tricks	

Table 22 *Linking learning methods to aims*

	Disseminate knowledge	Develop the student's capability to use ideas and information	Develop the student's ability to test ideas and evidence	Develop the student's ability to generate ideas and evidence	Facilitate the student's personal development	Develop the student's capacity to plan and manage their own learning
TEN COMMON LEARNING METHODS	1. Lectures 2. Up-to-date textbooks 3. Reading 4. Handouts 5. 'Guest' lectures 6. Use of exercises to find up-to-date knowledge 7. Develop skills in using library and other learning resources 8. Directed private study 9. Open learning materials 10. Use of the Internet	1. Case studies 2. Practicals 3. Work experience 4. Projects 5. Demonstrations 6. Group working 7. Simulations (eg computer-based) 8. Workshops 9. Discussion and debate 10. Essay-writing	1. Seminars and tutorials 2. Supervision 3. Presentations 4. Essays 5. Feedback on written work 6. Literature reviewing 7. Exam papers 8. Open learning 9. Peer assessment 10. Self-assessment	1. Research projects 2. Creative problem solving 3. Group working 4. Action learning 5. Lateral thinking 6. Brainstorming 7. Mind-mapping 8. Creative visualisation 9. Coaching 10. Problem-solving	1. Feedback 2. Experiential learning 3. Learning contracts 4. Action learning 5. Learning logs 6. Role-play 7. Structured experiences in groups 8. Reflective documents 9. Self-assessment 10. Profiling	1. Learning contracts 2. Projects 3. Action learning 4. Workshops 5. Mentors 6. Learning logs and diaries 7. Independent study 8. Work placement 9. Portfolio development 10. Dissertations

PAUSE FOR THOUGHT

For each one of the methods in the list on page 95 that you do not recognise, search the Internet for a definition and a working example. You could start with this: http://www.trainersnetwork.org/html/lrn-method.html.

In Figure 22, we see Martin and Jackson's (2002) illustration of three interconnected factors for consideration in the selection of training strategies.

How can this apply to the design decisions we are constantly having to make? In order to achieve learning outcomes and objectives, different methods are appropriate. For example, when I was undertaking a consultancy assignment at British Airways, they wanted to develop their senior purchasing manager's ability in advanced negotiating skills. I knew that this would involve a considerable amount of practice, skills development, and rehearsal. That takes time. My colleague and I resisted strongly the demand by the client to cut down on the length of time required for the learning event. In order to develop their negotiating skills, the learners needed time to practise these new skills in a relatively safe learning environment. Then they needed feedback, further input, and further opportunities to improve.

Increasingly, methods for learning will include not only face-to-face training, either on the job or in a training room, but organisations are increasingly using open, distance and flexible learning, which include among other materials, paper-based workbooks delivered to people so they can learn where and when they prefer. Perhaps there could also be the use of audio cassettes and videos, CD-ROMS, or DVDs, which people can have access to as they travel to work, or in their home.

Other methods will be appropriate to develop other knowledge, skills and attitudes. For example, in order to learn how to use a particular software programme, such as Microsoft® Access, we can watch somebody construct a database, or hear a lecture, read a book, study the manual, or watch a video. However, in the end, the learners need to actually use a computer themselves, in either a dedicated computer-learning suite or room, or better still, on their own machine in the workplace.

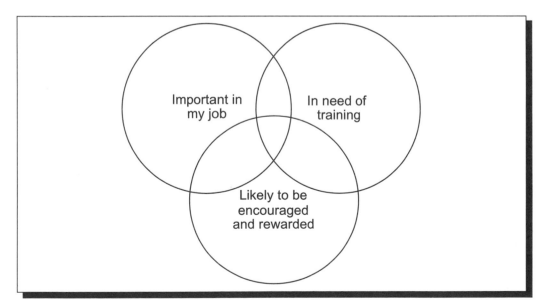

Figure 22 *Selecting learning strategies*

And how much will all this cost?

It is most important to be able to justify to all stakeholders the return on investment (ROI) that such a training design will achieve. There has been a history in training circles over many years of not addressing this major issue. Consequently, this has devalued its worth in the eyes of senior management in general, and the finance director in particular! Now, at last, there is a means of adopting an approach to assessing the ROI of training and learning with which senior executives are familiar and which they regularly use in other aspects of the organisation. There are two templates that need to be used together, which you will find in Figure 23. These have been adapted from groundbreaking work by Swanson (2001).

Selecting different training and learning methods

Cheetham and Chivers (2001) catalogue for us a useful list of on-the-job learning events:

- mentoring
- learning from complex to multi-faceted problems
- innovative and pioneering experiences.
- working above grade
- working alongside more experienced colleagues
- networking
- teamworking
- multi-disciplinary working
- switching perspectives
- learning from clients/patients/customers
- learning from para-professionals
- feedback
- learning from criticism
- self-knowledge and self-image
- simulation
- learning through articulation
- learning through teaching others
- cultural transfer/cross-cultural stimulation
- extra-occupational learning and transfer
- learning by linking
- mindset changes and 'Damascus Road' experiences
- mental models, imagery and other psychological devices
- reflection
- coping with professional stress.

Such methods would seem to go a long way towards meeting user needs. Although the majority of small and medium-sized enterprises appear to be resistant to education and training, a small minority – mainly those pursuing growth – embrace training. Their requirements are twofold: an immediate menu of technical fixes for current problems, and longer-term requirements, mainly for marketing and finance. Ideally, they would like one-to-one and face-to-face tuition. This is not feasible within the cost parameters of institutionally provided training.

The outcome/worth spreadsheet

Learning event: .... Training designer: .... Date: ....

Learning options	Option 1	Option 2	Option 3
Data			
a) What is the unit of performance?			
b) What is the financial value of each unit?			
c) What is the learners' initial performance?			
d) What is the performance target at the end of the learning event?			
e) How long will it take the learners to reach the target standard?			
f) What is the period of external validation? [Enter the highest value from e]			
g) How many learners will participate in the learning event?			
Calculations			
h) How many usable units do the learners produce during the learning event? $\frac{d + c}{2}$			
i) How many usable units are produced during the development period? $h \times e$			
j) How many usable units will be produced during the total external validation period? $[(f - e) \times d] + i$			
k) What is the value of the outcome during the external validation period? $j \times b$			

Figure 23 *The ROI of training and learning*

Figure 23 *continued*

The input/cost spreadsheet

Learning event: .... Training designer: .... Date: ....

Learning options	Option 1	Option 2	Option 3
Identify and analyse			
Diagnose performance			
Document expertise			
Contract with stakeholders			
Other			
Plan and design			
Diagnosis and feedback			
Off-the-shelf design			
Tailor-made design			
Pilot and improve			
Develop media and materials			
Other			
Implement and deliver			
Manage learning event			
Deliver learning event			
Fixed costs			
Opportunity costs			
Other			
Validation and evaluation			
Assess results			
Report results			
Follow-up performance			
Roll-out			
Other			

Figure 23 *continued*

TOTAL input/costs			

Analysis

Learning options	Option 1	Option 2	Option 3
TOTAL outcome/worth for all the learners [K]			
Minus **TOTAL input/costs**			
Result			

PAUSE FOR THOUGHT

Take a few moments now to reflect on a recent learning event.

Identify – for the trainer involved – the following elements, as if you were giving feedback to the trainer.

1. What did they do, in precise terms?

2. What did they do that was particularly successful?

3. What didn't work so well?

4. The next time they run this session:

   they should avoid:

   they should change:

   they should include:

Effah (1998) explores some of the avenues for training and staff development. Within limited financial resources, opportunities nevertheless exist for training and staff development at the universities in Ghana. These opportunities include:

- induction/orientation on first appointment
- in-service/on-the-job training
- study visits
- staff meetings
- informal discussions with colleagues
- seminars/workshops/conferences
- job rotation
- participation in activities of professional associations

- study leave/sabbatical/leave of absence
- consultancy
- in-house journals
- organised departmental research/individual research.

Interestingly, he sees the lack of training and learning in the higher education establishments in Ghana as not being due to the lack of opportunities:

> It would seem that the major problems rather relate to a lack of co-ordination, the unsuitability of courses, a poor incentive and reward system for individual learning effort, as well as cost considerations. But by far the biggest limitation seems to be the lack of a training needs analysis.

How can this be applied in reality? Well, for example, during a total quality management (TQM) training programme, learners spend most of their time, according to research by Vermeulen and Crous (2000), on:

> - communication skills
> - problem-solving techniques
> - quality service to customers.
>
> It is interesting that the real issues of TQM, namely the introduction to TQM and the use of TQM tools, receive less attention from certain respondents. Contents of a TQM training programme will differ from organisation to organisation. The contents of the training programme should however always be in line with the objectives of the overall TQM programme, which is actually aimed at improving business processes. Quality training programmes should therefore centre round the basic principles of understanding the different processes in the organisation, the relationship between different processes, and eventually the improvement of these processes. Top management should foremost establish the criteria (objectives) to be followed in the design of the training programme; for example, that the training courses should be job- and outcome-oriented. The main objective of any TQM training programme should be to achieve continuous improvement in all activities.

Another way to consider how to select learning methods and techniques is to see them in the context of a basic teaching process (Wilson 1999), as in Table 23 on page 103.

Selecting different training and learning media and materials

A very useful way to help you select appropriate learning media is to use the framework in Table 24 on page 104.

With the increasing use of broadcast technology at home and for leisure, learners' expectations are being raised all the time about the quality and standards of learning materials. A poor handout that's been photocopied many times will not only be difficult to read and understand, but will reduce in the learners' eyes the quality of all the training that's delivered. When it comes to distance, open and flexible learning materials, a great deal of thought must be given to layout and format; to the visual effect of the words on the page; to the use of pictures and icons; the use of white space; and the font used.

When I was preparing for this book, I needed to read a large number of different materials, and some of them were – to be frank – difficult and off-putting, simply because of the choice of the layout and the font size. My discussions with the commissioning editor for this book have, I hope, borne fruit. I hope you are finding this easier to read and more accessible than perhaps some materials. When it comes to training

Table 23 *Selecting learning methods*

1. Examine learning objectives	2. Consider learning styles and strategies	3. Select methods	4. Design techniques	5. Prepare materials
Performance criteria Learning outcomes	Trainer-centred Learner-centred Consider planned and emergent learners Consider needs of activist, pragmatist reflector and theorist	Case study Buzz groups Syndicate Lecture Fish bowl Action maze Outdoor management development	Ice-breakers Energisers Dice games Attitude scales Role hats Deconstructing skills Closers Road shows Market place Card games Score cards	Envelopes Masking tape Washable cards Layered flipcharts Coloured pins Video cases Post-it® labels

and learning we need to strive for excellence. We need not pursue perfection, but professionalism. We need to strive for standards and quality in our materials that would be acceptable to the board of directors, senior executives and our chief customers.

In the past I've been involved in commissioning training videos. We used a professional and commercial organisation to undertake the whole project. It was fascinating to work through all the processes from original scriptwriting and storyboarding, thinking about shots and scenes, and then moving through the stage of getting the right actors. We went through the location shots and the filming and the hectic nature of all of that. And then the hard graft of post-production work with editing and sound, all the graphics and the computerised effects. And then came all the tape duplication before we were ready to use the videos for product knowledge training in a financial services environment. All these steps helped me to see that a lot of hard work is undertaken over many, many months in order to produce just a half-hour video if we are to achieve the kind of excellence that is expected. We are not here to look slick, but to be professional with our learners in a way that doesn't cause problems, and helps them to achieve their potential. We are to be thorough, and well-prepared. So, an overhead projector transparency slide that we've been using for five years is unlikely to stand the test of acceptability.

Why do we use slides anyway; why do we use the overhead projector? The same question can be asked of many different kinds of media, because different media can be used in different ways for different kinds of learning. The size of group is important, and the message and learning outcome will also determine which media are best in any given situation.

Table 24 *Increasing retention*

Retention level (%)	Media	Learner involvement
10	**Reading** Books, handouts, journals, computer text	*Passive* *Visual receiving* *Sight*
20	**Listening** Lectures, audiocassettes, radio	*Passive* *Aural receiving* *Hearing*
30	**Looking** Charts, diagrams, flipcharts, whiteboards, slides, overhead projector transparencies, visualisers, data projectors	*Active* *Visual receiving* *Sight*
40	**Following** Computer graphics, transparency overlays, working models	*Active* *Aural and visual receiving* *Sight*
50	**Watching** Videos, DVDs, demonstrations, CD-ROMs, computer-generated animation	*Active* *Aural and visual receiving* *Hearing and sight*
60	**Writing** Reports, learning logs, tests, keyboards	*Active* *Verbal contributing* *Sight and touch*
70	**Talking** Discussions, 'telephone' simulator, audio cassette, computer voice recognition, DVD-I	*Active* *Oral and aural contributing* *Hearing and taste*
80	**Practising** Simulations, exercises, multimedia	*Active* *Participating* *Sight, hearing, touch, taste, and smell*
90	**Experiencing** The real job	*Active* *Doing* *Sight, hearing, taste, touch and smell*

If it's a small group of three, four or five people, an overhead projector will be intrusive. It is far better to use a flip chart. When the group is larger, with say 15, 20 or 30 people, an overhead projector then is essential.

How we use media is also important. I think it's important for many reasons for the trainer to be well versed in how to use a particular overhead projector, and if necessary to practise beforehand in an empty room. For the learner, there's nothing more dispiriting than for a trainer to say 'Now, where do I switch it on?' or for the projector to be switched on with no transparency being shown. Even worse is for the trainer to walk in front of the screen, or for the transparency to be put on upside down. We know these things, we've been there, and we've seen it. And our heart sinks, and we stop learning.

When the group increases beyond about 30 or 40 people, it's important to consider whether an overhead projector is going to be effective enough. Perhaps we need to consider using instead a video projector or data projector, linked to a laptop or console computer. That enables us to use perhaps PowerPoint® slides. But with every step up, there is increasingly the temptation to become more sophisticated and to invest many hours of preparation. This can unfortunately diminish the learning.

The problem is that we can spend a long time with, say, PowerPoint®, developing some really wonderful slides that may actually get in the way of the message we're trying to put across. Moreover, having invested so much time and effort in developing such slides, we're then determined to use them, not matter how inappropriate or ineffective they may be. The other problem with PowerPoint® is that many users don't realise that you can actually skip between slides – you aren't obliged to proceed from slide one to two to three to four. You can miss some out and come back to others. But if some trainers have developed 30 slides for a session, then unfortunately that's what the learners will receive!

In terms of media it's also important to consider e-learning. And while that will be dealt with later in a further chapter in this book, the increasing use of electronic media for learning has great implications for design and delivery. The biggest question here is, 'Are there resources available to develop learning in a package that will increase the employee's performance?' Many computer-based training programmes have cost thousands of pounds, and done a great disservice to the training function. It would be far better for the money to be spent in selecting an off-the-shelf programme that has already been developed and used by other customers, even if it's not wholly relevant or appropriate to the organisation. Because, if somebody else has spent a lot of time, money and effort in developing a package on, say, health and safety, teamworking, problem solving, how to use Lotus Notes®, or how set up a project management system – if that learning programme already exists, then the development costs will inevitably be dramatically reduced. Moreover, the very nature of e-learning means that it can be edited, and improved and adapted and made applicable to the organisation's needs.

And finally, while we're talking about e-learning, how will the packages be distributed? Will they be physically sent by mail, by way of CD-ROMs or DVDs, or floppy disks? Will they be available on an organisation's intranet? Or will the learners use the World Wide Web? Each of these has benefits and problems associated with it. But it's in the design stage that these factors need to be considered.

So, different learning will be accomplished by using different media and materials. Increasingly, I am tempted not to use overhead projector slides. Very rarely will I use PowerPoint®, and only occasionally will I get my learners to see the whole of a training video. DVDs offer more flexibility than linear video's. I think I prefer to use a flipchart or a whiteboard because they offer increased opportunities to be interactive and participative with the learners, rather than imposing on them my agenda, my transparencies, and my objectives.

Finally in this section, it's important to remember that certain methods and media are better for different learning outcomes. Role play or skills development is particularly good, not just for helping people to practise certain skills, but also for developing attitudes. Similarly videos, CD-ROMs and DVDs are excellent at helping learners to develop a different attitude.

Learning support processes

A learning support process involves a variety of different aspects of the training function. At one end it may include the tutor, the trainer, or the instructor, who is available or stands alongside the learner when they are being coached, or when they're developing a new skill on the job. At the other end of the spectrum it will include the whole of the training administration arena, such as the people, practices and systems that are used to facilitate the learning events. This will involve not just booking rooms and speakers, and making sure handouts and materials are available, but ensuring that the documentation is up to date with training records, and appropriate links are made to appraisals and performance management systems. In between, there's a whole raft of communication processes that needs to be undertaken in relation to the learner, the trainer and the line manager. Increasingly, this is done electronically by e-mail. But it's very important for effective communication to have back-up systems, team meetings, project teams, and written hard copy.

PAUSE FOR THOUGHT

Read through this case study and try the task at the end.

Focal Point Holidays is a company, which specialises in holidays for independent travellers. The company puts together holidays tailored to the individual traveller's requirements. It says no two holidays are the same!

Colin Johns and Mary Honey are the co-founders and directors of Focal Point Holidays, which they began in 1996. Initially it was just the two of them and as the business has grown, they have taken on more staff. They now have five shops in England. Each one of them has a manager and six members of staff.

You have been appointed recently as the personnel and training manager.

Colin, Mary and the shop managers form the Focal Point Holidays management team. Colin and Mary have realised that there may be some tensions in the team, as things don't seem as relaxed as they have been in the past.

Although the performance of the managers is acceptable, the directors are realising that there are areas for improvement. The level of experience and knowledge among the managers is varied. A recent incident of misconduct in one of the shops, which was not dealt with swiftly enough, has led to the directors having concerns.

Similarly, there are concerns about members of the teams working for the managers. Recently one or two of Focal Point Holiday's longest-standing customers have commented, to the directors, that service isn't what it has been in the past.

The directors, Colin and Mary, have asked you to address these issues as a matter of urgency.

You will need to look at the following areas:

■ the management team – ie the managers and directors

■ the branch managers

■ the branch members

The directors will be looking for practical and feasible recommendations if they are to accept your proposals – and agree to fund them!

Your task
You need to make detailed design proposals, outlining your recommendations to meet the training and development areas identified. Your recommendations should include details of the proposed solutions, costs, learning outcomes, and any constraints you have considered, and outline your recommended training design including the methods you propose.

SUMMARY

We have now covered all the components of a learning plan. You now need to draw the plan together and present it to all concerned to obtain their agreement. Let's recap on what you have learned as a reminder of the various components that you may need to include. The actions and decisions that we have covered in this section are:

1. Identify the performance aims/objectives that the organisation intends to achieve as a result of the training.
2. Decide the learning objective – training and enabling objectives.
3. Establish the entry behaviour of the learners.
4. Draw up and agree a specification of learning requirements to establish a design brief.
5. Decide how learners should be prepared.
6. Select suitable training methods.
7. Select and sequence the content.
8. Decide on the media to be used.
9. Decide on a time-table.
10. Decide how to ensure that the learning is translated into performance at the workplace.
11. Review the design for any errors or omissions.
12. Specify the resources required.
13. Evaluate the costs.
14. Specify the monitoring and control systems.

Remember that many of these issues are not mutually exclusive, nor must you consider them in any particular order. You may have to modify some of your early decisions because of constraints that become known later.

QUESTIONS

1. The main board of directors of a global organisation has decided to reduce the learning and development budget for next year by 50 per cent. Assess and evaluate a range of learning strategies to address this situation.
2. Critically analyse the return on investment of two different learning options with which you are familiar.
3. The personnel manager of a large retail company has written to you as part of a benchmarking exercise, asking for advice on how to use learning and development to manage diversity in her organisation. Write her a reply.

The delivery of training

> The biggest job we have is to teach a newly hired employee how to fail intelligently. We have to train him to experiment over and over and to keep on trying and failing until he learns what will work.
>
> **Charles Kettering**

LEARNING OUTCOMES

- Describe the implications for the delivery of training events of different trainer roles and styles.
- Outline the implications for the fair, accessible and timely delivery of training events of diversified types and categories of learners.
- Establish a climate conducive to learning.
- Tackle equitably and effectively the difficulties that learners experience in different types of training situation.
- Establish and maintain effective learning relationships with learners.

CHAPTER OUTLINE

- How to work with other organisational and external personnel in delivering training events. The range of trainer roles, styles and behavioural characteristics, and how to adapt these to learners' expectations and to the objectives of training events.
- The operation of effective learning and instructional processes during training events, including
  - how to build and sustain a conducive learning climate in short- and longer-term training events
  - how to establish and maintain effective learning relationships with a wide variety of learners
  - how to identify difficulties experienced by learners in different types of training and employment situation, and tackle these equitably and effectively.

INTRODUCTION

From the outset, we need to understand that the modern globalisation-driven notion that 'one size fits all' just doesn't apply to the design and delivery of training.

Ordinary packages delivered in a standardised way soon fall foul of even the least discriminating learner or manager. Perhaps this is the reason why so many people and organisations have found difficulty with, for example, NVQs and computer-based training courses. Even 30 years ago, when I was responsible for producing an annual training plan for a National Health Service region, there was a reluctance among many people to present themselves or their subordinates for the wonderful courses which I had so meticulously organised and planned on their behalf!

There is a notion, based on Tayloristic principles, that there is 'one right way'. Patently, this is not true, at least in terms of human resource development. Imposing solutions on others, forcing them to fit into our preconceived ideas of what is good for them, or making them participate in events which others consider would be good for them – such approaches are doomed to failure. There is an inner conflict in the employee between toeing the company line and following their natural inclinations. There will be a struggle between their head and their heart, between loyalty to the organisation and integrity with what they know to be true.

Often, the employees themselves may be unable to articulate this inner turmoil with any degree of accuracy, or it may be expressed as a concern with the trainer's idealistic approach. Nevertheless, whenever external agencies adopt a paternalistic or patronising stance in their attitude towards learners, there are likely to be difficulties in this crucial area of delivery. If people feel ignored through the process of learning design, then they will usually express their concerns later at the time of learning delivery.

Therefore, for delivery to be effective, it must be learner-centred.

I am constantly fascinated by the way in which a particular learning event can turn out quite differently for each set of learners. I am sure this is one of the ways that I am kept on my toes, and also one of the reasons why I enjoy this wonderful world of learning and development! In the end, it's about relationships, and the learning relationship must be one of the most worthwhile and beneficial ones with which to be involved at work.

As training facilitators, our aim must be to constantly strive to be servants of those we are seeking to help develop. Our focus must be on the learners and not on our own agendas, or programmes, or exercises, or perfectly produced PowerPoint® slides!

This chapter will seek to explore some of the ways in which we need to adapt our approach to various learners in different situations.

THE DELIVERY OF TRAINING – IN THEORY
Different trainer roles and styles

There appear to be five behavioural competencies essential for organisational success (Garavan and McGuire 2001):

- good interpersonal relationships among team members
- capacity for openness and willingness to discuss issues
- high levels of trust among team members
- discipline and cohesion in decision-making
- capacity to discuss and understand both long- and short-term issues.

Such qualities and characteristics are exactly those that need to be developed among members of the training team. In modelling such behaviours, the team of learning facilitators will convey to their learners the importance of such competencies to the organisation.

Diversified types and categories of learners

According to Wilson (1999), there will be four distinct types of required learning for the workers of the future:

- updating functional skills and acquiring new ones
- developing organisational and interpersonal skills
- developing positive traits and attitudes towards change and innovation
- cultural and multicultural acclimatisation.

As professional trainers, we need firstly to address these issues for ourselves, and then take them as starting points in the identification and analysis of training and development needs for our colleagues. Among other things, we must address the variety of their learning styles.

There has been much discussion of learning styles and preferences over the last quarter of a century. But Adey *et al* (1999) are keen to distinguish 'learning styles' from other terms used in a similar context. They provide the following definitions:

A *Learning Style* is a deep-rooted preference an individual has for a particular type of learning. One can think of this as being similar to the way one folds one's arms. Each person has a preferred way to do it even though they are quite capable of folding their arms the other way. However, in order to fold one's arms 'the wrong way' one has to think much harder about what one is doing, and it never feels quite as 'natural' ...

At the other extreme, *Learning Skills* are almost like 'tricks' which are specific, designed to do one job and can be taught. One example of a learning skill is the use of a mnemonic to help remember a series of facts, such as 'Richard Of York Gave Battle In Vain' in order to remember that the seven colours of the rainbow are red, orange, yellow, green, blue, indigo and violet ...

Somewhere in between these two extremes, the term *Learning Strategy* is used for groups of skills that a learner uses together for a particular purpose. Examples include setting objectives, selecting and formulating questions and comparing characteristics.

Clearly, different people learn different things in different ways! We can now combine the *stages* in Kolb's cycle of experiential learning, together with Honey and Mumford's four preferred learning *styles*, and the four classic *ways* of learning (Table 25). It follows, therefore, that different learning styles are better suited to different learning methods. For example:

- knowledge acquisition – reflector/theorist
- skills development – activist/pragmatist
- continuous professional development – reflector/theorist
- workplace learning – activist/pragmatist
- research and development – reflector/theorist
- evidence based practice – reflector/pragmatist.

Reynolds (2002) goes further (Table 26) by comparing the five major classifications of learners.

Table 25 *Ways of learning*

Stages in the learning cycle	Preferred learning styles	Ways of learning
Concrete experience	Activist	Imitation
Reflection	Reflector	Being told
Concluding	Theorist	Thinking
Testing	Pragmatist	Trial and error

Table 26 *Classification of learners*

Classification	Description
Myers-Briggs Type Indicator®	This model classifies learners according to their preferences on scales derived from psychologist Carl Jung's theory of psychological types: extroverts or introverts; sensors or initiators; thinkers or feelers; judges or perceivers
Felder-Silverman Learning Model	This classification has five categories – sensing or intuitive learners; visual or verbal learners; inductive or deductive learners; active or reflective learners; sequential or global learners
Hermann Brain Dominance Instrument	This method classifies learners in terms of their relative preferences for thinking in four different modes – left-brain cerebral (logical thinkers); left-brain limbic (sequential thinkers); right-brain limbic (emotional thinkers); right-brain cerebral (holistic thinkers)
Kolb's Learning Style Inventory	This classifies learners as having a preference for (a) concrete experience or abstract conceptualisation, or (b) active experimentation or reflective observation
Honey and Mumford's Classification	Developed from Kolb's inventory and learning cycle this model has four components – activists; reflectors; pragmatists; theorists

However, a major criticism of each of these approaches is that they are all founded upon purely cognitive psychological models. Other writers, though, have acknowledged the importance of different influences and models of learning in the social and emotional realms.

For example, when delineating the key differences between learning orientations and learning styles, Woods and Cortada (2002) show how the first set of propositions depends on a complex blend of interrelated influences, whereas in the second set there is dependence on the cognitivist school alone (see Table 27).

Table 27 *Orientations and styles*

Learning orientations	Learning styles
Considers how individuals learn differently, using a comprehensive set of influences and sources for individual learning differences, including affective, connotative, social and cognitive factors	Considers how individuals learn differently by focusing primarily on cognitive ability, preferences, and differences in how learners prefer to think or process information
Considers emotions and intentions as a dominant influence on learning (ie key influences that may develop, guide, or manage how we use cognitive ability)	Considers cognitive ability and preferences as the dominant influence on learning
Considers how learners generally relate and respond to key internal and external influences in their environment	Considers how learners use cognitive ability to process content, often regardless of the environment
Provides measures to assess online learning ability	Estimates cognitive preferences

These writers then describe (see Table 28) the implications of their analysis for mass customised learning environments by classifying the learning orientations of learners as being either transforming, performing or conforming.

Table 28 *Orientations and environments*

Learning orientations	Mass customised environments
Transforming learners	For transforming learners, design environments that are sophisticated, discovery-oriented, mentoring environments. They prefer loosely structured flexible environments that promote challenging goals; discovery, strategies, problem-solving and self-managed learning orientations. These learners want to be assertive, challenged by complex problem-solving, and able to control, self-manage, and self-monitor learning and progress to attain higher standards and long-term goals.
Performing learners	For performing learners, design semi-structured, interactive (hands-on) environments that stimulate personal values, encourage teamwork, and provide details, tasks, processes and project completion. These learners prefer task-oriented, energising and competitive environments. These environments should use coaching, practice and feedback to encourage self-motivation, problem-solving, self-monitoring and task-sequencing – while minimising the need for exploration, extra effort, and difficult standards.
Conforming learners	For conforming learners, design safe, low-learner controlled, structured environments that help learners achieve comfortable, low-risk learning goals in a linear fashion. These learners prefer environments that are simple, scaffolded, non-risk environments that use explicit, careful guidance that helps individuals learn comfortably in an easy, step-wise fashion.

From an examination of this typology, we can see that there are certain similarities here with the association of cognitive approaches and learning styles by Sadler-Smith (1996):

The two dimensions of cognitive style affect learning in two separate ways.

1. The verbal–imagery dimension has been shown to interact with the mode of presentation of information to affect learning performance. Verbalisers may be expected to benefit from the presentation of information in a textural form; imagers on the other hand may be expected to benefit from the presentation of information in a pictorial or diagrammatic form. Hence, the verbal – imagery dimension of cognitive style may be used to determine the most appropriate mode of presentation of information for a given individual ie the mode of presentation may be matched to the verbal–imagery dimension of cognitive style.
2. The wholist–analytical dimension has been shown to interact with the structure of presentation of information in affecting learning performance. Each aspect of this dimension has its strengths and weaknesses (analytics have difficulty 'seeing the wood for the trees'; wholists have difficulty 'seeing the trees for the wood'. In order to compensate for the weaknesses of each, some have suggested that:
   - Wholists may benefit from information in advance of learning which shows the structure of a topic to be learned in terms of its component parts. The advance information provides a structural, analytical map for the wholist.
   - Analytics, on the other hand may benefit from information in advance of learning that gives an overview of the whole topic. In this case the advance information serves as a map of the terrain in which the whole can be seen and provides the holistic approach that the analytical finds difficult.

Sadler-Smith (1996) also raises similar considerations about learning styles:

1. Should learners be exposed solely to the methods they express preferences for, as opposed to the methods which they learn most effectively from, but may not necessarily prefer? For example, learners on management or professional development programmes may often express an aversion to making formal presentations to their peers, but recognise that the skills to be gained from such an exercise outweigh their personal distaste for the exercise itself.
2. Should learners' preferences be matched with the teaching and learning methods used in anticipation of positive effects on motivation (or are there gains to be made through the tension of a mismatch of learner preferences and methods?

As facilitators, do we sometimes do our learners a disservice by avoiding potentially confrontational or conflictual situations in the learning event? Would there occasionally be greater learning through times when learners needed to be stretched out of their normal comfort zones of acceptance and tolerance?

Diversity in learning

The diversity of learners is of greater significance in group-learning situations. I feel that Harrison (2002) has highlighted a most important aspect of our practice when she describes the downward spiral of 'difference' in workplace learning (see Figure 24).

As professional HR practitioners, we need also to be very clear on the differences between 'equal opportunities' and 'managing diversity'. Personally, I like Wilson's (1999) explanation:

- ■ Equal opportunities
  - ■ concentration on discrimination/unfairness
  - ■ perceived as an issue for women and ethnic minorities and people with disabilities
  - ■ focuses on boosting proportion of minority groups in employment
  - ■ strategy has to be 'mainstreamed'
  - ■ emphasis on positive action rather than corporate vision

- ■ Managing diversity
  - ■ aims to ensure that all employees maximise their potential and contribution to the organisation
  - ■ concentrates on movements within an organisation, its culture and the meeting of business objectives
  - ■ concerns all staff and especially managers
  - ■ does not rely on positive action and provides a vision.

How we view others in the workplace will affect how we train them. How others treat them in the workplace will affect how they learn.

Establishing a learning climate

How can training practitioners establish an effective learning climate? Wilson (1999) shows the need for appropriate sequencing and pacing in the learning event:

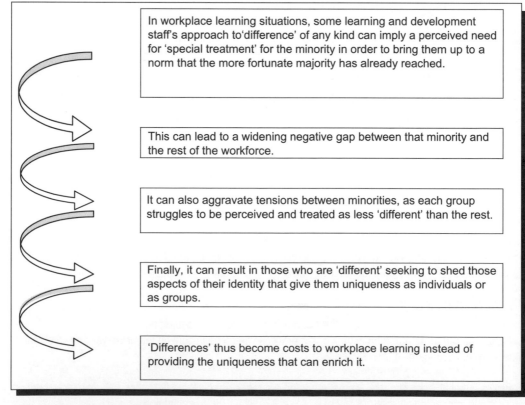

In workplace learning situations, some learning and development staff's approach to'difference' of any kind can imply a perceived need for 'special treatment' for the minority in order to bring them up to a norm that the more fortunate majority has already reached.

This can lead to a widening negative gap between that minority and the rest of the workforce.

It can also aggravate tensions between minorities, as each group struggles to be perceived and treated as less 'different' than the rest.

Finally, it can result in those who are 'different' seeking to shed those aspects of their identity that give them uniqueness as individuals or as groups.

'Differences' thus become costs to workplace learning instead of providing the uniqueness that can enrich it.

Figure 24 *Downward spiral of 'difference'*

- Set the scene and establish climate.
- Start from participant levels of skill, knowledge and attitudes.
- Introduce subsidiary essential skills and knowledge.
- Allow regular practice after input.
- Allow student-directed enquiry and study.
- Regularly review the key learning or principles.
- Introduce composite/complex skills and knowledge.
- Relate/apply the learning to other situations and focus on transfer.

We must at all times remember that we are dealing with adults. It is imperative to note that the differences in experience between children and adults have at least three consequences for learning (Wilson 1999):

- Adults have more to contribute to the learning of others; for most kinds of learning, they are themselves a rich resource for learning.
- Adults have a richer foundation of experience to which to relate new experiences (and new learnings tend to take on meanings as we are able to relate them to our past experience).
- Adults have acquired a larger number of fixed habits and patterns of thought, and therefore tend to be less open-minded.

Such a view is developed by Chawla and Renesch (1995), who believe that adult learning communities are places where:

- invisible fabric of relationships are tended to and cared for.
- vulnerability and diversity are welcome.
- curiosity reigns.
- experimentation is the norm.
- enquiry is practised with compassion.
- questions can go unresolved.

Therefore, the people within such learning communities:

- communicate with each other honestly and openly
- offer themselves and others honour and respect
- value and seek feedback
- are challenged to see themselves and others with new eyes
- encourage each other to sense, see, listen to, and speak of the whole system
- are free to be completely themselves, with no masks.

As a result, here is a clear agenda for the development of the training function in most organisations.

Now contrast the roots and effects of favourable and unfavourable training climates with the Lynton and Pareek (2000b) model depicted in Figure 25.

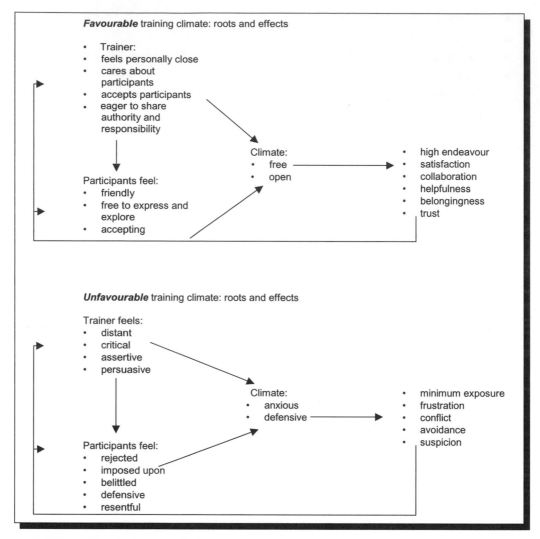

Figure 25 *Favourable and unfavourable climates*

What can we do to establish a helpful connection with our learners? Over 40 years ago, Carl Rogers (1961) explored the *transactional* nature of this adult, respectful, dignified learning relationship between the trainer and learner:

If I can create a relationship characterised on my part:
– by a genuineness and transparency, in which I am my real feeling
– by a warm acceptance of and prizing of the other person as a separate individual
– by a sensitive ability to see his world and himself as he sees them

Then the other individual in the relationship:
– will experience and understand aspects of himself which previously he has repressed
– will find himself becoming better integrated, more able to function effectively
– will become more similar to the person he would like to be
– will become more of a person, more unique and more self-expressive
– will be more understanding, more acceptant of others
– will be able to cope with the problems of life more adequately and more comfortably.

I agree wholeheartedly with Rogers when he further declares that:

> I believe that this statement holds true whether I am speaking of my relationship with a client, with a group of students or staff members, with my family or children. It seems to me that we have here a general hypothesis, which offers exciting possibilities for the development of creative, adaptive, autonomous persons.

This can be contrasted with the individual's readiness to learn and the organisational response. In Figure 26, we can see a gradual maturing and developing in the individual as they are allowed and encouraged to take greater responsibility for their own learning (McGoldrick *et al* 2002). From this we can detect certain essential elements of the learning organisation where the learner and the organisation interact and mature in a mutual, symbiotic relationship. So what can be done to overcome learning difficulties?

Individual learning ability	Organisational response
Continuation stage The individual is self-motivated; has achieved independence as a learner; has developed a questioning approach; demonstrates autonomy at a group and individual level	**Independency** Organisation offers linked career planning; shared responsibility for production and investment goals; broad commitment to work group autonomy
Formation stage Self-development; independent learning; role interdependence; interest in teamwork	**Transitional** The organisation offers job rotation and shadowing; wider industry training; opportunities for teamwork; experiential learning
Foundation stage The individual is ready to learn; shows interest in acquiring the skills to learn; involvement in learning activities	**Dependency** The organisation offers formal job training; remedial education; introduction to teamwork

Figure 26 *Taking responsibility for learning*

Tackling learning difficulties

It is most important to stress from the outset that we are here concentrating on *learning* difficulties, not on *learner* difficulties. Too often in the past, trainers have blamed learn*ers* when the learn*ing* has been difficult.

We must remember also that there are any number of ways of looking at intelligence. Wilson (1999) cites Howard Gardner, who proposed seven forms of intelligence:

1. linguistic
2. logical/mathematical/scientific
3. visual/spatial
4. musical
5. bodily/physical/kinaesthetic
6. interpersonal
7. intrapersonal.

Handy (1997) seems to support such a view when he posits that each one of us is good at something, and that there are multiple intelligences to be seen among our colleagues:

- factual intelligence
- analytical intelligence

- numerate intelligence
- linguistic intelligence
- spatial intelligence
- athletic intelligence
- intuitive intelligence
- emotional intelligence
- practical intelligence
- interpersonal intelligence
- musical intelligence.

This approach tends to be more inclusive, holistic and accepting than the unidemensional, exclusive, normative typology of intelligence developed early in the last century by, say, Eysenck. But more than this, the very means of attaining such intelligences are profoundly different.

This has great importance for training design and delivery. The *way* people learn mathematically is quite different from how those same people learn linguistically or musically. And attainment in the spatial realm is somewhat dissimilar to the methods of accomplishment in the athletic or practical realms.

Of relevance here to the context of difficulties in training design and delivery, we need also to consider with Wilson (1999) various barriers to learning:

- psychological issues
- practical issues
- institutional barriers
- financial concerns
- personal and social factors.

Although perhaps jaundiced in his observation, another commentator (Reynolds *et al* 2002) provides an analysis of some of the problems he has encountered with training instruction. Instead of merely dismissing such views, it would be salutary for us to consider them soberly:

The conventional idea of instruction, as exemplified by the 'tell and listen' classroom lecture, dates back to the medieval period when books were in short supply and learned men were given the task of reading extracts to their students. While nothing has replaced it yet, especially in terms of cost-efficiency, the model does suffer from some fundamental deficiencies:

- Information flows largely in one direction: insufficient attention is given to the contributions of participants or the formation of constructive dialogues.

- The experience can be largely theoretical: few opportunities exist for action and experimentation.

- Topics may be disconnected from actual challenges and tasks, even when described as work-related.

- Opportunities for social interaction are limited: relationships with peers are established but not cultivated.

- Courses can be blunt and unwieldy, often too large, too late, and of varying relevance to participants.

- Learning is a continuous process, whereas instruction is discrete.

- There is a tendency for instruction to react to gaps in capability rather than encourage self-development.

- Instruction can foster a dependency relationship in which the learner waits for instruction rather than takes charge of their own learning agenda. Effectively this presents a barrier to self-directed learning.

Nevertheless, Harrison (2002) gives evidence for her ideas of the causes of learning difficulties in the workplace, which typically arise in relation to:

- task performance, where they are connected with difficulty in carrying out one or more specific tasks related to the job
- task management, where they are connected with difficulty in general planning, problem-solving and decision-making in the job
- boundary management, where they are connected with difficulty in operating confidently and effectively in the role and job by reference to the social and political environment in which the job-holder must operate
- motivation, where they are connected typically with mistaken expectations about the job, or its level and content, or with unsatisfactory training, support and rewards, or with poor supervision and feedback on performance.

Such difficulties can be increased or reduced by:

- the learner; who needs the right level of competence, motivation, understanding, support and incentives in order to perform effectively
- the learner's workgroup, whose members will exercise a strong positive or negative influence on the attitudes, behaviour and performance of each new recruit
- the learner's manager, who should act as an effective role model, coach, stimulus and communicator related to performance
- the organisational context, which may product barriers to performance. For example, there may be a lack of any compelling vision and leadership; there may be an ineffective or inappropriate structure and culture; there may be poor management or a lack of motivating and supportive human resource policies and practice in the workplace.

Establishing effective relationships with learners

The six core assumptions of adult learning are:

1. Adults need to know why they need to learn something before learning it.
2. The self-concept of adults is heavily dependent on a move toward self-direction.
3. Prior experiences of the learner provide a rich resource for learning.
4. Adults typically become ready to learn when they experience a need to cope with a life situation or perform a task.
5. Adults' orientation to learning is life-centred, and they see education as a process of developing increased competency levels to achieve their full potential.
6. The motivation for adult learners is internal rather than external.

Taken together, we can synthesise such dignified statements into an undergirding view of how we treat learners.

PAUSE FOR THOUGHT

Writing value statements

A statement that I would feel happy to adopt might be along the lines of:

'I will adopt a learner-centred approach in all learning events. This will mean that I will behave towards learners with respect and dignity, listening to them and treating them as individuals who have specific needs and motivations.'

Write a similar statement that trainers in your organisation could adopt.

THE DELIVERY OF TRAINING – IN PRACTICE

Different trainer roles and styles

From the very outset of this section, we need to be honest about our own professional practice. So here are three self-completion questionnaires for you to complete.

First, how good are your facilitation skills? Have a go at this quiz from *Assessments A to Z* (2000 Jossey-Bass/Pfeiffer). Tick those statements that you agree with:

✓

__ One of the most important skills for facilitators is the ability to ask good questions.

__ Facilitators plan questions in advance of a meeting.

__ Facilitators know that specific questions obtain better results.

__ One responsibility of a facilitator is to gain involvement and participation from all group members.

__ A facilitator provides both structure and methods to move a group towards consensus.

__ To encourage discussion, facilitators are expected to arrange appropriate seating and other aspects of the physical environment for a meeting.

__ When beginning discussion on a topic, facilitators ask a question of the entire group, rather than direct it to any individual.

__ Facilitators avoid asking questions that can be answered with a response of 'yes' or 'no,' which may limit discussion.

__ Facilitators may say, 'That's a good point' or 'That's a good idea' to encourage more people to offer their comments.

__ Facilitators ask clarifying questions such as, 'Who can summarise the group's position?'

__ Facilitators carefully monitor their own body language to avoid appearing to disapprove of something that would discourage discussion.

The more answers you ticked, the more you understand about the role of facilitators! Now, see how well you do on this trainer's self-assessment questionnaire (Rae 2002b).

Consider each of the paired polarised statements and allocate 10 marks between the two, giving neither statement more than 9 marks, and with the total adding up to 10 marks. The higher marks will be given to the statement that you most closely (but don't necessarily completely) agree with. For example in statements (a)/(b), 7 marks may be allocated to (b) leaving 3 marks for allocation to (a). Place your marks alongside the relevant letters.

___ a. It is the trainer's sole responsibility to decide on and set the agenda for training.
___ b. The learners should decide what they learn.

___ c. It is the trainer's sole responsibility to decide how the learners will go about learning.
___ d. The learners should decide how they learn.

___ e. People learn best by doing and perceiving the consequences of their own actions.
___ f. People learn best by watching, copying and listening to experts.

___ g. Learners must be trusted to find the answers for themselves and encouraged to question perceived wisdom.
___ h. The trainer should always be an expert in their subject and know all the answers.

___ i. The trainer's status must always be higher than the learners' because trainers are experts in their subjects.
___ j. The learners needs must always take precedence because they are the important people in the learning process.

___ k. The trainer must take the lead and be an exceptional presenter and communicator.
___ l. The trainer should act as a resource and facilitator, providing the environment the learners need to succeed.

___ m. It is best that learners organise their own route to achieving their goals.
___ n. It is best that all learners do the same things at the same time so that the trainer can keep control of what is being learned.

___ o. It is impossible to match everything taught to everyone's needs, so it is best to aim training to the average level.
___ p. Learners should be allowed to work at their own pace which reflects their level of ability.

___ q. Learners should develop their own procedures and methods of working from scratch.
___ r. Experts should work out the best methods of working before training learners in the procedures etc they have developed.

___ s. Learners should be encouraged to experiment and take risks which can lead to failure as well as success.
___ t. Training programmes need a rigid and well-defined structure that has been tested to ensure consistency of approach and success.

___ u. People enjoy learning for its own sake.

___ v. People need to be taught or made to learn.

___ w. It is the trainer's responsibility to make decisions about people's abilities and competences and what further training they need.

___ x. Learners are the best judges of their own abilities and competences and are in the best position to decide on their training needs.

___ y. Learning can take place wherever the learner is, as people have the capacity to learn all the time.

___ z. Training can only take place where the trainer is, as people only learn when they are taught.

Now, transfer your score for each statement into the appropriate column below and obtain total scores for each of the two training styles.

<table>
<tr><td>Trainer-centred style (T)</td><td>Learner-centred style (L)</td></tr>
<tr><td>A __</td><td>B __</td></tr>
<tr><td>C __</td><td>D __</td></tr>
<tr><td>E __</td><td>F __</td></tr>
<tr><td>G __</td><td>H __</td></tr>
<tr><td>I __</td><td>J __</td></tr>
<tr><td>K __</td><td>L __</td></tr>
<tr><td>M __</td><td>N __</td></tr>
<tr><td>O __</td><td>P __</td></tr>
<tr><td>Q __</td><td>R __</td></tr>
<tr><td>S __</td><td>T __</td></tr>
<tr><td>U __</td><td>V __</td></tr>
<tr><td>W __</td><td>X __</td></tr>
<tr><td>Y __</td><td>Z __</td></tr>
<tr><td>Total ____</td><td>Total ____</td></tr>
</table>

Subtract the lower total from the higher and enter the result on the T–L continuum.

Trainer-centred   Learner-centred
130 120 110 100 90 80 70 60 50 40 30 20 10 **0** 10 20 30 40 50 60 70 80 90 100 110 120 130

Your position on the continuum suggests your tendency towards learner- or trainer-centred attitudes and style.

Thirdly, rate your skills by using the inventory of trainer skills that follows on page 123 (Rae 2002b). Place a tick in just one column against each of the 41 skills.

	No problem or not relevant	Satisfactory	Should improve	Must improve
1. Listening actively				
2. Expressing myself clearly				
3. Being brief and concise				
4. Taking up views expressed				
5. Using relevant humour				
6. Using real-life anecdotes				
7. Avoiding jargon				
8. Fitting my language to the learner				
9. Using my voice efficiently				
10. Helping learners understand the difficult points				
11. Not forcing my own views in discussion				
12. Asking open questions				
13. Answering questions effectively				
14. Using appropriate non-verbals and gestures				
15. Identifying the learners' learning preference styles				
16. Using relevant visual aids				
17. Using clear and readable visual aids				
18. Using clear, readable writing on posters				
19. Adding *all* comments by learners to posters				
20. Using videos when relevant				
21. Using videos effectively				
23. Using of other visual aids				
24. Being able to use range of techniques and methods				
25. Being aware of own behaviour				
27. Giving instructions effectively				
28. Being enthusiastic				
29. Coping with conflict within the group				
30. Coping with conflict between me and group				
31. Handling difficult participants				
32. Handling too-high-contributing participants				
33. Handling too-quiet participants				
34. Knowing how to 'mix' groups effectively				
36. Setting up activities effectively				
37. Taking feedback/report-back after activities				
38. Commenting appropriately after case-study interviews				
39. Being able to introduce spontaneous input				
40. Being able radically to modify programme during the event to satisfy the needs of the learners				
41. Other training activities not included in above (please state)				

PAUSE FOR THOUGHT

Using the information from these three questionnaires, reflect on your current professional practice.

What are your strengths and weaknesses?

Who could you discuss these findings with?

How will you change your own personal development plan?

Which trainer roles and styles could you adapt or adopt?

How can we select people for trainer roles? Phillips and Stone (2002) advocates using a number of criteria:

Selection criteria for the trainers included technical skills, exemplary work performance, and the judgement of the operations manager. In 1991, operations managers at the USA National Academy for Nuclear Training used a guide, which listed qualities to consider when selecting employees as a trainer or evaluator. These included the following:

- **recognition of responsibilities**

- **personal standards of performance and commitment to quality**

- **professionalism**

- **technical knowledge of the tasks to be evaluated**

- **maturity, judgement, integrity**

- **conservative approach toward nuclear safety**

- **industrial safety awareness**

- **communication and observation skills.**

More specifically, Darling and her colleagues (1999) found six significant organisational factors affecting the role of trainers in delivery:

- increase in outsourcing
- impact of structural changes on delivery
- emphasis on consultancy/advisory role
- emphasis on research
- increase in work-based learning approaches
- diversified types and categories of learners.

How could these criteria be utilised both in your organisation and for your own personal continuous professional development?

Diversity in learning

In order to clarify some of the issues of diversity as they affect trainers and developers, I want to present a scenario developed a number of years ago by one of the world's leading exponents in the field, Jane Elliott (http://www.horizonmag.com/4/jane-elliott.asp):

> 'I am better than you. I am smarter; I am more attractive. You are stupid and lazy. Your children are dirty and rude. I and my kind will always be superior to you and yours. I am White.'

Jane Elliott says that, regardless of whether I voice these thoughts or even acknowledge thinking them, as a white person, I have been raised with a myth of white superiority. Elliott, a retired school teacher, originated the 'blue eyes brown eyes' exercise in the 1960s to demonstrate to her fourth-grade students how harmful the myth of white superiority is and what, as a result of this myth, it meant to be black in America.

In 1968, Jane Elliott was an elementary-school teacher in her all-white hometown of Riceville, Iowa. Dr Martin Luther King Jr had been a 'hero of the month' in Elliott's fourth-grade class, because Elliott believed that 'what he was doing was right for all of us, not just for Blacks.' When King was shot, her students wanted to know why their 'hero' had been killed. Elliott took the opportunity to discuss race with her students.

She queried the kids on what they knew about black people (none having ever met a black person). Their responses were bile-laden: 'They're dirty,' 'They stink,' 'They don't smell good,' 'They riot, they steal,' 'You can't trust them, my dad says they better not try to move in next door to us.'

Elliott decided to administer a racial reality check. She divided the class into two groups: the brown eyes and the blue eyes. Anyone not fitting these categories, such as those with green or hazel eyes, was an outsider, not actively participating in the exercise. Elliott told her children that brown-eyed people were superior to blue-eyed, due to the amount of the colour-causing-chemical, melanin, in their blood.

She said that blue-eyed people were stupid and lazy and not to be trusted. To ensure that the eye-colour differentiation could be made quickly, Elliott passed out strips of cloth that fastened at the neck as collars. The brown eyes gleefully affixed the cloth-made shackles on their blue-eyed counterparts.

Elliott withdrew her blue-eyed students' basic classroom rights, such as drinking directly from the water fountain or taking a second helping at lunch. Brown-eyed kids, on the other hand, received preferential treatment. In addition to being permitted to boss around the blues, the browns were given an extended recess.

Elliott recalls, 'It was just horrifying how quickly they became what I told them they were.' Within 30 minutes, a blue-eyed girl named Carol had regressed from a 'brilliant, self-confident carefree, excited little girl to a frightened, timid, uncertain little almost-person.'

On the flip side, the brown-eyed children excelled under their newfound superiority. Elliott had seven students with dyslexia in her class that year and four of them had brown eyes. On the day that the browns were 'on top', those four brown-eyed boys with dyslexia read words that Elliott 'knew they couldn't read' and spelled words that she 'knew they couldn't spell'.

Seeing her brown-eyed students act like 'arrogant, ugly, domineering, overbearing White Americans' with no instructions to do so proved to Elliott that racism is learned. Prior to that day in 1968, her students had expressed neither positive nor negative thoughts about each other based on eye colour. Yes, Elliott taught them that it was all right to judge one another based on eye colour. But she did not teach them how to oppress. 'They already knew how to be racist because every one of them knew without my telling them how to treat those who were on the bottom,' says Elliott . . .

Despite the milestones achieved through years of struggle for racial equality, people of colour are still discriminated against because they are people of colour.

If you think that a single black person has gone through life without ever being judged negatively because of the colour of his or her skin, you are wrong. No, not all of us whites are racist. But yes, all blacks are subjected to racism . . .

Elliott has a 'laundry list' of things white people can, and *should*, be doing to end racism. She says that first, like so many alcoholics, you need to admit you have the problem and take ownership of it. Then educate yourself about the problem. Thirdly, realise that you weren't born racist; you learned to be this way and, you can unlearn it. Lastly, you must follow her marching orders to actively protest racism in all its forms, subtle or blatant. You must take a risk and stop racism.

It is not a black problem, says Elliott: Racism is a 'White attitudinal problem.' For too many years, we have been blaming racism on people of colour, says Elliott. We have thought, 'If you people would just get White we'd all be all right.' Wrong. If *we* people would just accept that, as Elliott says, 'we are all different and have the right to be so,' it will all be all right.

PAUSE FOR THOUGHT

Show this scenario by Jane Elliott to three people in your organisation and discuss with them the implications for training and learning.

Investigating multicultural training practices Lee and Chon (2000) found that:

. . . heterogeneous teams perform better than homogeneous ones in the long run because of the learning experiences associated with cultural differences.

They continued with respect to the hospitality industry:

The lack of understanding of different cultures may lead to ineffective management techniques in directing, motivating and rewarding culturally diverse employees. On the other hand, diversity enriches a hospitality organisation by adding new cultures, ideas and alternative methods for solving problems.

It is therefore imperative that all training professionals examine closely not only their style and practice but also their underlying attitudes. Let's strive towards a situation where we actually treat all people – learners, stakeholders, and colleagues – with dignity, rapport and respect. In part, at least, this can be accomplished by establishing a healthy and effective learning climate. How can this be done?

Establishing a learning climate

Here is an instance from Beech *et al* (2000) of how the creation of an appropriate and relevant learning climate was fundamental not only to the satisfactory achievement of the learning objectives in the programme, but also to its bottom-line impact in the organisation:

'Transfusion' was a major training event comprising a series of three-day workshops, held during 1997, which utilised dramatic techniques in order to break the old norms of rule-following and cautious task-orientation. The aim was that individuals should develop a more holistic view, organisational commitment and entrepreneurial ethos ... Transfusion represented a major departure from traditional systematic training. Needs were not formally analysed and delivery was high on emotion and low on rational engagement ...

There are two alternative models for changing cultures through training – either starting with behaviour and expecting that new behaviour will impact on values and attitudes, or starting with training for new values and attitudes and expecting behaviour to change subsequently. Transfusion was working in both directions at once, and more. It engaged people emotionally and psychologically as well as behaviourally and attitudinally. In doing so it adopted what can be termed an 'evangelical' approach ...

Transfusion was an innovation in training and development for Tamara plc, in that it incorporated drama, excitement and norm-breaking activities. The aim, for the organisation, was to access the 'whole person' and to involve staff at all levels in the process of changing the culture ...

While there are theoretical and ethical objections to this type of employee development, its impacts cannot be ruled out, or ignored, at a pragmatic level. Eighteen months after the initial study there has been significant positive change and development in the organisation, as reported by focus groups of employees at all levels, and Transfusion is seen to have played a part in this. Participants themselves reported enthusiasm, greater mutual understanding and a feeling of integration ...

Transfusion represents a displacement of traditional, systematic training, but it must be questioned as to whether it can be a total displacement, as it does not focus on the outcomes of skill, competency or knowledge development. It can, however, be seen as strategic at two levels of analysis. First, and overtly, the organisation strategy makers are seeking to create a workforce who understand, commit to, and know their part in, strategic goals. Second, and perhaps unconsciously, there is an organisational desire to have an integrated workforce in both rational and emotional senses.

Such specific, noble aims for an acceptable learning climate as these can also be seen in the Canadian International Development Agency (CIDA) cross-cultural training programme's focus on achieving seven skills:

1. Communicate respect.
2. Be non-judgemental.
3. Personalise knowledge and perceptions.
4. Display empathy.
5. Practise role flexibility.
6. Demonstrate reciprocal concern.
7. Tolerate ambiguity.

Would I be right in assuming that such dignified aims reflect how we would like to be treated? These also appear to be echoed in the USA, where the Peace Corps training has the following objectives (Wilson 1999):

■ Prepare the volunteer to accept and be tolerant of values, beliefs, attitudes, standards, behaviours, and a style of life that might be quite different from one's own.

■ Provide the skills to communicate this acceptance to another person.

■ Provide the sensitivity and understanding necessary to effectively interact with a person from another culture.

- Teach appropriate behaviour responses in situations where characteristics of the other culture prevail.

- Prepare the volunteer to understand, anticipate, and cope effectively with the possible reactions to him or her as a stranger or as a stereotype of his or her own culture.

- Provide an understanding of one's own culture and problems cultural bias might create.

- Provide the adaptive skills to cope with one's own emotional reactions in the new and strange situation and to satisfy one's own culturally-conditioned behaviour.

- Provide the skills needed for continued learning and adjustment in the other culture.

- Help develop an orientation towards the sojourn in the other culture as a potentially interesting, enjoyable, and broadening experience.

In concrete terms, and as far as learning is concerned, researchers have found that owners/managers generally reflected the idea that courses/programmes need to be pitched at a level that they can understand, and with which they can identify. They would listen to someone who knows what they are talking about, with regard to running a small business, rather than someone from a large company or a consultant preaching a message that is over their heads (O'Dwyer and Ryan 2000).

Moreover, Lawless *et al* (2000) found similar outcomes in their research in Limerick. It showed that the preference of small and medium-sized enterprises was for one-to-one training, but resource constraints meant that this was not a viable option. Instead, managers chose the second preference of workshops, with a structure reflecting their views. The pedagogical aspects that were therefore adopted in this approach, involved collaborative learning with some mentoring:

The workshops are to be held on a weekly basis in the evening, covering more popular topics identified by the SMEs. There will also be an element of one-to-one tuition within the workshops. The format will include the following:

- **Group discussions. This will be used to aid reflection and application to the managers' own environment, etc, as well as providing support and motivation. For reflective learning to take place in a face-to-face situation, it is necessary to build in time for reflection and group discussion.**

- **Group activities. These will apply theory to real life situations in order to promote active and collaborative learning.**

- **Tutor support. Tutors will be at the workshops to facilitate and guide learning, as well as providing some one-to-one tuition.**

- **Synchronous tuition. There will be a need for some subjects to have a 'mini lecture' form of tuition, but this will be embedded by group discussions.**

Tackling learning difficulties

Let's now take a long, cold look at the following example from Phillips (2002). A typical on-the-job training event in a manufacturing setting begins with the trainer:

- Trainer shows the trainee the machinery.
- Trainer describes what the machine does.
- Trainer shows the trainee how to turn the machine on.
- Trainer says, 'I'll be working at another machine. Call me if there are any problems.'

This leads to the following results:

- Trainee tries the steps.
- Trainee feels awkward about asking questions because it's human nature not to admit failure.
- Trainee has performance problems and trainer spends time retraining the trainee.
- Trainer feels that the trainee should have 'gotten it the first time'.
- HR wonders why so much effort is being spent retraining the individual.
- The production manager is displeased with the overall performance drop in the line.
- The trainee feels added pressure to perform because it seems to be his or her fault.
- The trainee finally learns the job through trial and error, becomes experienced and trains a new employee in the same manner.

If we are brutally honest with ourselves, how true has that been of much of the training with which we have been associated? So, what can we do to prevent or pre-empt such dreadful delivery problems?

Establishing effective relationships with learners

Here is an interesting example from Lynton and Pareek (2000b) of how important it is to establish effective relationships with learners:

> Once, a tradition-laden East Asian participant came up after a session to ask one of us a personal question: 'Professor,' [sic!] he ventured, 'is trial and error your method of teaching?'
> Trainer: 'You are very uncomfortable with what has been going on … [pause] If you thought I had planned this chaos, you would be able to accept it.'
> Participant: 'Yes.'
> Trainer: 'Maybe you are not quite sure just now whether I, your professor, know what I am doing?'
> The man looked as if his heart had missed a beat, then he turned and literally bolted from the room. For two days, he did not speak in a session. After that, he participated more than ever before, and became more personally free and involved.

One of the most important elements to consider when establishing relationships with a group of learners is the physical environment or ergonomics of the training situation. At one level, obvious barriers like sitting on opposite sides of a desk during a mentoring session hardly need to be mentioned. At another level, I personally always arrive in plenty of time before a group of learners so that I can rearrange the training room furniture myself. Desks and chairs laid out in neat rows will add nothing to the situation; in fact, it could be argued that such a configuration will actually detract from the potential amount of learning gain. Despite this, most universities still use, on occasion, large lecture theatres where one 'expert' (Master) will hold forth in front of 200–300 students (Bachelors). This may be a model of education acceptable to a few traditional pedagogues and accountants, but I suggest it has little or nothing to do with a learner-centred approach to training and development.

Instead, depending on the space available and the numbers of learners, I prefer to arrange the furniture either in a hollow 'U' formation or in 'islands' of desks where four or six are grouped together. Consequently, the learners can actually face each other; this will support the (unstated) assumption that I want them to learn from each other.

The use of names is another important consideration. Nameplates always help, and I strive early in a course or a session to use their names frequently. Learners are, in the end, individuals – albeit as part of a group – and they not only like to be treated as people but they will also learn more if that happens. Residential programmes are ideal for getting to know learners more; there are informal opportunities to become acquainted with them on a one-to-one basis. You can more easily enter into a conversation about the person's home, family, hobbies or holidays. By taking an interest in *them* as a unique human being, rather than merely as a representative of the marketing department or yet another new graduate, they will feel respected and treated with dignity. Following from that, they will accept as being true your assertion that you actually want them to participate and contribute in the sessions, and that you think that what they have to offer to the group is important.

The use of power in training is probably one of the taboo areas that is very rarely discussed in polite training circles. Once the training room door is closed, the trainer is all-powerful, and can ask the group to do almost anything – and they will duly oblige! Unfortunately, some trainers have abused such power, and I'm sure we all know apocryphal stories of awful things being undertaken in the name of training. I prefer instead to focus on the huge amount of good that can come from this powerful relationship being channelled towards the gain in learning. When I am often asked why I am a trainer, or what I get out of it, I usually reply to the effect that I have been very privileged to be part of changing many people's lives, for ever! That's good enough for me.

Therefore, I try to hold in mind an adaptation of just part of the model of personal relationships that are based on the **PARENT–ADULT–CHILD** notion of transactional analysis (see Figure 27). Put very simply, and just to restrict it to the learning situation for our purposes, the model proposes that there can be a wide variety of relationships between the trainer and participant in workplace learning events.

Let's have a look at just one typical application. If the learner feels that the trainer is adopting a patronising, supercilious, arrogant approach and undermining the integrity of the learner by appearing all-knowing and condescending, then the participant could easily become angry, antagonistic or openly aggressive. This can so quickly descend into what is known as an 'attack–defend' spiral, where nobody wins (Figure 28).

Consequently, the trainer needs to take responsibility by being the first to change. They need to take the initiative by adopting a much more 'adult' style of approach, by listening more, by treating the learner as an equal, and by respecting their contributions. It is very difficult under those circumstances for the learner to remain in 'parent' mode, and usually they follow by taking a more 'adult' approach themselves (Figure 29).

When the trainer and participant are responding as 'adults', the learning gain will be greatly enhanced.

PAUSE FOR THOUGHT

Reflect on a situation in a learning event with which you felt uncomfortable. Why was that? Using the simple adaptation of part of the transactional analysis model shown in Figure 27, try to assess the causes of the problem, and how they could have been overcome. If you were personally involved in the situation, how could you prevent it in the future?

SUMMARY

We have seen that the effectiveness of training delivery depends on many things apart from, and in addition to, the mere mechanics of presentation skills. Being able to relate to a wide range of learners is paramount. Delivery and diversity are interlinked. Consequently, HRD practitioners are required to be both flexible and adaptable. Above all, trainers must be learner-centred in order to focus squarely on the needs of each individual.

The effective planning and delivery of training will in the end be seen in performance development and bottom-line improvement.

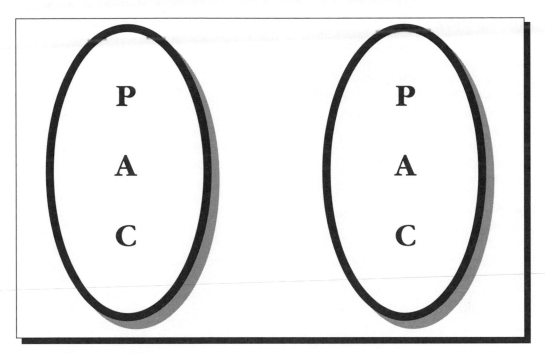

Figure 27 *Parent – Adult – Child*

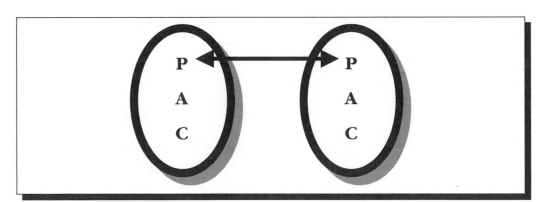

Figure 28 *Attack / Defend*

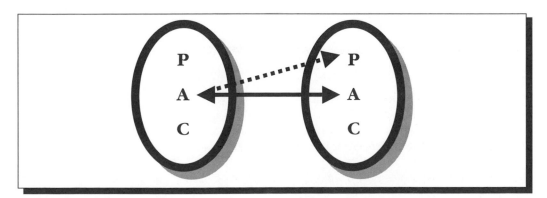

Figure 29 *A more adult approach*

QUESTIONS

1. What are the major causes of difficulties in learning events?
2. Discuss, with reference to examples from your own organisation, situations in which there has been an abuse of power in learning events.
3. What can trainers do to improve access to training and development?

Incorporating new technology into the training process

> Before you become too entranced with gorgeous gadgets and mesmerizing video displays, let me remind you that information is not knowledge, knowledge is not wisdom, and wisdom is not foresight. Each grows out of the other, and we need them all.
>
> Arthur C. Clarke

LEARNING OUTCOMES

- Apply technology to training plans, designs and delivery.
- Describe electronically based assessment of training and trainees.

CHAPTER OUTLINE

- How to incorporate new technology in the design of training events.
- The uses of electronically delivered methods and media in the delivery and assessment of training and learning.

INTRODUCTION

Isn't it depressing that by the time you get your new computer home from the shop it is already out of date! And by the time you read this chapter, it will be out of date too! The use of technology to enhance the training and learning experience is changing at a phenomenal rate. The chapter aims to explore the benefits of a blended approach to learning.

INCORPORATING NEW TECHNOLOGY INTO THE TRAINING PROCESS – IN THEORY

Applying technology to training

Cheetham and Chivers (2001) assert that there has been a shift in traditional views on the psychology of e-learning:

> Earlier, it was stated that the design of computer-based training had been influenced by behaviourist principles. That was certainly true until quite recently. However, shifts in psychological orthodoxy, supported by advances in technology, have led to the use of more cognitive design approaches.
>
> Cognitive principles are now being applied to screen design, for example through the use of icons instead of text. More flexible architectures, such as Hypertext and Windows, also enable less structured approaches, allowing trainees to explore sources of knowledge and information in their own individual way, with help and tutorial facilities available if and when required, and tests offered to trainees as an option, rather than being automatically administered to them.

This approach has led to a number of e-learning benefits, both for the organisation and for the learner (Harrison 2002):

- There will be an increasing alignment of e-learning and e-commerce.
- Effective e-learning is fast learning.
- E-learning can be highly efficient.
- E-based technology connects to the knowledge process.
- Online training networks can help the organisation to build intellectual capital.
- Computer-based assessment (CBA) allows instant scoring and feedback of results to learners.

Such a view would appear to be supported by Reynolds *et al* (2002) who catalogue an impressive array of advantages for any organisation adopting e-learning as part of its overall HRD strategy:

- easy access to and interrogation of high volumes of diverse-learning resources, including texts, pictures, library materials, learning tools and other aids to learning selected by the instructor
- ease of access to other materials from other sources, including non-educational sources
- ease of access to experts, inside and external to the institution
- interaction in various modes: teacher–student, student–student, and student–learning materials
- interaction in various time dimensions: in real time (synchronous) or over a period (asynchronous)
- access to a range of personal support: by e-mail with tutor and mentors, or through peer group discussions
- ease of navigation to sources and persons within and outside the training course or materials
- logging or tracking of activities for personal records, sharing or assessment
- multiple levels of engagement to different depths of understanding, different volumes of data, difficulty of learning activities, according to individual capacity or interest
- feedback loops, either from teachers, peers or others, or from within the materials themselves through progress checking, quizzes and online assessment
- linkages to other media, such as sound, video and TV
- ease of access to simulations of dangerous or complex activities for learning purposes
- choice of learning styles within the same package according to the needs of the learner
- global connectivity and collaboration opportunities
- flexibility of access from different locations.

However, it is important for the training practitioner to recognise that there are eight critical distinctions between traditional approaches to training and innovative aspects of e-learning (Woods and Cortada 2002). These are presented in Table 29.

Training professionals need to work hard to counter such discrepancies in their efforts to embrace all the benefits of blended learning. Before doing so, however, they need carefully to distinguish between various aspects of different types of e-learning, which are often confused (Reynolds *et al* 2002), as shown in Table 30.

Table 29 *Training and e-learning*

	Training	E-learning
Delivery	Push – instructor determines agenda	Pull – student determines agenda
Responsiveness	Anticipatory – assumes knowledge of the problem	Reactionary – responds to problem at hand
Access	Linear – has defined progression of knowledge	Non-linear – allows direct access to knowledge in whatever sequence makes sense to the situation at hand
Symmetry	Asymmetric – training occurs as a separate activity	Symmetric – learning occurs as an integrated activity
Modality	Discrete – training takes place in dedicated chunks with defined stops and starts	Continuous – learning runs in parallel and never stops
Authority	Centralised – content is selected from a library of materials developed by the educators	Distributed – content comes from the interaction of the participants as well as the educators
Personalisation	Mass produced – content must satisfy the needs of many	Personalised – content is determined by the individual user's need to know in order to satisfy their needs
Adaptivity	Static – content and organisation/taxonomy remain in their original authored form without regard to environmental changes	Dynamic – content changes constantly through user input, experiences, new practices, business rules, and heuristics

Table 30 *Types of electronic learning*

Web-based learning	Supported online learning	Informal e-learning
Content-focused	Learner-focused	Group-focused
Delivery-driven	Activity-driven	Practice-driven
Individual learning	Small-group learning	Organisational learning
Minimal interaction with tutor	Significant interaction with tutor	Participants act as learners and tutors
No collaboration with other learners	Considerable interaction with other learners	Multi-way interactions among participants

Therefore, the components of e-learning could be defined as (Reynolds *et al* 2002):

- multi-way communication among learners, and between learners and experts
- hypertextual, rather than linear, presentation of material

- integrated access to resources both inside and outside the e-learning package
- multimedia forms of interaction and presentation of material.

These authors point out that information may be accessed and delivered online by using a variety of devices:

- lecture notes
- hypertext
- slides
- multimedia CD-ROMs
- World Wide Web
- conferencing
- newsgroups/communities of practice
- virtual reference rooms
- streaming audio and video
- question and answer assignments
- real-time study sessions and peer tutorials
- online 'office hours'
- e-mail
- FAQs
- file-sharing
- access to commercial databases.

However, Sadler-Smith *et al* (2000) urge caution against training professionals being swept up in the all-pervading tide of enthusiasm that often accompanies technology-based learning:

> Telematics, using the convergence between information and communications technologies (for example, video-conferencing), provides training that is both distributed and synchronous and permits interaction-at-a-distance. However, the method has yet to establish itself as a mainstream training technology, particularly in the small firm section.

Electronic assessment

One of the main drivers behind e-learning and electronic assessment has been the growth of knowledge workers in many economies (see Figure 30, Stewart and Tansley 2002). Consequently, an assessment of the contributions that knowledge workers make to their organisation's performance would appear to be increasingly important. Such an assessment needs to be integrated within the overall electronic production and distribution of training and learning media and materials. (see: Kworx.net)

Looking at many companies today, we can see these changes starting to take place (Wilson *et al* 2001). There has been a significant growth in interest in e-learning. Learning programmes are being tied into competency frameworks, and into performance measures. E-learning is growing rapidly as a delivery model, and trainers are becoming interested in using 'blended' or integrated learning programmes.

You can use the checklist shown in Table 31 on page 138–139 to avoid common mistakes and oversights associated with developing electronic assessments:

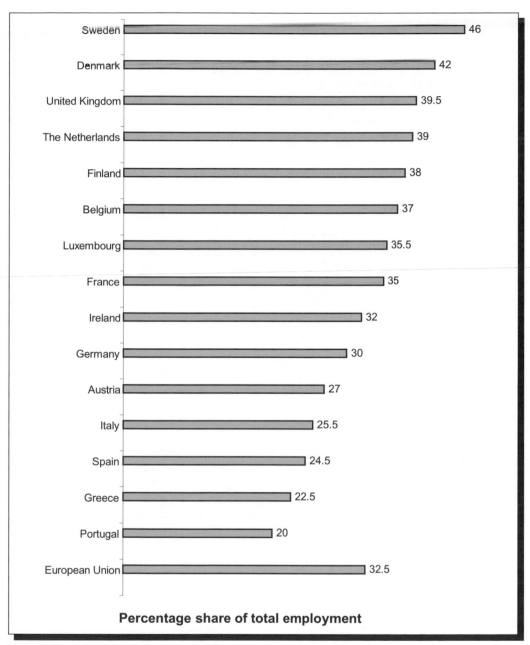

Percentage share of total employment

Figure 30 *Knowledge workers in European economies*

Table 31 *Electronic assessment checklist*

	YES	NO	COMMENTS
QUESTIONS			
Will the questions collect the required information?			
Is the question type appropriate?			
Are the questions clear?			
Have abbreviations been spelled out and jargon been eliminated?			
Do the questions cover a single topic?			
Are any scales comprehensive?			
Are the questions arranged logically?			
Are the questions free of bias?			
Is the question wording simple and unambiguous?			
Do closed questions use a yes/no format?			
Do the criteria specified for questions require ranking?			
Has negative wording been omitted?			
Is every question linked to the learning outcome?			
Are all the answers feasible in multi-choice questions?			
DIRECTIONS			
Are the directions clear and complete?			
Do the examples illustrate how the answer?			
Do directions explain how to complete and submit the assessment?			
Is contact information provided?			
FORMAT			
Are similar question types arranged together?			
Does the assessment start with easy questions?			
Has sufficient space been allowed for answers to open-ended questions?			
Are the questions and screens numbered?			
Do graphics intrude or add emphasis?			
Has colour been used appropriately?			
Do subheadings group questions on the same topic?			
Are pop-up screens minimised or even eliminated?			
Can the respondent complete the assessment later?			
Is confidentiality ensured?			
Does the respondent know when to expect feedback, and in what format?			

	RESPONSE	COMMENTS
ASSESSMENT CONTENT		
Mission		
What is the purpose?		
What is important to the organisation?		
What is important to the training and development function?		
What is important to the learner?		
What is the focus?		
What are the results or outcomes?		
Measures		
What measurement methods will be used?		
How will the measurement approach be balanced?		
What is important about the measurement approach for the organisation and the individual?		
How will data from the measures help the learner and the training function?		
Structure and scope		
What will be considered part of the assessment products and processes?		
How far will the assessment impact on the performance of the learner, the business unit and the organisation?		
Integration		
Which processes will the assessment complement?		
Roles and responsibilities		
Who is the owner of the assessment?		
What do other stakeholders expect?		
Resources		
What are the resource requirements for the assessment?		
What are the technical requirements for the assessment?		
How will resources and technical assistance be approved and provided?		
Action		
Who needs to take action?		
What actions need to be taken?		
What is the timeframe?		
What are the key deliverables?		

INCORPORATING NEW TECHNOLOGY INTO THE TRAINING PROCESS – IN PRACTICE

Applying technology to training

Unfortunately, e-learning may not be the cure-all panacea for which some had hoped:

Why Europe spurns e-learning

'Europe has problems with e-learning.'

That was the message from consultant Jane Massy in her opening remarks at OnLine-learning 2001 Europe Conference & Expo in London. For one thing, learning in Europe is more a part of the social fabric and less business-driven – in contrast to the United States, with its faster-and-cheaper corporate ethos. In Europe, the public sector dominates training and lifelong learning. That constitutes 'a powerful driving role', Massy told attendees. E-learning, she added, 'is not strictly a business proposition.'

Massy, from Cambridge, listed these further constraints on European e-learning:

E-learning so far hasn't been very good. That highlights a key difference between Europe and North America: Europeans want to know if it works before they try it, said Massy. In contrast, she said, the US tendency is: 'Great! Go for it! Just do it and see if it works.'

Any claim that an e-learning product complies with a widely accepted standard is 'a load of bananas,' Massy said. 'There is no existing standard that somebody can comply with at any level.' The closest thing to a standard, she added, is the work of IEEE LOM the Institute of Electrical and Electronics Engineers Inc.'s Learning Object Metadata working group (http://www.ltsc.ieee.org/doc/wg12/LOM-WD3.htm).

Europe doesn't expect learners to learn independently. Online mentoring and other support tactics that 'seem to be a relatively new discovery in North America', Massy said tartly, have long been European priorities.

Learning from stand-alone computers was ill suited to those priorities – until the emergence of the Web made community and support available.

However, providing support for e-learners will add to costs. 'I'm an e-moderator,' she said. 'It takes a huge amount of time.'

A shortage of good instructional designers limits growth of e-learning in Europe. Few learning professionals have the know-how 'to innovate using pedagogical technology,' said Massy. 'And most people currently selling e-learning are pretty green around the ears when it comes to pedagogical knowledge' (http://www.trainingvillage.gr).

Trainers aren't ready to make a business case for e-learning because trainers don't think in business terms. An Electronic Training Village survey of European trainers found that 25 per cent of respondents didn't even know their organisation's annual revenue. 'I haven't a clue,' one responded. Massy called that 'really quite shocking'.

Learning professionals tend to be 'very bad at managing time, very unfocused – they let the hours slip, they don't manage groups well,' said Massy. 'And if you don't have these skills in a Web environment, then it will cost vast amounts of money – and it will be ineffective.

The conclusions from the CIPD's own research (Sloman and Rolph 2003) are also not as positive as one might expect:

> The main conclusion of our study [of 10 organisations] is positive. All the organisations believe that e-learning has an important (and in some cases pivotal) role to play in their future business and learning strategies. No one is seeking to cut back on their commitment to e-learning, still less withdraw. Many can demonstrate considerable resource savings that have arisen from the introduction of e-learning. It should be apparent by now that e-learning has much to offer and there is potential for further progress. Our review has demonstrated examples of creative thinking and radical innovation among our study group of 11 organisations. The organisations vary tremendously in their strategy for learning, their pace of change, and their desire to be ahead of the field. Each has defined an approach based on a vision of where they want to be and how they can utilise e-learning to help meet their goals. Some want to be radically ahead, while some want to temper enthusiasm with the benefit of lessons gained from others. As was emphasised earlier, every organisation must progress along its own learning curve in what is essentially a change management process. Evidence shows that organisations are not taking a herd-like approach to the adoption of new technologies. Recognition of the potential is balanced by reflection on what is needed by the individual organisation, and what can be prioritised and achieved within the many business constraints that accompany sound business practice. Process innovation is happening. Variation in delivery methods and creative combining of alternatives is addressing the problems of wavering commitment, motivation and learning style on the part of learners. As with most new topics, time spent defining and agreeing terms and outcomes should ensure a common understanding. At present the term 'blended learning' means different things to different people but, as examples of good practice become more widely available, then clarity of purpose will follow.
>
> So what has emerged from our survey in terms of practical guidance to others? Although generalisation is difficult, a number of propositions that have emerged from the study are set out in the appendix. Not all organisations would agree with all these propositions, but they can be regarded as received wisdom at this stage in the development of e-learning. More generally, respondents see motivation as crucial for effective learning. Support can enhance this tremendously and again we have examples of good practice. There is a lot of scope here to develop the workplace as an appropriate and supportive environment for learning as well as for working. Line managers play a decisive role in fostering learning, and they in turn deserve support as they undertake a task for which they may get little acknowledgement. New initiatives and recognition for line managers in supporting learners might be the next step for many organisations.
>
> While there is no universal blueprint, organisations stand a much better chance of making e-learning work if they approach the change management process systematically. Hard questions must be asked and appropriate steps taken in each of the areas considered in the main body of this *Change Agenda*: strategic intent, introducing the system; blended learning, content, supporting the learner, and measurement and monitoring. It's difficult to see how anyone could make e-learning a success if any of these critical areas are neglected.
>
> One final conclusion is obvious, yet it seems to have taken an age to penetrate. E-learning is about learning and not about technology. A recognition of this fact is fundamental to the success of the e-learning strategies of our participant organisations.

The majority of Open University Business Studies management students have access to a computer. Those that did not were asked if they would buy one if the course required one – 48 per cent of the respondents said 'yes', leaving just over half preferring not to use a computer. This suggests that, for the present at least, there is a core of individuals who are averse to using ICT for learning.

Nevertheless, despite all such concerns, there is much positive anecdotal evidence, as this example from Philips and Jacobs (2002) shows:

The training solution

SubmitOrder chose its Learning Management System (LMS) based on the functionality of the software, the vendor's application of e-learning methodology in its creative services offering, and the vendor's reputation for follow-through after the implementation.

The system's non-disruptive Web-based training platform supports recurrent-learning instructional methodology by providing training in smaller 'chunks' to enhance the trainee's retention of the material while decreasing overall training time. *SubmitOrder*'s training director describes the LMS as 'a very educated learning-delivery system that uses triggers from quality monitoring systems and workforce management systems to enhance a manager's ability to deliver targeted training.'

Design process

SubmitOrder had performed a complete overhaul of its training materials during the year prior to the LMS implementation, which greatly simplified the transition from a facilitated training format to an e-delivery format. With these changes already in place, the next step was to apply e-learning instructional design principles to the existing courses. To co-own the project, the LMS vendor played a large part in the development of templates and initial courseware. Consultants visited *SubmitOrder* to research the call centre's 'pain points' then recommended courseware that would directly and quickly address these issues. This early effort on the part of the vendor helped internal champions of the project demonstrate the system's effectiveness.

Electronic assessment

Online instruction has two principal advantages over traditional classroom-based learning. It enables learners to spend more time on the task and it provides more opportunities for collaborative interaction, both of which, research has shown, are correlated with higher learner achievement. The point here is not that learners with online access to information will necessarily learn more than learners without access to online resources. Instead, network-based instructional resources provide learners with increased and enhanced *opportunities* for learning. The flexible *availability* of online course materials provides learners with an expanded range of opportunities for acquiring, exchanging, and reflecting on the significance of information.

However, as Mazoué (1999) propounds, mere exposure to online learning is insufficient:

What the critics and proponents of online instruction both agree on is that improved learning does not merely depend on exposing students to technology, but on their using technology in ways that enhance learning. Instructional designers need to keep in mind that technology promotes educational achievement only when it is meaningfully utilised. Technology is simply a tool that, when used to augment learning, crucially depends on its being used in ways that intelligently organise information. The goal of online course design, then, should be to create a learning environment that assists students in using information in ways that promote the instructional objectives of a given course.

Successful online instruction, then, depends on:

- an adequately equipped and supported network learning infrastructure
- the capabilities of existing hardware, software and personnel

- existing resources being evaluated
- the degree of institutional commitment to providing a revenue stream for continued equipment upgrades
- adequate user support services.

Any lack of IT literacy skills will undermine the effectiveness of online instruction, even if all the other pre-requisites, like equipment and support services, are present. The curriculum itself, therefore, may need fundamental revision if it fails to provide users with adequate training in core skills such as how to use word-processors, e-mail, Web browsers, graphics, databases and spreadsheets, and how to conduct computer-based information searches.

Organisations should therefore provide:

- a network learning infrastructure
- institutional support for IT-based instruction
- adequate access to equipment and support personnel
- curricular support and basic computer literacy skills.

Nonetheless, Mazoué (1999) goes further still in stressing the need for *fit*, or congruence, between the message and the medium:

> The adoption of an instructional strategy should be based on the cognitive capabilities and needs of the learners, as well as an understanding of the extent to which the course material lends itself to electronically mediated instruction. Different populations of learners and academic disciplines require different instructional approaches. Younger learners, for example, may benefit from drill-and-practice teaching methods, whereas older students may not. Adult learners may benefit more from instructional approaches that emphasise the development of higher-order critical thinking and meta-cognitive skills. And, although multimedia and game simulations may have a useful instructional role in some disciplines, they may not in others. The nature of the discipline under study and the course content itself will often determine the extent to which particular forms of instructional media can be adopted. One of the initial tasks, then, in designing an online course should be an analysis of the degree of fit between its content, its instructional aims, the anticipated level of student preparation, and applicable and available technological resources.

In sum, then, online-learning environments are effective when they are:

- informative
- accessible
- navigable
- interactive
- collaborative.

Therefore, in an effective online course, learners must be provided with appropriate electronic assessment. This will include resources for:

- *analysis* – active acquisition of information
- *integration* – schema modification

- *application* – understanding and extending conceptual relationships
- *collaboration* – information-sharing and relevance-testing
- *self-assessment* – monitoring, measuring, and tracking successful performance.

Although there is still a large investment needed in the underlying infrastructure, such as organisational intranets, increasing network bandwidth, and global systems, there has been significant activity around learning management systems (LMSs) as a core component of the e-learning infrastructure to manage and provide access to learning. There has, in addition, been an explosion on the supply side of the industry. Virtually every training company seems to have its own e-learning story, even if it is still limited in terms of its real e-learning experience and products. The e-learning marketplace is starting to mature, and companies are growing organically. We are starting to see a number of significant drivers for change in training and learning.

These will in turn facilitate the introduction of e-learning and its assessment:

- a shift in responsibility for learning from the organisation to the individual
- a restructuring of learning delivery away from courses to developmental learning programmes, learning on demand, and learning communities
- the development of centralised mechanisms for providing access to, and management of, learning
- a restructuring of learning delivery away from classroom-only models to integrated/blended learning models
- a rapid growth in the use of e-learning delivery components
- an increased use of work-based assessment and developmental objectives managed and facilitated remotely using technology-based mechanisms.

The shift has started to take place. It is hard to see how it cannot but transform the shape of organisational learning and development for ever. There are a number of important features to consider when exploring the possibilities of such virtual learning environments (VLEs).

- They are created when distance, information and telecommunication technologies are used to provide educational services that transcend barriers of time and place associated with traditional lecture-type teaching. Technologies unite the learner and the teacher, carry course content and information and provide the opportunity for two-way interaction.
- They are supported by a virtual learning system which is composed of two co-dependent infrastructures: a services support network (soft infrastructures which include educational products, instruction, and learner services) and an electronic network linking learners and educators with services (hard infrastructures which include sending, receiving and carrier technologies.)
- They serve individuals and groups, facilitate synchronous (same time) and asynchronous (different time) learning, and provide educational services that can be accessed from homes, institutions, communities and workplaces.
- They provide opportunities for learners to increase their participation in the management of the e-learning process, often creating changes in the relationship between teachers and learners.
- They challenge educational organisations and bureaucracies to modify or remove formal and informal restrictions that have traditionally limited learner access and institutional responsiveness eg transferability, geographic and programmatic jurisdictions, attendance and residency requirements.

It is salutary to remember, however that e-learning has yet to fulfil the dreams with which it has tantalisingly excited so many training designers. For example, look at this press release from ICUS (http://www.icus.net/media/PDF/survey_press_release.pdf):

E-learning fails to deliver

According to a survey by the e-learning firm ICUS, online learning is failing to deliver the promised benefits.

Almost half of the 275 HR professionals who responded to the survey claim that online learning has not been a success in their company.

A third cited poor content as a major problem, while a quarter felt that there is a high drop-out rate for e-learning because it does not engage staff and leaves the learners feeling isolated.

A third of those questioned believe that e-learning must include discussion forums and interaction to motivate staff to continue with the-learning.

Surprisingly, one in three said that they adopted e-learning as a way to cut HR costs!

Electronic Assessment

And so we come to the crucial area of assessment by using electronic media, known as computer-assisted assessment (CAA). From the training perspective, perhaps the question is: do we want human markers to become more machine-like, or computers to become more human? Alternatively, can we use our analysis of the strengths and weakness of each to help us to define an improved middle ground of marking reliability and efficiency?

The benefits of computer-based assessment, both for staff and students, are now well documented (see examples that follow, from http://www.lboro.ac.uk/service/ltd/flicaa/conferences.html). They include rapid formative feedback to students, reduced marking load for staff and a closer match between the assessment and learning environments. However, it has been shown that issues relating to student performance should be carefully considered whenever CAA is introduced.

Using computers to mark essays

C-rater[TM] *(concept-rater)*

An additional area of inquiry is the feasibility of automating the scoring of short answer content-based questions such as those that appear in a textbook's chapter review section. To date, we have developed an automated scoring prototype, *c-rater*[TM], using natural language processing technology, and evaluated its effectiveness at producing 'credit/no credit' ratings. Results of an initial, small-scale study with a university virtual learning program were encouraging: c-rater[TM] achieved over 80 percent agreement with the score assigned by an instructor. This research has the potential to evolve into an automated scoring application that would be appropriate for evaluating user-constructed responses in online instruction and assessment applications.

C-rater[TM] is related to e-rater in that it uses many of the same natural language-processing tools and techniques, but the two differ in some important ways.

Holistic scoring versus content scoring: E-rater assigns a holistic score. That is, it assigns a score for writing skills rather than for specific content. There is no correct answer in a holistic scoring rubric, only a description of how to identify good writing. Concept-rater needs to score a response as being either correct or incorrect and to do this, it must identify whether a response contains specific information in the form of some particular concepts. If the response expresses these concepts it is correct, and if it does not, it is incorrect, without regard to writing skills.

Rhetorical structure versus predicate-argument structure: E-rater identifies, and gives a grade based, in part, on the rhetorical structure of an essay. Rhetorical structure shapes and organizes the main points of the essay. C-rater™, on the other hand, needs to identify specific content. In order to do this, it generates a fine-grained analysis of the predicate-argument structure, or logical relations between the syntactic components (e.g. subject, verb, object) for each sentence in the response.

Training materials: E-rater is trained on a collection of 270 essays that have been manually scored by trained human raters. C-rater™ does not require a large collection of graded answers for training. Instead, it uses the single correct answer that is found in an instructor's guide or answer key. C-rater™, takes this approach because it is unrealistic to require extensive data collection for the purpose of grading relatively low stakes quizzes, especially given that there is often a set of short questions at the end of each chapter in a textbook.

The ability to use automatic essay scoring in operational scoring environments reduces the time and costs associated with having multiple human readers score essay responses. The agreement between two human readers, and between e-rater and one human reader has been noted to be comparable. E-rater scores are comparable to human reader scores, and automated scoring procedures can reduce the time and costs involved with manual essay scoring. Therefore, automated essay scoring would appear to be a favorable solution toward the introduction of more writing assessments on high-stakes standardized tests, and in a lower stakes environment ñ for classroom instruction. Moreover, the availability of these technologies may well provide incentive for making more assessment and instructional materials available online.

Peer assessment with computers

The Computerised Assessment and Plagiarism system provides an online means of students assessing the essays of their peers, and providing formative feedback. This system has been successfully used at levels one, two and three of an undergraduate programme in the field of computer studies at the University of Glamorgan. It has been used for continual assessment at level one, a combination of multiple choice/peer assessment at level two, and for self, peer and reflective self-assessment at level three. The use of this networked tool has produced major positive benefits both for the students and staff. Its acceptance has not only provided an efficient method for formative/summative assessment, but has also aided in developing the students' essay-writing skills. From a lecturer's point of view, those who in the past have been sceptical of the use of peer assessment and the more general use of objective testing have become much more receptive to the introduction of these innovative assessment methods.

http://www.lboro.ac.uk/service/ltd/flicaa/conferences.html

PAUSE FOR THOUGHT

Selecting Internet or other multimedia programmes

The instrument (Rae 2002b) shown below can be used when a decision has to be made about the method of training/learning to be offered to meet identified training needs. It suggests a number of questions that should be asked before a decision is made, particularly where Internet or other media-based training methods are being considered.

- What is the e-learning medium being considered?

- Has this package/medium been used previously? With what results?

- Why is this medium being considered in preference to any others?

- What is the target population of this programme?

- Are the programme's objectives stated? What are they and do they cover your needs?

- Does the e-learning environment have the necessary technological equipment and back-up services available?

- If this is not complete, what additional facilities need to be obtained? At what cost? Is this cost budgetable?

- Is the hardware capable of running the installed package in the most effective manner – from the hard drive or a CD-ROM?

- Where technological equipment is involved in following the programme, do the learners have the necessary skills in operating the equipment?

- Is all the information in the site correct, clear, intelligible and comprehensive? Describe any feature that is not.

- Is the language used in the programme appropriate to the materials and the target audience?

- To what extent is the programme interactive? Do you consider this to be sufficient?

- To what extent do the graphics or other site additions enhance the site or interfere with the learning?

- How easy is it to move about the site to areas required?

- Does the site have (a) internal links, (b) external links?

- How effective are these links?

- Is video included in the programme? If so, how efficient and effective are these videos?

- Does the programme give clear, sufficient/comprehensive, logical instructions on the use of the equipment
  - as equipment?
  - for the learning programme purposes?

- What is the minimum operating knowledge necessary?

- To what extent is a trainer's/supervisor's presence necessary?

- What is the cost of the programme?

- Is this within your budget?

SUMMARY

The exponential growth of e-learning has met, as yet, neither the needs nor the expectations of trainers and learners. More work is required before the full benefits of blended learning are fully exploited. According to Peter Honey (2003), e-learning is a welcome addition to a long and varied list of learning opportunities, but he makes four suggestions:

- Stop pushing text down a telephone line and calling it learning.
- Have more sympathy for the learner's situation.
- Stop behaving as if it is 'The Answer', a panacea.
- Show far more interest in learning as a process and in how to tailor information to meet the needs of learners with different learning styles.

QUESTIONS

1. 'I set about devising an online questionnaire to investigate the existence or otherwise of e-learning styles ... My initial survey may have failed to reveal e-learning styles as such, but I am confident that it shows up some important differences about how people approach online learning.' Discuss this statement by Peter Honey.
2. Make a case for the introduction of e-learning in an organisation with which you are familiar.
3. Evaluate the ways in which e-learning could contribute to the induction process.

The transfer of learning

> A certain awkwardness marks the use of borrowed thoughts; but as soon as we have learned what to do with them, they become our own.
>
> **Ralph Waldo Emerson**

LEARNING OUTCOMES

■ Describe the implications for trainers, learners and other stakeholders of positive and negative transfer of learning into and out of the training situation.

■ Work collaboratively to achieve or improve the positive transfer of learning.

CHAPTER OUTLINE

■ The theory and practice of transfer of learning; ways of tackling problems that can arise in the transfer of learning into and out of the training situation.

■ How to involve stakeholders in

   ■ gaining commitment to achieve effective transfer of learning into and out of the training situation, including the provision of support systems for learners

   ■ identifying major issues of concern related to learning transfer

   ■ reaching agreement on how these should be tackled in current and future training initiatives.

INTRODUCTION

For too long, training was left in the training room, and any benefit from it was lost on both the employee and the organisation. Fortunately, many training professionals are now seeing the need to contextualise the learning event squarely within the organisational strategy and the individual's performance development plan. The trainer must take responsibility for designing into the programme opportunities to enable the transfer of the working experience into the learning event, and vice versa. This chapter will help you accomplish such an aim.

THE TRANSFER OF LEARNING – IN THEORY
Transferring learning into and out of the training situation

Having learned to drive a particular model of car, we expect to be able to drive different models; although some of the controls may be alien to us, we can adjust ourselves to them without having to repeat the entire learning process. This is because of *positive learning transfer*, which is said to occur when learning that has already taken place on one task assists later learning on another. (Reid and Barrington 2000)

For too long training and learning have been separated from the working environment physically or at least emotionally. For learning to be effective it needs to be applied, and then for that to be demonstrated and proved in increased job performance, however that may be measured. Different organisations may have different goals or targets or performance measures. Some will have key results areas, and so on. But, for training to be effective, for learning to be increased, there needs to be a transfer of that learning, from the learning environment, from the learning event, back into the situation in which it is to be applied.

Hodges (2002) offers us some definitions of learning-transfer factors (see Table 32). However, Billett (2000) explores some of the difficulties facing the training professional working in an increasingly knowledge-related economy:

> Engagement in everyday activities in the workplace provides ongoing access to goal-directed activities and support that are instrumental in assisting individuals constructing or learning new work-related knowledge as well as the strengthening of that learning … However, the learning accessed through participation at work alone may not be sufficient for developing the requirements for expertise at work … As well as having benefits for individuals, in terms of enhancing their vocational practice and its scope of applications, this kind of transferable knowledge is required to enable enterprises to respond to new demands and challenges such as the ever-changing nature of work tasks and dealing with new problems.

He continues by showing the importance of making the links between the employees' existing and new knowledge:

> A rich base of transferable knowledge, including conceptual knowledge, in a workplace provides at least one sound basis for enterprises' survival and growth … The act of engagement in workplace activities is associated with ongoing and constant learning through everyday problem solving, supported and guided by contributions from the workplace. This engagement actively mediates between what the learners currently know with what they encounter through engagement in workplace tasks… This interdependence is also energised or de-energised by individuals' interest and commitment to the knowledge to be learnt.

I feel very strongly that, as training practitioners, we need to assist our colleagues to gain that most important of skills, namely *to learn how to learn*. This will be one of the most crucial abilities for managers in the next decade. Moreover, to be able to learn, employees will need to develop habits of reflection. That is to say, for learning to be complete, the worker requires opportunities to reflect on the learning event and then to implement the developed knowledge in the working environment.

Or to put it another way, *action without reflection does not equal learning*. This can be expressed as an equation:

$$A - R \neq L$$

> Reflection is a key element in the learning process. It converts informal and perhaps accidental opportunities into efficient learning. A major task of trainers and developers is therefore to get people to recognise and use opportunities for learning and to help to develop their skills of reflection. (Barclay 1996)

Table 32 *Definitions of training transfer factors*

Transfer factor	Definition
Learner readiness	The extent to which individuals are prepared to enter and participate in training
Motivation to transfer	The direction, intensity, and persistence of effort towards utilising in a work-setting the skills and knowledge learned
Positive personal outcomes	The degree to which applying training on the job leads to outcomes that are positive for the individual
Negative personal outcomes	The extent to which individuals believe that not applying skills and knowledge learned in training will lead to outcomes that are negative
Personal capacity for transfer	The extent to which individuals have the time, energy, and mental space in their work lives to make the changes required to transfer learning to the job
Peer support	The extent to which peers reinforce and support the use of learning on the job
Supervisor support	The extent to which supervisors/managers support and reinforce use of training on the job
Supervisor sanctions	The extent to which individuals perceive negative responses from supervisors/managers when applying skills learned in training
Perceived content validity	The extent to which trainees judge training content to reflect job requirements accurately
Transfer design	The degree to which (1) training has been designed and delivered to give trainees the ability to transfer learning on the job, and (2) training instructions match job requirements
Opportunity to use	The extent to which trainees are provided with, or obtain, resources and tasks on the job enabling them to use training on the job
Transfer effort – performance expectations	The expectation that effort devoted to transferring learning will lead to changes in job performance
Performance – outcomes expectations	The expectation that changes in job performance will lead to valued outcomes
Resistance – openness to change	The extent to which prevailing group norms are perceived by the individual to resist or discourage the use of skills and knowledge acquired in training
Performance self-efficacy	An individual's general belief that he is able to change his performance when he wants
Performance coaching	Formal and informal indicators from an organisation about an individual's job performance

This is no more important than in our current economic climate. To ensure sustainable competitive advantage, we must ensure regular opportunities for employees fully to undertake their roles as knowledge workers. This will entail them in not only reflecting on their own actions to become new learning, but also in sharing that new learning with others in a spontaneous exchange of information, wisdom and understanding. When considering the emergence of strategic training in a global economy, Horwitz (1999) comments that:

> ... transfer of learning, new knowledge and the notion of intellectual capital become as important to levering competitive success as does sensitivity to local conditions ... An expectancy theory understanding of HRM focuses on motivation and rewards. SHRD provides the capacity to enhance individual abilities and competencies as a necessary requirement for effective performance. The latter is therefore a combined function of ability, motivation and opportunity.

Horwitz goes on to stress the importance of the application of new skills gained during the learning event to increased job performance:

> ... transfer of learning is only likely if the employee has the opportunity to use newly acquired skills in his/her job ... If the learning derived from training is not associated with enhanced job performance or raised capability, then the credibility of both HRD specialists and the process are at risk ... A strategic approach to transfer of learning raises important but often situationally contingent questions regarding roles, responsibility, accountability, performance management and reward systems for training ... Management support (job linkage), relevance of training to current work, links to managerial performance management, career advancement, rewards and performance measures are important prerequisites for effective transfer of training.

Achieving improved transfer of learning

Research demonstrates that US organisations spend a staggering $30 billion a year on training. Even more surprising is the estimated wastage of $27 billion, since only 10 per cent of the $30 billion investment is actually transferred back to the workplace in the form of improved skills and knowledge.

To establish strategies for ensuring transfer of learning, Hodges (2002) proposes five important approaches:

1. Market the programme.
2. Design transfer strategies into the programme.
3. Ensure involvement by all players before, during and after the programme.
4. Demonstrate the extent to which transfer takes place by summative evaluations.
5. Communicate programme successes (and failures) to the organisation, so that the lessons learned can be used for future programmes.

On the other hand, Harrison (2002) feels that, in her opinion, to ensure transfer of learning, it is just as important to give learners opportunities to transfer their experience *into* the learning event:

> There are two points at which transfer of learning must be effective – transfer of learning into a learning event, and from it upon its completion. Past learning will transfer positively into the event if that learning can be used in the new situation. It will transfer negatively if it seems to the learner impossible to apply or if it contradicts what is being taught in the new situation.

Interestingly, Lynton and Pareek (2000b) point to the need to attend to changing patterns of work performance over a period of time after the learning event, in order to determine the effectiveness of training transfer:

1. If performance stays in the expected range or better and keeps improving with further practice, this means the program was sound, that both participants and their organisations were ready to use the training, and that participants learned enough during training to keep on improving their performance.
2. If performances tend to decline, this means participants and their organisations found the training less useful than expected, or that participants did not have sufficient training during the program and/or support on the job to carry on successfully. But wait, and continue watching, because ...
3. ... If the results show a sharp drop at first and then a rise, this shows that the transfer from training to action was unexpectedly difficult, but that participants and their organisations have overcome the difficulties and are making headway.
4. If the results show a sharp drop and stay down, this means the organisations and/or the participants were not prepared to make the change on the job or that the training objectives were not realistic.

This has been illustrated diagrammatically (see Figure 31) by Lynton and Pareek (2000b). Conversely, Darling *et al* (1999) focus on the need for both challenge and support in work-based learning. They stress the need to develop mechanisms to integrate learning into the organisation. Figure 32 on page 154 shows a model of what happens to individuals in organisations where there is a different balance between challenge and support for work-based learning. The challenge dimension considers the extent to which people are stretched and extended in their work roles, while the support dimension reflects the degree to which support such as training, development, mentoring etc is provided.

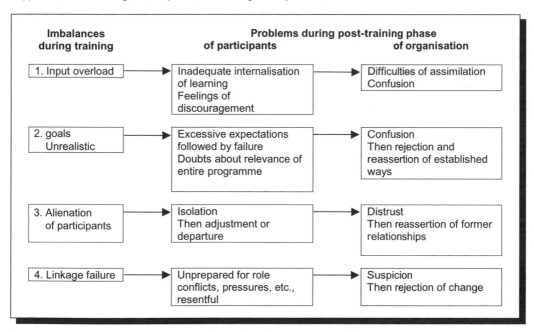

Figure 31 *Training transfer problems*

THE TRANSFER OF LEARNING – IN PRACTICE
Transferring learning into and out of the training situation

One of the best ways for training transfer to be accomplished is through the use of learning contracts, or *learning plans*. Out of and through an effective appraisal or performance management system there may

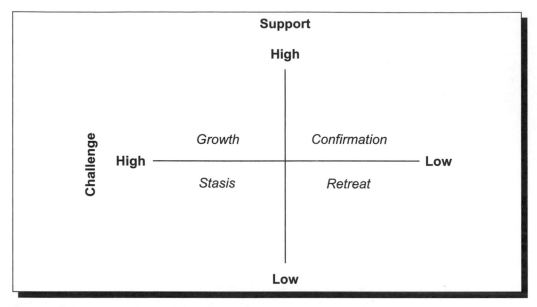

Figure 32 *Challenge and support in learning*

be a whole range of different outcomes. These could include elements applicable to personal development plans, career development plans and succession plans. For an individual it may be linked to continuous professional development. More specifically, there will be individual learning plans. These will be based on a conversation between the employee and their supervisor or line manager where specific learning objectives can be identified.

Here are some examples of learning plans that have been used, and you will see that, for the best learning plan, the trainer is also involved in signing off what is to be achieved, because it's the trainer rather than necessarily the learner or even the line manager who has the technical expertise to know how best to meet the learning needs.

The learning plan
The learning plan is essential for effective learning to take place. It will provide a structure for a conversation between you and your learners and their line manager. It will enable you to establish and agree some meaningful objectives. Second, it will help you to see where this fits into their personal development plan. And finally, it will assist you in identifying how this learning will help them meet local and organisational goals.

The learning plan requires a semi-structured conversation between the learner and yourself. It also helps to address the divergent needs of the learner, the organisation and the wider community. For example, the learner might want to develop their computing skills, whereas the organisation has a pressing need to complete a special redevelopment scheme by the end of the year. The department, meanwhile, may be attempting to encourage its regional offices to achieve Investors in People recognition.

Most important of all, the learning plan forces you to meet together, and to decide what learning is needed, and how it can be applied. Too often in the past, training has been ineffective because the wrong people have been on the wrong courses, at the wrong times, and for the wrong reasons!

See Figure 33 for an example of a completed learning plan.

LEARNING PLAN

Learner: *Surinder Patel*
Manager: *Lesley Smith*
Department: *Marketing*
Trainer/mentor/coach: *Vanesssa James*

1. Which specific learning need has been identified?
     To improve my influencing skills

2. What other learning needs does this relate to, either for yourself or others you work with?
     Assertiveness; time management

3. What is your learning objective?   *To influence the group to change their work pattern*

4. What is your preferred learning style?   *Thinking*

5. By when would you like the learning to be completed?   *Before Easter*

6. What constraints can you identify that could limit the effectiveness of your learning?
     Quarterly returns; Pat is on maternity leave

7. What will you do after the training in order to implement your learning, and so improve your work?
     Have individual and group discussions

Signatures

Employee: ....

Date: ....

Manager: ....

Date: ....

Trainer: ....

Date: ....

Figure 33 *Learning plan – example*

The best learning plans and contracts are those that enable the learning to be *applied and implemented* after the learning event. But too often in the past the employee who comes back after a course is asked by the manager, 'so how did you get on with the training course?' and before they've even had time to reply, the manager will say something like, 'Well, you can forget that lot now, you're back at work'. Many learners return to their working environment full of enthusiasm and new ideas, only to find their hopes dashed through cynicism, sarcasm or intransigence.

Therefore, if the line manager, the employee and the trainer have a three-way conversation before the learning even takes place, there will be agreement about how the learning can be implemented afterwards.

A further aspect of transfer of learning is to transfer experience from the workplace into the learning event. It doesn't matter how good the case studies or scenarios used by the trainer may be, the best examples are those that the learners themselves bring to the learning event. Obviously some situations have to be made anonymous or confidential, but nevertheless, many situations can be used to great effect, both for the individual learner and the other people on the course or programme.

PAUSE FOR THOUGHT

Take a look at the following questions. They may help you to write your own learning plan:

- Where am I now – from a personal and professional perspective?

- What are my strengths?

- Where are my gaps (strengths for the future)?

- What are my personal objectives for the programme?

- What will I do to meet my objectives?

- How will I know that I have succeeded?

- What do I hope to learn from the programme?

- What are my objectives? ie What do I hope to be able to <u>do</u> as a direct result of the programme?

- What other opportunities to learn am I likely to find in my workplace?

- What is the situation/issue/problem/group of people that I most want to do something about?

- What targets/standards should I set myself?

- Who might help me if I get stuck? (ie at work/at home/elsewhere)

When you have given some thought to the answers to the questions above, refer to your most recent appraisal or personal development plan. Identify just one specific learning objective. Now complete a learning plan for yourself, using one of the templates on pages 156 and 157.

LEARNING PLAN

Learner: ....
Manager: ....
Department: ....
Trainer/mentor/coach: ....

1. Which specific learning need has been identified?
2. What other learning needs does this relate to, either for yourself or others you work with?
3. What is your learning objective?
4. What is your preferred learning style?
5. By when would you like the learning to be completed?
6. What constraints can you identify that could limit the effectiveness of your learning?
7. What will you do after the training in order to implement your learning, and so improve your work?

Signatures:
Employee: .... Date: ....
Manager: .... Date: ....
Trainer: .... Date:................

Name: Date: Page ___ of ___

Learning plan

TASK NEEDED	PROPOSED LEARNING	PROPOSED ACTION	TIMESCALE	RESOURCES AND RESPONSIBILITIES

Increasingly, this method is used in reflective learning practice, such as with clinical supervision in health and social services. But it can also be used in a wider variety of different learning events than is normally supposed. Many trainers spend many hours designing a case study, a problem situation, a role-play or an exercise.

Instead, it would be far better for the trainer to spend that time developing a model, a means, a method for developing a particular skill, and for the learners to bring the content, the material, based on their own experience.

A number of years ago, I was involved with helping some middle and senior managers in Glaxo to develop problem-solving techniques. On the first of the two days in the workshop I helped them to understand, use and develop a particular problem-solving model that was found to be effective. On the second day, we then used that approach to solve real-life problems from the learners' own working environments. The amount of learning was dramatically increased, because they were able to apply the model to difficult situations that had arisen in their own working situations, and they could immediately see how a problem that was relevant and important for them could be dealt with.

I remember one particular scientist who had been struggling with an exacting problem for over 18 months. He brought his problem to the group. I didn't pretend to understand half of what he was talking about, but by applying the problem-solving model to his situation, he suddenly said, 'Ah, now I've got it! So you mean, I could put the radioactive isotope on the other end of the molecule! That's fantastic!' The light dawned, the penny dropped, and he was able to find a solution to his own problem, which had clearly cost the organisation many of hundreds of thousands of pounds in time, effort and resources.

Therefore, it's better for individuals to bring their own material, content, and experience. And talking of experience, I tend to lean a lot on the learners themselves. If a particular person in a group says to me, 'Well, David, what would you do about so-and-so, or such-and-such?' sometimes I will bounce it back to the individual and say, 'What do you think?' or 'What have you already considered?' or 'What do you think you could try?' Alternatively, I will bring in the rest of the group and say, 'Well, who else has considered this or tackled that or encountered it?' Because, if there is one trainer and 15 learners, there is 15 times the amount of experience in the group than in the trainer!

Using the experience of others is one of the best ways to transfer the learning from the individual to the group and vice versa. Moreover, it helps to bring the workplace into the learning event and for the learning event to be taken back into the workplace, because people are better able to see how to generalise and contextualise the specific learning into their own situation. If it's an example in a book, or even a video, it is easy for employees to dismiss it as being unrealistic, fictional or perfectionist. But if somebody else has brought a situation, then they are able to see how *their* work could also be changed, *their* performance also improved, and *their* behaviour altered for the better.

Transferring learning out of the learning event can be achieved in a number of ways. If there is a culture within the organisation of using learning plans or learning contracts aligned to personal development plans or appraisal systems, and if there is also a culture of learning logs, diaries or journals, then people will be used to reflecting, thinking and writing, whether with their mentors or otherwise. It will be much easier for them – towards the end of a learning event – to begin to start to think about how the learning can be applied.

> As the process of learning grows in significance in the workbased learning context, instruments such as learning logs, diaries and learning journals are playing an increasingly important role. Each offers the student the opportunity of reading and reflecting on the learning process as well as noting more context-based matters. (Shaw and Green 1999)

So, transfer is best handled during the learning event itself, rather than leaving it till afterwards, and one of the best bridges that I have found for helping learners to take what they've learnt and apply it after the learning event is through the use of action plans. Here are some examples of action planning tools that could be used.

The action plan

The value of any learning event can only be measured once it has been completed. The results depend entirely on what happens when it is over. And this will largely be determined by the learner's ability and opportunity to *apply* the learning to the job. Applying learning implies doing things differently.

Therefore, the manager needs to discuss with your trainees *before* the training exactly how they expect to implement their learning. And *during* the training itself, the trainer or manager will develop that discussion based on the actual learning that has been gained. After the learning event, the trainer and manager must be actively involved in providing opportunities and support for the learner to apply their increased knowledge, skills and attitudes.

This method of transferring learning to work is called an *action plan*. An action plan involves addressing issues of change:

- change in the learner
- change in the job
- change in relationships
- change in the organisation.

Learning is all about managing those changes, so that the work, systems and relationships can become more effective. Ideas for the action plan will come to the learners from themselves, the manager or trainer, and also from:

- the knowledge gained
- the skills improved
- the attitudes developed
- the learning tasks undertaken
- the other learners
- the opportunity given to think reflectively about the job.

The purpose of the action plan is to:

- help build a 'bridge' between the learning and the job
- provide the motivation to overcome any resistance from work colleagues who have not had the opportunity to gain from the training and learning
- predict possible difficulties in implementing changes, and to allow you to consider possible options and solutions
- offer a record to help review performance at a later stage
- provide a clear and concise list of parts of the job currently requiring time and attention
- enable the learner to identify further changes and training needs.

In one organisation, the trainees were asked to write out copies of their personal action plans at the end of the learning event. These plans were then given to the trainer, who kept them and subsequently returned one copy to the learners approximately a week later. Two months after that, the trainer sent out the second copy of the action plan, and the learners were asked to comment on their performance against those objectives. A certificate of completion for the training was issued only after the trainer received evidence of this discussion between the trainee and their manager.

However, the vast majority of organisations do not use these. Consequently, when, at the end of a programme, the trainer tries to encourage the learner to use an action plan in order to transfer the learning from the event into the workplace, such a suggestion is often greeted with dismay or concern. Therefore, the manager must be involved in providing opportunities, support, motivation, encouragement and resources, so that the learner can take time out from what they would normally be expected to accomplish, so they have a chance to carry out the new learning.

Knowledge management

Another effective way of transferring the learning into the working environment is by means of helping others, to share that understanding, which forms some of the basic elements of knowledge-management strategies. So, for example, if the learner has been to a seminar or conference, they could be encouraged to write a paper, deliver a presentation, hold a briefing session, or lead a focus group with their peers and colleagues when they return to work. Alternatively, if they have developed a new skill then they may be asked to cascade that through their department or office. One of the best ways of learning is by having to train others.

But for learning to be effective, it must be in the context of departmental and organisational strategies and plans. And so the best form of transfer of learning is where the learning is essential to the development of the organisation. Single-, double-, and deutero-learning have been developed as concepts to encourage this. Another way of looking at this is where the individual needs to grow, change, mature and develop, in relation to the changing context and environment of the workplace. And meanwhile the organisation is adapting and improving, in the context of different forces for change, including political, economic, social, technical, legal and environmental.

But the magic happens when one interacts with the other, so that the individual in their very growth, development and learning changes the organisation and where the organisation changes the individual, Suddenly, you have a figure of eight, a double-loop:

8

And if you put this figure of eight on its side, you can see the similarity to mathematical sign for infinity:

∞

Because learning never ends, learning is a process, a journey, a becoming – it's not an achievement! Reid and Barrington (2000) point out the importance of the HRD manager in training transfer:

As a general rule, the more the HRD manager can take part herself in the mainstream organisational activity and can involve the sources of power in the actual training, the greater the likelihood of learning transfer. Examples might be:

- organising learning sessions as an integral part of mainstream events

- emphasising the personal responsibility of managers in training their subordinates, and assisting them to do this

- assisting managers to coach their subordinates

- ensuring that managers are directly involved in briefing and debriefing sessions for staff undergoing training

- if the occasion is appropriate, arranging for top management to attend a course first

- developing managers and supervisors as trainers in their own departments

- asking senior managers to lecture or lead session on in-house courses

- the use of mentors.

The learning log
Here are some guidelines (Barclay 1996) for planning and completing a learning log:

- *Preparation.* Before embarking on your personal development plan, spare some time to assess your present situation, your strengths and weaknesses, and future aspirations. Ask yourself
    - What do I do well in my present job?
    - What could I do better?
    - Where, and in what roles do I see my future?
    - What new knowledge and/or skills will I need?
    - What support might I need from colleagues?
    - What constraints or problems do I foresee?
    - How could these be minimised?
    - What resources are available to me?
- *The action plan.* You should now be able to set about creating a personal development plan, to address your development goals. Ideally you should consider
    - the objectives you aim to achieve
    - the activities which will allow you to develop the skills identified
    - developing contacts with others who may help (other managers, colleagues, mentors)
    - an appreciation of any constraints
    - the time by which you will have achieved your objectives.
- You should try to carry out and write up one new activity per month. You should also review your plan regularly (and discuss and revise it with your mentor if necessary). In completing the log, the key points to ask yourself are
    - What did I do?
    - What will I get from doing it?
    - What will I do differently/better as a result?
- For each entry, the log should
    - identify the learning/development objectives
    - outline the processes involved
    - analyse the learning, and explore any difficulties
    - evaluate how far the objectives were achieved
    - identify areas for future development.
- The log should also include an introduction and summary which includes discussion of
    - what you were trying to achieve in your plan at the outset
    - how you felt about the elements of the plan
    - what aspects of the development activities you most/least enjoyed, and why
    - what you have learned about your learning style
    - what you have learned about your own strengths and weaknesses
    - the main areas you need to work on in the future.

Achieving improved transfer of learning

Achieving improved transfer of learning will come as and when there is effective stakeholder analysis, or 360-degree feedback, linked to the learning event, so that the learner is no longer an individual on their own, keeping the learning to themselves. Instead, the learning is shared with peers, colleagues, managers, subordinates, mentors and coaches. The learning can even be shared with competitors, suppliers and customers. Increasingly there are partnerships and alliances that are cutting across, and doing away with, traditional barriers of demarcation and separatism, so that people are finding that investment in training and learning can also affect other relationships and social links in the value chain.

From their study, Read and Kleiner (1996) analysed the factors ensuring the effectiveness of training transfer:

> When possible, it is best to pick a method that encourages active participation by the trainee and provides adequate feedback. This increases the likelihood that what is taught in training will be retained and later applied. Of the training methods discussed, one-on-one instruction, role-plays, games/simulation, case studies, and computer-based training all rank high in both trainee activity level and feedback. The other methods are inherently passive but can be made active without additional effort on the part of the trainer . . . Measuring post-training behaviour also indicates how well the information learned is transferred to the job. For training to be beneficial to the company, it must be applied. This transfer is dependent on both the training and the work environment.
>
> For example, a bank sent its tellers to product training so that they could sell customers additional services. After training, the tellers could not risk low performance ratings by putting their new skills to work and taking time to discuss the bank's other products and services, because their performance was still measured by the number of transactions handled. People will do what they are rewarded for doing. In this case, the environment did not give the tellers the opportunity or incentive to use their training on the job. Even though the training itself may be effective, if employees cannot transfer what they have learned, training is wasted.

Therefore, training practitioners must consider learning transfer strategies right at the design stage of the programme (Hodges 2002):

1. Ensure that the programme designers or developers develop realistic exercises.
2. Provide a positive training environment.
3. Design a peer-coaching component for the programme.
4. Anticipate barriers and be prepared to assist participants in developing methods for overcoming those barriers.
5. Use action planning.
6. Tell the participants they will be tested not only at the end of the training but on the job as well.
7. Conduct follow-up sessions.
8. Encourage support groups.
9. Develop job aids and use them during as well as after the programme.

When considering issues of training transfer, Philips and Jacobs (2002) studied aspects that contributed to its effectiveness:

The course design was customised to support full transfer of skills to the workplace through high levels of participant interaction, peer coaching and feedback skill practices, involvement in real-time action-learning scenarios, and regular reference to action planning as a training outcome. Production management agreed to be available to help introduce the program and its desired results, as well as to emphasize the importance of successful completion of the qualification and the action plan. Management also attended a summation 'issues' review during the closing on day three.

Following the three-day program, participants were immediately scheduled to meet with the senior training consultant or the training specialists for a one-hour individual follow-up session. During this time ATs were audited on successful completion of the qualification and asked to initiate their 30-day action plan. The focus of the action plan was for each participant to identify two to three specific structured OJT [on-job-training] skills learned from the train-the-trainer program, which they would then apply to their structures OJT processes during the next 30 days.

On the other hand, research by Barclay (1996) centred on learning from experience by using learning logs. He had hypothesised that using a learning log would suit 'reflectors' more than those with other learning styles, because keeping a log reinforces the reflector's favoured mode. Surprisingly, the results did not support the hypothesis.

Q. Do you think you will continue to keep using some form of learning log?

	Yes (%)
Activists	20
Reflectors	63
Theorists	80
Combined styles	67
(n = 30)	

To ensure that a training programme offers an integrated learning experience leading to the desired individual performance, we must deliberately create transfer of learning opportunities from the beginning. Otherwise, we risk an unstructured approach in which the learner fails to recognise and apply the learning that has resulted from programme activities, and so they forget.

There is also the likelihood that both learners and their managers will see training as being confined purely to those off-the-job parts of the programme. The fewer opportunities there are to practise and build upon knowledge, skills and attitudes acquired through a training programme, the less effective the training is likely to be. Each training programme will allow a different range of transfer of learning opportunities to be used, depending upon the circumstances.

We can help overcome these difficulties by ensuring continuing opportunities for learners to apply, practise and develop their knowledge and skills by:

- obtaining management support for training, as reflected in the organisation's training policy
- commitment to integrated rather than unstructured training: this will not eliminate resistance based on pressure of work, precedent or cost, but it will help to reduce it
- discussing with learners and supervisors their roles in the training programme and their responsibilities for being active rather than passive participants in the learning process. This allows the supervisor to plan work allocation to accommodate the follow-up activity. Discussions between learner and supervisor establish a 'learning contract' for exploiting the learning opportunity

- designing the transfer of learning opportunities to fit in with the aspirations and abilities of the learners and their supervisors: consultation with both will help in deciding the most useful transfer of learning mechanism and should result in the design of an effective training programme.

The effective transfer of learning from an off-the-job training course to the job situation does, of course, require the course content to be based on an accurate identification of need. If the original identification of need was wrong, then the transfer of learning activity should help to identify this when it is established that the learning cannot be applied to the job. This means trainers need to be involved at some stage in monitoring the transfer of learning.

Activities to help transfer of learning

There are many techniques that we can incorporate into a training programme to assist the transfer of learning from off-the-job training into the job situation. They can also help involve line management more fully in the training programme, and may provide information to monitor the effectiveness of the specific training courses and the overall training programme. Information may be generated on what has been learnt as well as on the organisational impact and results of training.

You can incorporate the following activities into a learning event, either individually or in a combination, depending on the constraints and resources you have available.

Individual projects

A project is similar to an action plan but it is usually broader in scope. Completion of the project may be a major part of the learner's entire job for a considerable period after the training course. For example, a supervisor who has just completed a safety course may be given a project that includes an immediate survey of the entire work area in order to identify hazards. The supervisor may then systematically take steps to eliminate existing hazards and formulate rules and procedures to minimise the risk of accidents. In effect, the learner becomes a 'safety officer' for a period of weeks. Having completed the project, the learner then returns to a standard supervisory position where safety is only one of their responsibilities.

To complete an assigned project, a learner must: review, consolidate, and apply material learned during training. The learner is then more likely to use this learnt material on return to his or her own job. In addition, the on-the-job project can be used to measure learning and also to generate tangible benefits (for example, a lower accident rate) for the organisation.

Group projects

A group project is similar to an individual project, but the difference is that several learners co-operate in the project. This follow-up activity is particularly useful where one of the objectives of training is the development of interpersonal skills.

Group projects have been used widely in management training. For example, junior managers who have just completed a course on planning may be formed into a taskforce to plan the introduction of a new product. The organisation receives a plan of action relating to a real business problem and the learners apply their new learning in a practical, and therefore satisfying, way.

Individual guidance and coaching

Potentially, this is one of the most potent follow-up techniques. Its effectiveness, however, depends almost entirely on the development skills of the learner's supervisor, who is usually given the role of coach. This potentially very effective method of follow-up will fail if the supervisor is an inadequate coach or does not have the time or inclination to co-operate.

Individual guidance and coaching is not the same as 'looking-on', where a learner watches what to do and then does it. Guidance and coaching involve progression through a thoroughly planned set of learning experiences with the learner receiving individual attention from the coach.

This type of training is often used at upper levels of organisations where individuals are appointed to 'understudy' or 'shadow' the occupants of key positions by working through a carefully selected set of projects, programmes and other learning experiences.

A trainer can assume some aspects of the coaching role through a series of scheduled follow-ups. If used primarily for monitoring and helping learning, rather than evaluating, this is useful, but not as effective as frequent coaching by the supervisor.

Formal review sessions
This kind of session is a mini-course. It is run some time after the training programme and can be used to re-examine material that learners have reported as being difficult. Or, it can be used to motivate learners to continue to use the concepts and skills learnt in the main programme. It can also serve as a useful review of the original programme, but may not adequately serve the differing needs of individual learners.

Seminars and guest speakers
In seminars, learners can be brought together to extend their knowledge of topics of mutual interest. They can prepare seminar papers themselves, or guest speakers can be invited. Success depends on the effectiveness of the speakers and the importance of the topic to the learners. For example, the speaker may be asked to present a subject without going into the theory in any depth. Often, however, enough is included to gain the interest and attention of learners. Trainers then find that follow-up seminars on further aspects of the subject will be well received. These extend the learners' knowledge while reiterating the core concepts of the training. Through e-learning, communities of practice can be adopted to extend this method of learning transfer.

Workshops
Workshops are a very popular and often effective way of following up training. At regular workshop meetings, learners take turns at presenting their current work problems. Group members draw on the training materials, plus their own experience, to propose solutions to the problems. Workshops thus reinforce concepts and skills learnt in training, and can contribute significantly to the reduction of organisational problems.

Personal development plans
A personal development plan is completed before an off-the-job training course is undertaken, and can greatly assist the transfer of learning. The plan should be used in such a way that the learner can be directed through the course content and thereby establish the relevance of the subjects and the priorities for study. By talking through the learning to be achieved with their supervisor, the learner can gain commitment to, and support for, the learning objectives from the supervisor, as well as increase his or her own commitment to the training. This discussion should also establish the requirement for post-course review, leading to individual guidance and coaching on return from the training course.

SUMMARY

In summary, therefore, you should try to minimise all external factors that inhibit transfer of learning. Provide resources to help transfer of learning and build transfer of learning into training programmes at the design stage. Involve learners' supervisors in training programme design: negotiate their help and support for the training activities and for enabling the learners to perform differently after the training. Minimise factors inside training courses that might limit transfer: instead build job-related issues into all courses and encourage learners to assume responsibility to use and develop their learning. Finally, organise and implement the transfer of learning activities and monitor the implementation of transfer of learning activities.

QUESTIONS

1. To what extent are organisations rather than individuals able to learn?
2. You have recently been appointed as the personnel and training manager for a large recruitment agency. Your HR director has made it clear that one of your first priorities is for the company to become a learning organisation. What steps should you now take?
3. Argue the case for the introduction of personal development plans in an organisation with which you are familiar.

The evaluation of training

Measuring more is easy, measuring better is hard.

Charles Handy

LEARNING OUTCOMES

- Identify the stakeholders in the evaluation of training events, and ways of reconciling differing stakeholder goals.

- Ascertain criteria for the selection of evaluation processes and methods.

- Work collaboratively to monitor, evaluate and continuously improve training events.

CHAPTER OUTLINE

- Differences between monitoring, validation and evaluation and

  - how to establish the monitoring process and gain agreement on how to operate it

  - formative and summative techniques for validating the learning of trainees

  - evaluation models, approaches and methods, and their application to different kinds of training event

  - criteria to apply in designing and implementing monitoring, validation and evaluation of training outcomes (eg information needed, purpose, expectations of stakeholders).

- Ways of responding to contingencies affecting training

  - typical organisational and individual issues, problems and responses

  - planning and carrying out training audits and ensuring action on outcomes.

INTRODUCTION

A great deal has been written about evaluation for many years. One of the fundamental planks of the systematic approach to training is the need for evaluation of the learning objectives. More recently, Investors in People has, as one of its four major components, the need for evaluation and review. And a foundational part of the whole total quality management approach is based on evaluation and review, assessment and feedback.

However, evaluation of training, while being acknowledged for many years as having great importance, is rarely carried out to any degree.

Most of us have been on courses where, at the end of the day, the trainer suddenly says, 'Ah, just before you go, I wonder if you could help me? I've got a little form here. Now I wonder if you could take a few moments, just to put a few ticks in some boxes, and that would help us greatly with the next time we run the course.' Unfortunately, the learners' minds are already on the motorway, what they're going to have for their evening meal, or the latest episode of their favourite soap. So, they fill in the form – the happy sheet, the course review, the 'reactionnaire', but reluctantly, and with no great conviction or motivation. And in that frame of mind they'll tick any box just to keep the trainer happy. Reality, honesty and truth rarely come to the fore.

What the learners may not realise is that, in some organisations at least, the performance of the trainer or external consultant is assessed in great detail, but based purely on these most dubious of measures. Indeed, their future livelihood could depend on getting a mean score of, say, 4.5!

Many such forms are badly designed, and are often full of leading, loaded or ambiguous questions. Many of them have boxes to tick on a scale of one to five, and so, in a typically British or western approach, people will tick box number three, in order not to upset the trainer. As soon as the learners have fled from the training room, the trainer pounces upon these happy sheets, and gets a wonderful glow of warm affirmation. And such a collusive, shallow, superficial approach to evaluation does little to change the learners, the organisation, or the trainers!

Shaw and Green (1999) posit that the key to effective evaluation lies in the demonstration of learning outcomes.

Individual programmes of learning do not lend themselves to traditional assessment methods. It would be difficult indeed to write an examination paper for a diverse group of work-based learners! Increasingly a portfolio approach of the demonstration of involvement is being adopted in which a variety of materials are presented. These may range from the more traditional project report to team meeting minutes and tapes of presentations. The key is the link between the learning undertaken and the appropriateness of the demonstration tool.

THE EVALUATION OF TRAINING – IN THEORY
Reconciling different stakeholders' goals

O'Donnell and Garavan (1997) advocate the use of three categories of evaluation criteria, namely criteria of suitability, feasibility and acceptability. Suitability will determine the fit with the organisation's goals; feasibility can assess the practicality of HRD plans and policies; and acceptability requires an analysis of the overall organisational mindset and cultural web.

And Garavan *et al* (1995) had earlier identified eight contextual factors, which impact on the form of the HRD function, and the type of activities in which it engages. These are the external environment and the organisation's stakeholders, culture, technology, structure, change, size and power.

There are a number of reasons why training and development programmes are not evaluated:

- People are not convinced of the purpose or benefits of evaluation.
- They feel it will be too time-consuming.
- They believe that the costs of evaluating a training event will outweigh any benefits.
- No training objectives have been identified.
- Appropriate assessment criteria have not been agreed.
- People have difficulty in selecting key areas for assessment.

- They are unaware of the methods of evaluation and how they can be used.
- They do not have the time, expertise or resources to analyse the learning results of any evaluation.
- People feel threatened.
- They may not actually want to hear any bad news.
- They may feel they are above such considerations.
- The organisation or union has no agreed policy for evaluation to take place.

Consequently, evaluation has seven purposes:

1. to validate tools and methods of training needs analysis
2. to confirm or revise the options available
3. to confirm or revise the training strategies chosen
4. to determine the trainee and trainer reactions
5. to assess the acquisition of knowledge, skills and attitudes
6. to assess the trainee's performance in the workplace
7. to determine whether organisational goals are being met.

Therefore, what should training evaluations evaluate? As Mann and Robertson (1996) put it:

> The most common form of evaluation consists of trainee reactions that are written at the end of the course. Relatively few use pre- or post-tests or follow-up questionnaires or evaluations by participants. This means that few companies, despite massive investment in training, are actually determining whether the training produced the desired results.

The authors address the issue of the threat posed by evaluation:

> There is a commonly held view that training evaluation can be a risky and expensive enterprise. There is a fear that an evaluation may indicate that a publicly endorsed programme is not meeting its objectives. This view is an unfortunate misunderstanding of the purpose of evaluation which should be to provide the information to help improve programmes rather than to declare them to be good or bad.
>
> Training evaluation can serve as a diagnostic technique to permit the revision of programmes to meet the large number of goals and objectives. Thus, the information can be used to select or revise programmes. Good evaluation information can demonstrate the usefulness of the training enterprise. This type of information can actually show the benefits of the training in terms of cost. The data can be very useful when economic realities force difficult decisions on how organisational budgets should be allocated.

Moreover, effective training evaluation can have beneficial legal implications. Legal issues have become important considerations in human resources. Employment tribunals often question the criteria for entrance into training and the value of training, especially when it is used as a requirement for promotion or recruitment. In those cases, evaluation data are required to show the relatedness of the training programme to the job.

Another benefit gained by evaluating training includes more effective decision-making. Evaluations can help decide between alternative training programmes and who should participate in future programmes. If an evaluation can show which trainees are likely to benefit most, then it will be more cost-effective to offer future programmes to those types of trainee. In addition, evaluations assess the clarity and validity of tests, questions and exercises. They must measure the skills, knowledge and attitudes the programme is designed to develop.

I am also a strong advocate of learning through assessment. Evaluation can reinforce to the participants major points made in the learning event. A follow-up evaluation can reinforce the information covered in a programme by attempting to measure the results accomplished by participants. It reminds the participants of what they should have accomplished, or should be accomplishing.

According to Lewis and Thornhill (1994), ineffective training evaluation is directly related to organisational cultures. In order to attempt to counteract this problem, and to change an organisation's culture, those responsible for training evaluation should carefully consider the following action points:

- Attempt, first, to understand the organisation's culture and organisational attitudes to evaluation.

- Recognise all levels of the organisation's culture in order to consider how positive attitudes can be fostered at all of these.

- Determine measurable goals for changing attitudes to evaluation in the organisation in relation to time.

- Utilise Lewin's forcefield analysis to analyse the extent of the problem and the task to be undertaken and his approach to bringing about change.

- Adopt a proactive approach to the advancement of organisational-level training evaluation by promoting this to senior management and by forging links with line managers and other key players in order to effect new organisational beliefs towards training evaluation.

- Choose a suitable change strategy or strategies to promote new organisational beliefs towards training evaluation, through seeking answers to a number of critical questions.

- Seek to involve a wide range of organisational participants in the implementation stage, in an attempt to change attitudes towards training evaluation.

- Actively evaluate the results of this culture change attempt.

Selecting different evaluation processes and methods

After the pioneering work by Bloom (1956) on the need for trainers to establish behavioural objectives for the purpose of performance management, over the next 10 years there was a steady stream of research into training evaluation by, among others, Cronbach (1963), Hesseling (1966), Oppenheim (1966), Scriven (1967), Pym (1968), Jones and Moxham (1969), Garbutt (1969), Kohn and Parker (1969) and Jackson (1969).

Out of this early work there emerged several classical approaches to the evaluation of training and learning:

Table 33 *The Kirkpatrick model*

Evaluation level	Questions
Reaction	Were the participants *happy* with the training?
Learning	What did the participants *learn* from the training?
Behaviour	Did the participants change their *behaviour* based on what was learned?
Results	Did the behaviour change have a positive *effect* on the organisation?

The Kirkpatrick model (1967)
Despite the fact that most trainers espouse this classic approach (shown in Table 33), almost unquestioningly, we must be aware that there are nevertheless important criticisms of the Kirkpatrick model (Swanson and Holton 2001):

Not supported by research. Research has consistently shown that the levels within the taxonomy are not related, or only correlated at a low level.

Emphasis on reaction measures. Research has shown that reaction measures have nearly a zero correlation with learning or performance outcome measures.

Not used. The model is not widely used. Despite decades of urging people to use it, most do not find it a useful approach.

Can lead to incorrect decisions. The model leaves out so many important variables that four-level data alone are insufficient to make correct and informed decisions about training program effectiveness.

The Warr et al model (1970)
Again, there were four categories of evaluation (CIRO):

1. context
2. input
3. reactions
4. outputs.

The Hamblin model (1974)
Hamblin developed Kirkpatrick's model slightly by adding a level of 'ultimate value':

1. reactions
2. learning
3. job behaviour
4. organisation
5. ultimate value.

The Easterby-Smith model (1986)
Easterby-Smith's model uses not only a different approach and more levels, but causes the evaluator to consider their perspective and purpose more thoughtfully:

1. context
2. administration
3. inputs
4. process
5. outcomes
6. organisational change.

Rae's model (2002a)
More recently, Rae has developed his own, more complete, model of the evaluation process:

1. training needs analysis leading to training objectives
2. design of the evaluation process
3. establishing the business base level for post-training implementation to determine the return on investment or other cost- and value-effectiveness
4. pre-course testing of knowledge, skills and attitudes
5. line manager pre-course briefing
6. start-of-course testing or assessment
7. interim assessment and validation
8. end-of-programme testing or assessment of learners
9. end-of-programme validation of training and learning objectives
10. end-of-programme reaction review
11. learner action plan at end of programme
12. line manager post-course debriefing and support for implementation of learning
13. medium-term follow-up and review of implementation of learning
14. long-term follow-up and review of implementation of learning
15. cost- and value-effectiveness analysis by line manager
16. assessment and report on achievement of the programme.

The essential difficulty with much that underpins many of these approaches, however, is that they tend to be systems-based in their origin and linear in their application. Line managers in general, and financial directors in particular, have demanded more robust measures of efficiency and effectiveness from trainers for many years. Those in training departments have often just shrugged their shoulders at the impossibility, the enormity, or the difficulty, of such a task.

Now, at last, in the USA, Phillips (2002) and Swanson (2001) have led the profession in attempts to determine vigorous approaches to the analysis of return on investment (ROI) of training and learning. Over the years, there has been much debate about the difficulty of assessing the effectiveness of training and learning at these upper or wider levels. In this context, Phillips' ROI model (2002) for collecting level-five evaluation data is a major contribution (see Figure 34).

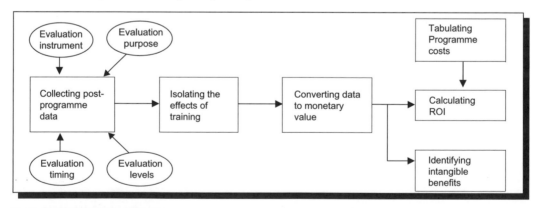

Figure 34 *ROI of training and learning*

We shall take a closer look at the complex area of cost analysis later in the chapter. From all these many and various approaches, we can synthesise a composite model for the evaluation of training and learning (see Table 34).

Finally, let me offer a development of this approach, which I have called the ripple model of evaluation, which you can see in Figure 35 on page 174.

Table 34 *A composite model for the evaluation of training and learning*

LEVEL (Where?)	INDEX (Which?)	QUESTION (What?)	METHODS (How?)	TIMING (When?)	OUTCOMES (How much?)
1. REACTION	Happiness	What were the *reactions* of the learners to the training activity?	Training records Learning styles Verbal questioning Observation Visual assessment Body language Interpersonal relation-ships Reaction questionnaire	Before During Immediately afterwards After a month	Are the trainees still motivated to learn? Has the credibility of the trainer/the programme been maintained or increased? What needs to be changed?
2. LEARNING	Learning	What *learning* was accomplished?	**Head** – assessing recall, understanding, application, analysis **Hands** – assessing manual, intellectual, and communication abilities **Heart** – assessing rel-evance, sincerity, and durability of attitudes **Holistic** – assessing integration of learning to the whole self	Before During Immediately afterwards After a month After three months After nine months	*Internal validation* of changes to knowledge, skills and attitudes: What has still to be learnt? What has been remem-bered? What needs to be changed?
3. JOB PERFORMANCE	Application	What direct *changes* have there been to job performance?	Self-appraisal Peer appraisal Supervisory appraisal Subordinate appraisal Stakeholder analysis Activity sampling Interviews, discussions, and questionnaires Observation Performance indicators/targets	Before Immediately afterwards After a month After three months After nine months	*External validation* of training and learning objectives: What improvements to performance have been measured? What changes have been sustained? Any further changes?
4 DEPARTMENT/ ORGANISATION	Bottom-line value	What was the ultimate *value* of the training and learning?	Reporting processes/systems Performance indicators Cost–benefit analysis ROI Human capital investment analysis Strategic change	Before After three months After nine months	**Evaluation** of training and learning objectives: What has been the (financial/non-financial) benefit to the department/organisation? What still needs to be changed?

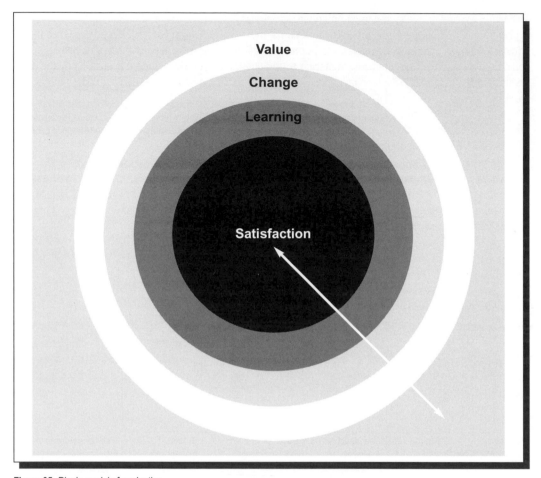

Figure 35 *Ripple model of evaluation*

Unlike in other models of training evaluation, which is too often viewed as linear, static or progressive, I believe evaluation should be perceived as a reflection of the people, systems and process in which it takes place. Consequently, it is constantly moving, dynamic, and organic.

In the centre is the requirement for the learner's needs to be satisfied. This becomes translated into learning, which in turn is transferred to the job and to the changed job performance. Finally, we determine its value to the wider organisation.

As the ripples flow out, so different parts and aspects of work performance are impacted. Moreover, the greater the learning, the greater will be the ripples, creating wider and wider waves. These will impact on an ever-widening group of others. For organisational change, therefore, there needs to a much larger impact from the learning than for individual change.

However, evaluation occurs in more than one direction, for the ripples also flow back towards the centre. Since learning always takes place within a context, the learning itself will be constrained and affected by, say, the organisational culture, financial imperatives and stakeholder expectations. These will cause classic interference patterns to be set up. Consequently, the organisation will also affect the rate and scope of change and learning in the department and the individual.

Therefore, evaluation measures must be undertaken, before, during and after the learning, by the learner, by the trainer, and by the manager. Job performance must be measured *before* the learning takes place, against whatever criteria or measures are normally used in the working environment. For example, this could be how much HR are spending in placing a job advert; how quickly a student is enrolled by the postgraduate office at a university; how much time is spent in servicing a gas central-heating boiler; or how late the trains arrive!

And then, *during* the training, people's reactions are assessed, and the learning can be measured. Later in this chapter I will develop the means and methods of accomplishing that.

At the *end* of training, and through the transfer of learning, including action plans, projects and assignments, the learning can be taken into the workplace and applied in a realistic environment, resulting in improved and changed job performance. This can then be measured using the same criteria and metrics as before the learning event.

The extent to which this impacts on the business unit, the shop, department, office or factory will be the degree to which the ultimate *value* of the learning will be accomplished.

Validation and evaluation

Internal validation of learning and training is a measurement of the extent to which the objectives have been accomplished. And this is tested in a number of different ways, but preferably during the learning event itself. *External* validation on the other hand is a measure of how far the learning has impacted on job behaviour and job performance. Evaluation, however, is a measure of the worth or value of that learning to the wider organisation, often in economic and financial terms, and this will include cost–benefit analysis and ROI measures.

It is appropriate at this point to offer a health warning! It must be remembered that, in an organisation which has little or no background or experience of effective evaluation systems, to introduce such an approach will necessitate a great deal of time, effort and resource – probably at least 18 months. Moreover, some evaluation systems that I've encountered in the past have become so elaborate and intricate that their benefit is questionable in relation to their cost.

For evaluation to be effective it must be seen to be part of a continuous cycle of improvement which includes training as well as every other function and department in the organisation. Where there is a history and a culture of change and quality improvement, this will be easier. Deming, Juran, Crosby and Ishikawa are well-known names in the development of quality management approaches. But fundamental and imperative to each of their systems is the need for evaluation, review and feedback. Training is central and fundamental to any change management system and process, and evaluation is foundational to effective training and learning.

Training itself must, therefore, include within it elements of review and assessment, change and continuous improvement. These must be built into each learning event, each programme, each course, seminar, workshop, conference, mentoring or coaching session. There need to be milestones for review, appraisal, assessment and evaluation. Feedback – honest, transparent, criterion-based feedback – is essential for improvement. Unless the trainer is open to receiving feedback on their performance, which is realistic, sincere and truthful, then their own performance is unlikely to improve, becoming stuck in traditional methods and media. They will use tried and tested exercises, old jokes, and tired case studies that have long passed their sell-by date, because it's easy and comfortable, because the trainers haven't been told, they do not know, and are unaware of the consequences, outcomes and responses to such methods and media.

Training professionals need – through continuous professional development, quality circles, and reflective practice – to lead in the development of professional practice.

For our organisations to be able to change, and to make change happen, training is central and core to the achievement of that purpose. But it's not linear, it's not a straight line, it's not about cause and effect any more. Change and learning are not two-dimensional; it's about a multidimensional, dynamic, organic approach, where there are webs, links, interfaces, relationships and social connections. And it's difficult for us to even name all the parts, let alone understand the connections. Instead, the role of the training practitioner is to facilitate and enable the generic transferability of skills, knowledge and attitudes so that employees can function more effectively. We must model such behaviour. Essential to that is the need for evaluation.

Interestingly, Wilson (1999) believes that, no matter which level you are evaluating, there are always basic questions you need to ask:

- Why are you undertaking the evaluation?
- Who are the stakeholders?
- How will you gather information?
- Who will have access to it?
- How will it be analysed?
- How will it be used and why?
- Is there a pre-designed or standard instrument available? (This may be particularly relevant for computer-based training.)
- Have you got the time and resources to pilot your methods?
- Can you anticipate the time and resources needed to complete the evaluation?
- How accurate does the information need to be, and if very accurate, how are you going to deal with error and bias?
- When, how often and over what period of time will it be undertaken?

He suggests that you then need to look at the types of evaluative method or instrument you think are most suitable or available. They may well include:

- personal inventories
- attitudinal diagnostic questionnaires
- factual written tests
- observations of practice or of interpersonal skill
- group discussion or analysis
- focus groups
- observation of work performance
- analysis of documentation according to pre-defined or open criteria
- portfolio of evidence
- individual or group interviews.

We need, therefore, to see evaluation in the context of normal performance-measurement approaches. Here are just a few of the ways in which people's work is measured today in, say, an HR department:

- labour turnover rates
- number of customer complaints
- cost, size and effectiveness of recruitment adverts
- speed of replacing staff
- uptake of new initiatives, such as 360-degree feedback
- implementation of appraisal
- accuracy of payroll and pensions administration
- results of employee relations negotiations.

PAUSE FOR THOUGHT

In what ways can the work of your HR department be assessed?

- Which yardsticks are used?
- Who is responsible for measuring performance?
- What standards and targets are set or agreed?
- How do you know when they have been reached?
- When was the last time there was a meeting to review your current working practices?

Collaborating in the continuous improvement of training

At this stage, it would pay us to review the total quality management process (Wilson 1999) (see Figure 36 on page 178). Such a process view of quality management undergirds the analysis of Hyland and his colleagues (2000) of the links between learning strategies and continuous improvement (CI):

Much of the task of converting information into action, which is the process of management, can be described with the simple concept of the feedback loop. Managers develop policies that enable the organisation to effectively respond to the outcomes of the process that is being managed. These rules, which enable appropriate responses, are contained in policies and the process of developing these policies is the process of learning. The effectiveness of a CI program in an organisation is related to the level of integration between the CI process and the learning within the organisation. CI requires a long-term commitment to a course or action and the development of a set of beliefs. If CI is developed in a vacuum, isolated from the main strategy of the company, then even though it may flourish for some time, it is unlikely to achieve general acceptance across the different functions of the organisation. Part of that strategy must be to invest in the people within the organisation. The companies that are prepared to equip staff at all levels of the organisation with the skills necessary to create and thrive on change, including CI, will be well placed to survive and grow ... Continued efforts to develop the learning environment for successful CI should allow firms to improve their feedback loops for organisational learning and create the possibility for more emergent strategic approaches within their structures.

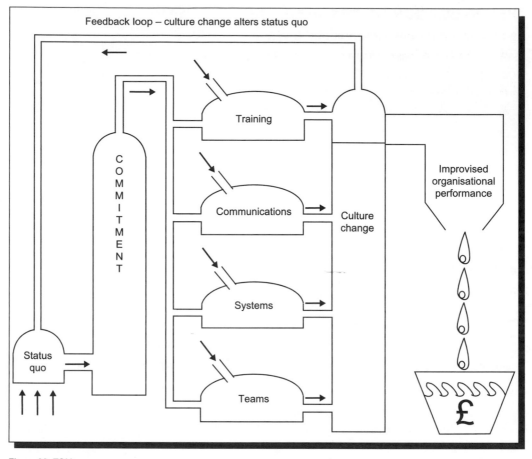

Figure 36 *TQM process*

The authors believe strongly that the feedback loop (see Figure 37) enables the identification of skills that employees will require if they are empowered to develop policy and responses within the CI process. The most fundamental of these is the ability to measure the performance of the process and so measure the success of learning strategies.

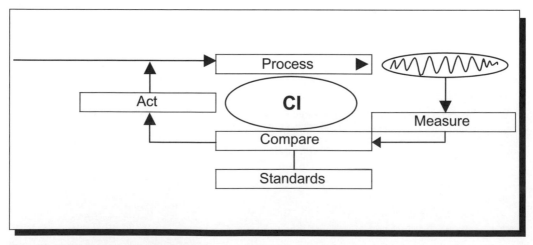

Figure 37 *Continuous improvement feedback loop*

THE EVALUATION OF TRAINING – IN PRACTICE
Reconciling different stakeholders' goals

Assessing the effectiveness of training and learning has a number of benefits. It:

- helps the learner to change performance
- confirms the extent to which the objectives have been achieved
- rewards the learner with knowledge of results
- assesses competence
- gives certification of competences for qualification purposes
- provides evidence of learning as a basis for further training
- identifies the need for remedial training
- identifies the learning gained
- provides evidence to revise the training design
- justifies use of resources (money, people, space, time, equipment)
- demonstrates the benefits of investment in training
- compares the costs/benefits of different training and learning methods
- provides evidence for marketing the training
- enables the credibility and profile of the training function to be raised.

Such benefits can be used to inform discussions between stakeholders and trainers.

At this point, there is a useful distinction to be made between 'pay-back' and 'pay-forward'. Pay-back means a return on training investment measurable in financial terms, such as profit or similar terms eg increases in sales, conversion of leads to sales etc. Pay-back evaluation suggests that the option to invest in training can be directly compared with other investment options using standard investment appraisal techniques. Pay-forward, on the other hand, means a benefit flowing from investment in training that cannot be expressed directly in financial terms. This may be in the form of cultural/behaviour change, increased identification on the part of staff with business objectives, or observed changes in individual or team behaviour.

There are, therefore, a number of necessary steps in gaining agreement with stakeholders in the evaluation process (see Figure 38 on page 180). As a result, training professionals must collaborate with stakeholders in agreeing:

- that an identified problem represents a training need, and what the real goals are
- the most appropriate training strategy
- if the chosen strategy has been successfully implemented
- if learning occurred, and to what extent
- the use of learning outcomes (at an individual level)
- the impact and worth of the learning (at an organisational level).

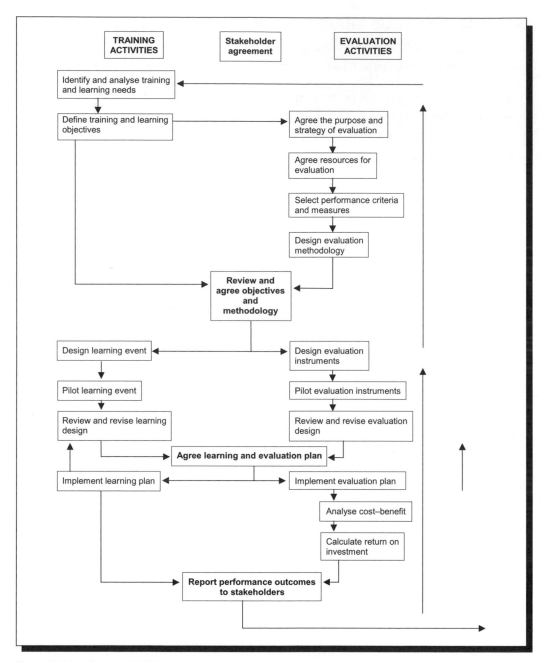

Figure 38 *Evaluation and stakeholders*

Selecting different evaluation processes and methods

Before contemplating how to select different evaluation processes, it is important firstly to remember some of the differences in the underlying learning processes. In considering the relative merits of various formative experiences, Cheetham and Chivers (2001) found the contribution to competence of diverse forms of informal learning varied considerably (see Figure 39).

Many of the respondents in their research highlighted the importance of repetition and practice, or 'iteration', in becoming proficient in any particular area. A number of more general comments were made by the

On-the-job learning
Working alongside more experienced colleagues
Working as part of a team
Self-analysis or reflection
Learning from clients/customers/patients etc
Networking with others doing similar work
Learning through teaching/training others
Support from a mentor of some kind
Use of a role model(s)
Pre-entry experience

Figure 39 *Contributions to competence*

respondents about other factors they considered important to becoming a competent professional. Taken together, these suggest five general factors:

1. the opportunity to experience a wide range of developmental experiences
2. the motivation to acquire the necessary competencies and to improve these continuously
3. adequate practice in carrying out the various key tasks and functions in order to master the requisite competencies
4. persistence in overcoming difficulties and in persevering when things are not going well
5. the influence and support (when needed) of others.

One further point was repeatedly made in relation to more formal training. This was having the opportunity to put something into practice immediately (not at some time in the future). Perhaps training professionals must in future consider this as a crucial area for assessment. Lange and Pugh (1997) determine that learning-by-doing benefits are not necessarily confined to the individual firms that expand output over time:

Labour turnover is one way in which knowledge obtained within one firm can be communicated to other firms. In this case, learning-by-doing within firms entails a positive externality i.e. learning spillovers – by increasing the stock of knowledge available to all firms within the economy. Accordingly, economic growth is a learning process that enhances productivity: i.e. learning and productivity increases are endogenous to growth. Learning-by-doing effects are not just a once-and-for-all source of growth but are a potential link in a process of unbounded growth. This process or cumulative causation sustains a virtuous circle – i.e. a self-expanding process – in which increased output induces productivity increase and thus further output increase (in principle, for ever).

Higson and Wilson (1995) bemoan the fact that managers are often promoted before they receive any management training:

Their training teaches skills which they are later unable to transfer to the workplace. For example: leaders are trained in how to help a group of people escape from being lost in the desert or on the moon. Expensive management games are used to train people in coaching and time management. Managers are trained to give presentations in the expectation that their confidence will improve … Because training courses in the main are not evaluated and because the trainee reverts to being supervised/managed by someone not trained to evaluate anyway, much of the value of training courses is lost.

One prevalent method for aligning learning and performance improvement is through organisation-wide mentoring programmes. But even here, it is imperative that appropriate records are kept. See Figure 40 for a sample mentoring session record. Such a record will not only help both the learner and the mentor, but also others who work in the same operational spheres of both. Such self-assessment is becoming increasingly recognised as being among the most effective methods of evaluating the learning process.

Mentoring session record

Date:

1. Status of items on which I've worked since the last meeting

2. Goals for today

3. Current issues

4. Options based upon current issues

5. Proposed actions (what, by when, resources needed)

6. Things to think about or work to do in the future

Figure 40 *Mentoring session record*

Fitz-enz (2000) has proceeded to amalgamate many of these approaches into a 'composite human capital scorecard', which could become a most useful tool for all HR practitioners, and for those in HRD in particular (see Table 35).

From these approaches, we can easily construct appropriate measures of training and learning that will be congruent with not only the organisation's purpose, function and culture, but also with its people and their many expectations.

Helpfully for the training practitioner, Fitz-enz (2000) has also tabulated a number of process and function metrics (see Table 36 on page 184). Taken together, these can be used to apply different evaluative measures in various organisational settings. It is imperative that HRD professionals adopt a client-centred approach to evaluation, and employ measures of performance such as those shown in the table that are known, transparent and applicable to the appropriate function or department.

Table 35 *Human capital scorecard*

CORPORATE		
Human capital revenue Revenue divided by FTEs*	**Human capital ROI** Revenue minus (expense minus total labour cost) divided by total labour cost	**Human economic value added** Net operating profit after tax minus cost of capital, divided by FTEs
Human capital cost Average cost of pay, benefits, absence, turnover and contingents	**Human capital value added** Revenue minus (expense minus total labour cost), divided by FTEs	**Human market value added** Ratio of market value to book value, divided by FTEs

FUNCTIONS		
Exempt percentage Number of exempt FTEs as a percentage of total FTEs	**Readiness level** Percentage of key positions with at lest one fully qualified person ready	**Satisfaction percentage** Percentage of employees scoring in top quintile of satisfaction survey
Contingent percentage Number of contingent FTEs as a percentage of total FTEs	**Commitment level** Percentage of employees committed to the corporate vision and expecting to stay at least three years	**Corporate climate** Percentage of employees scoring in top quintile of culture and climate survey
Accession rates Replacement hires and hires for new positions as a percentage of the workforce	**Depletion rate** Percentage of exempt separations among top-level performers	**Outsource ratio** Ratio of employee pay and benefits to outsourced and contingent worker cost
Total labour cost revenue percentage All labour costs as a percentage of total revenue	**Performance level** Average performance score compared to revenue per FTE	**Training ROI** Return on training investment

HUMAN RESOURCES			
Acquisition	*Maintenance*	*Development*	*Retention*
Cost per hire Time to fill jobs Number of add hires Number of replacements Quality of new hires	Total labour cost as percentage of operating expense Average pay per employee Benefits cost as percentage of payroll Healthcare cost per employee	■ Training cost as percentage of payroll ■ Total training hours provided ■ Average number of hours of training per employee ■ Training hours by function, job group	Total separation percentage Voluntary separations: exempt/non-exempt Exempt separations by length of service Cost of turnover

*FTEs = 'full-time equivalents'

Table 36 *Metrics for evaluation*

MARKETING	CUSTOMER SERVICE
Marketing costs as percentage of sales Advertising costs as percentage of sales Distribution costs as percentage of sales Sales administration costs as percentage of sales	Service costs as percentage of sales Mean time to respond and repair Service unit cost Customer satisfaction level
INFORMATION SERVICES (IS)	FINANCE
IS costs as percentage of sales Percentage of jobs completed on time and within budget Overtime costs Backlog hours Value of regular reports (use paired comparison)	Accounting costs as percentage of sales Ageing of receivables Accuracy of cost accounting Percentage of filings on time Percentage of on-time closings
FACILITIES	SAFETY and SECURITY
Work order response time Work order completion time Level of employee complaints Maintenance costs as percentage of sales Recycling percentages	Safety and security costs as percentage of sales Accident rates Lost days level Worker compensation costs Security incident rates
PURCHASING	ADMINISTRATIVE SERVICES
Purchasing costs as percentage of sales Average cost to process a requisition Average time to process a requisition Inventory costs Percentage of purchases defective or rejected	General and administrative costs as percentage of sales Outsourcing cost–benefit Average project response time Internal customer satisfaction level Percentage of projects completed on time and within budget

Collaborating in the continuous improvement of training

Here is an example that demonstrates the real costs of investing in people:

The, then, Department of Transport, Local Government and the Regions (DTLR) achieved Investors in People (IiP) recognition in mid-1999. They chose to be re-assessed in October 2001 so that – should they fail in the reassessment – they still had six months to reach the required standard. The Government had instructed each department to achieve IiP status by December 1999, and to retain accreditation. As the only political party at the time to hold accreditation, the Labour Party was satisfied with the benefits of IiP. The costs involved therefore tended to be regarded as almost immaterial. In the grand scheme of government and departmental expenditure, they are also insignificant.

On the surface, it would seem, the only **direct** measurable cost of reassessment was the fee paid to the assessor. This was £550 per day, and the assessment and report took 18 days = **£9,900**.

However, there were many hidden costs. A total of 180 staff from all grades were interviewed. An average cost of one hour each and an estimated on-costed salary of £30 per hour = **£5,400**. These are not fully on-costed values; for example, they do not include accommodation.

Preparing for the reassessment included conducting an internal 'healthcheck' carried out by staff from each division – 35 in the DTLR. The training of a member of staff from each division took two days. The average time spent on the 'healthcheck' was eight days, plus three person-days of interviews. The cost of 13 days × £30 × 7 hours x 35 divisions = **£95,000**.

In addition, there is a three-person team in HR whose sole function is liP matters, and a considerable part of their time was focused on these 'healthchecks', and then the reassessment. An estimate of their time commitment would be two months = **£28,000**.

The production of action plans in the department as a whole and then in each division took yet further time. The identified actions from these plans would require further time still to implement. An estimate might be three days in each division = **£22,000**. Note: if an 'action' involves 'all staff' this is a huge underestimate.

In addition, there are supplementary costs that have not been calculated. Each division was required to brief the staff and in particular the senior team – any of whom might have been selected. Each division produced its own briefing, since the liP position and actions within each are different. Distribution varied from an e-mail note to full divisional meetings.

ESTIMATED TOTAL COST OF REASSESSMENT = up to **£200,000**! (*plus* accommodation and other on-costs).

The costs of continuous improvement are considerable!

PAUSE FOR THOUGHT

Bellco

Bellco is a retail company with 73 supermarkets nationwide in the UK. The stores are typically located on the high street, selling a range of food and drink products, and fill the void in the market left by the larger supermarket chains that have focused their business around large stores in out-of-town settings. Bellco's stores are proving increasingly popular and profitable, and the company is embarking on an expansion programme, which involves the opening of another 45 stores over the next three years.

Each store has a manager, deputy manager, between three and five section managers depending on the size of the store, and between 25 and 40 staff (including, for example, checkout staff and shelf-stackers). The head office is in Dudley in the West Midlands and employees a total of 120 people in core management functions (for example human resources, finance, marketing). There is also a storage and distribution centre, also in the West Midlands, which employees 75 people including drivers. In total, Bellco employs just over 3,000 people.

Initially, Bellco recruited experienced store managers and deputies from the external labour market. Subsequently the company initiated a development programme for deputy managers to prepare them for store management posts. Store management posts continue to be resourced from both these sources; however, with the imminent expansion and with an eye on the quality of senior managers in the long term, Bellco has decided to introduce a graduate management training scheme. The company aims to recruit 10–12 bright and ambitious graduates each year. After a period of familiarisation, each graduate would spend some time as a section head in a store, progressing to deputy manager within around two years, spend a period in a chosen head office function and then progress to managing a small store within a total of three years. Progression thereafter to a regional management role or a post in a head office would be expected to be swift.

(contd)

The programme was designed by the HR department at head office and marketed on the 'milkround'. The 740 applications were whittled down through shortlisting and first interviews to 24. The final selection will be made by assessment centre. Selection at the assessment centre will be based around the competencies (below), which have been identified by the HR department in conjunction with existing store managers.

Graduate management trainee scheme competencies
Interpersonal effectiveness. Communicates clearly, lucidly and enthusiastically. Shows awareness of impact of actions and communication on others. Able to understand and interpret objectives and feelings of others. Persuades others of point of view. Motivates and inspires others. Able to say 'no' under pressure but willing to concede if necessary.
Written communication. Communicates clearly and concisely in writing. Adopts appropriate format and tone for the audience and subject matter. Able to persuade the reader. Uses facts to support arguments.
Analytical skills. Deploys high-level reasoning abilities to solve problems. Able to understand and interpret complex written material and to evaluate competing proposals critically. Able to understand, manipulate and evaluate complex numerical data.
Stress tolerance. Ability to maintain composure and effectiveness under pressure. Retains effectiveness when fatigued. Recognises effects of pressure on self and others, and reacts accordingly.
Planning and organising. Anticipates problems and plans to avoid them. Uses time and resources (including the abilities of others) effectively to meet future objectives. Willingness to change course if necessary.
Business awareness. Awareness and understanding of the business environment. Able to identify and capitalise on business opportunities. Understanding of how actions of self and others impact on business performance.

Your task
Design an assessment centre that will effectively identify those graduates who are suitable to be offered a place on the graduate management training scheme.

Author: Ben Lupton, Manchester Metropolitan University

SUMMARY

As training professionals we must be very clear on the differences between the validation and evaluation of training and learning. To implement a comprehensive, organisation-wide evaluation scheme from scratch will necessitate a considerable release of resources and determination. Nevertheless, if our learning events are to achieve their goal of performance improvement, then it is only responsible of us to undertake an assessment of their effectiveness. For too long, HRD practitioners have escaped from an appropriate financial analysis of their work. However, now you have a means of establishing the ROI of training in terms that middle and senior managers can accept.

QUESTIONS

1. In what ways are performance management and training linked?
2. Discuss ways in which your college or university could evaluate the course you are undertaking.
3. Critically analyse the return on investment of two different learning events with which you are familiar.

The management and marketing of training activities

> Coaching requires the manager to replace authority with a strategy that lets the employee take control.
>
> **Neil Stroul**

LEARNING OUTCOMES

- Explain the main tasks involved in ensuring well-managed and well-marketed training activities.

- List databases and advisory sources that explain the legal and ethical responsibilities of the managers of training events.

CHAPTER OUTLINE

- Effective and efficient management of training events, including

  - the management of training services for various training events

  - managing finances for learning events

  - dealing with issues concerning equality of access, confidentiallty and ethics, related to training events.

- The main tasks involved in organising and delivering effective and well-marketed training events and

  - how to obtain resources to facilitate those tasks

  - how to position and market training events to ensure they meet needs

  - how to collaborate with stakeholders so that training events achieve their desired outcomes.

INTRODUCTION

Work is a dynamic, organic inter-relational set of activities, relying on a multitude of connections in an ever-changing environment of political, economic, social, technological, legal and environmental influences. In an increasingly knowledge-based economy, it can be useful to see both learning, work and knowledge management as being similar – if not the same.

One way of viewing these overlapping activities would be to borrow a model from neuroscience (see Figure 41).

The basic structure of a brain cell can be thought of as being comparable to a tree: it has a trunk (axon), a system of roots (synapses) and a network of branches and twigs (dendrites) (http://science.howstuff works.com/brain1.htm).

Figure 41 *Brain cell*

However, for our purposes here, the astonishing feature of our brain function is not so much in the structure of the cells themselves but in the amazing *connections between them*!

These connections don't actually meet, for there is a minute gap between them, and the body produces hormones (neurotransmitters) to facilitate the electrical flow from one cell to another. Most adults have about 20–50 billion brain cells, and each cell has about 2,000–5,000 synapses. Therefore, the potential number of *connections* between these is ... HUGE! – approximately 6×10^{23}. To put this in context, the population of the whole world is currently only about 6 billion (6×10^{12}).

For me, the wonder is to be found in this enormous creative potential in just one person! If you then add to this the fantastic opportunities you have to make connections with other people, then the possibilities are as awesome as they are endless!

So, taking this metaphor, this chapter is concerned with the responsibilities of managing such possibilities in the context of individual and organisational learning! It is about the optimum utilisation of resources, but it is also about enabling learners to make full use of the infinite number of connective opportunities to develop, grow and mature.

THE MANAGEMENT AND MARKETING OF TRAINING ACTIVITIES – IN THEORY

Ensuring effective management and marketing of training

Wilson (1999) provides us with a useful overview of leadership roles as applied to the HRD function:

- the professional expert
- the provider of vision
- the modeller of the process
- the internal consultant
- the organisational politician.

He continues by pointing out that there are in fact four groups of decision-makers in training and develop-ment, who have a variety of different expectations:

- directors – who need their organisation to perform
- department managers – who seek efficiency
- training professionals – who rate cost-effectiveness highly
- trainees – who are concerned with personal performance.

The writer shows us that the purpose of marketing the training function is to inform stakeholders of:

- the service provided
- the benefits of those services
- the next steps needed to turn interest into business.

He delineates the factors leading to potential loss of existing customers:

- They are dissatisfied with the product you supply.
- They can make significant cost savings with another supplier.
- There is political pressure to try another supplier.
- There is a company policy to try another supplier and/or go out to tender after a set period.

There are a number of marketing streams available to the training manager:

- direct mailing
- telephone sales
- brochures and inserts
- HRD newsletters
- corporate newsletters
- Internet and intranet
- seminars and conferences
- focus groups
- media
- advertisements on television and radio
- advertisements in journals and newspapers
- articles or case studies
- customer visits and consultancy
- word of mouth.

So, how can we ensure effectiveness in the management and marketing of training? Some of the answers at least can be found in the report by Guile and Fonda (1999), which was commissioned by the New Learning for New Work consortium and published by the CIPD. The authors suggest a new paradigm for learning, which provides a most useful overview of organisational learning.

They propose seven guiding principles for management:

1. Management respects the workforce's perspective.
2. Management is clear about the kinds of capabilities expected of the organisation's whole workforce.
3. Management has recognised that the development of these capabilities depends fundamentally on creating an environment where people experience appropriate and relevant performance challenges.
4. Management is working to the principle of 'subsidiarity'.
5. Management understands that people need access to timely, relevant and competent support in identifying and responding to challenges and issues.
6. Management is acutely aware that everybody has their own talents and interests.
7. Management is conscious that this 'challenge and support' environment does not just happen.

The writers then suggest six new imperatives for development that follow from these guiding principles:

1. Focus on the performance challenges for individuals and teams.
2. See performance challenges as encompassing tomorrow's employability as well as today's work.
3. Recognise that most development is the result of social experience and interaction.
4. See development needs and development pathways as contingent.
5. Assume everyone has rights as well as responsibilities.
6. Collaborate for capability development.

The authors develop their hypothesis further by promoting a new development partnership between the four main stakeholders:

1. top managers
2. senior managers
3. front-line managers
4. front-line staff.

They then complete their innovative paradigm by advocating a new learning cycle, which works through social, cultural and collective processes, and depends on the commitment and competences of the four stakeholders (see Figure 42).

Guile and Fonda (1999) believe that this shift from task management to value-added management involves the introduction of both new management strategies as well as people management and development chal-

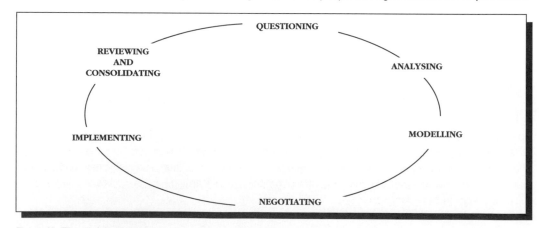

Figure 42 *The new learning cycle*

lenges. Taken together, these 'building blocks' can help organisations to develop their employees in an integrated, organic manner, in order that they can achieve the goal of taking responsibility for adding value. Figure 43, which shows their new learning paradigm, provides a coherent framework in which the goal can be achieved. They feel that such a dynamic partnership is qualitatively different from traditional, hierarchical 'command and control' approaches.

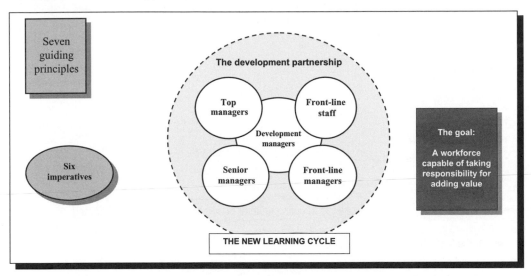

Figure 43 *The new learning paradigm (adapted from Guile and Fonda 1999)*

Interestingly, Bahar *et al* (1996) found the training and development situation in Bahrain not dissimilar to that proposed by Guile and Fonda. The training culture was characterised by eight binary variables:

1. existence of top management support for training
2. involvement of line managers in training programme selection
3. existence of formal training objectives
4. integration of training plans with business plans
5. training manager, not higher manager, matches employees to training
6. training manager, not higher manager, approves requests for training by individuals
7. training utilised for career development, rather than general knowledge acquisition
8. positive attitude to training needs analysis (willingness to identify weaknesses).

Training management and training leadership
It is important to briefly review the nature, function and purpose of training management and training leadership. This will help to inform those in positions of responsibility for training and development in any organisation.

According to Campbell (1996), twenty-first-century human resources trends require new management skills:

> During the past 20 years, human resources management has developed into a sophisticated and important organisational tool. A 1996 study identified the most important trends affecting the future of human resource management. The study also describes HR strategies and competencies necessary to cope with the anticipated changes.

She goes on to assert that:

Six major trends are expected to drive workplace change during the next ten years and into the 21st century. To meet the challenge of managing and growing companies in this environment, business managers and human resources professionals will need to be adroit strategic planners with the skill to transition ideas within their operations.

These trends are:

- globalisation
- technology
- change
- knowledge capital
- speed in market change
- cost control.

She found in her study that unique trends affecting smaller businesses were also highlighted:

- managing change
- speed of change
- using technology to advantage
- application of technology
- excellence of product/service.

Such outcomes appear to be supported by Robinson and Stern (1995), who charted the history of the Management Training Programme (MTP) in Japan, which was introduced by the US Air Force during the occupation period after the Second World War. The Japanese Federation of Employers' Association and the Ministry of International Trade have since taken responsibility for the programme. They observe that many 'Japanese' management practices are in fact based in the originally-American MTP or its offshoots, but that it is virtually unknown in the west, despite its roots.

They give an outline of the course, which included:

- theory of organisation and management
- job-instruction training
- job-methods training
- job-relations training.

They maintain that the MTP's influence on Japanese management has been higher than the Training Within Industries (TWI) programmes because it is taught at a higher level. Although quantitative evidence is scarce, MTP has been essential in promoting the practices of continuous improvement and the 'plan–do–see' approach, which enabled the development of quality control. The authors considered the implications for HRD, concluding that success will depend on:

- the importance of a common training platform
- government support

- regular revisions of the programme
- implications for management training in developing countries.

Their fascinating and illuminating article ends by asserting that it is impossible to understand Japanese management without understanding the MTP! Nearer to home, Sayers (1999) delineates Covey's four management paradigms (see Table 37). Such an analysis has much to offer organisations in general, and training managers in particular. To contrast with this, Cohen and Tichy (1997) discovered a model for organisational leadership, based on their examination of a number of successful businesses in the USA, including one successful non-profit organisation. They make five observations on successful leadership and how it can be developed:

- Good leaders should be judged on the performance of their organisation in adding value for shareholders.
- Successful organisations have leaders at every level within the company.
- Leaders are the best people to develop new leaders.
- Leaders need to understand, and be able to communicate, what it is that makes them good leaders.
- Good leaders are able to communicate their vision of how they see the organisation develop.

They use the story of Shell Oil, under the leadership of Phil Carroll, to illustrate how this kind of leadership can turn a company around, also explaining the contribution made by Shell's Learning Centre to the successful development of leadership within the company as a whole.

Critiquing the need for adequate paradigms of leadership and management in organisations, Thomas (1999) explains that:

The perception of many people in Europe is that the European Community is dominated by skilled incompetence. The perception is that highly paid and well-trained people run administrative machines that are just doing the wrong things.

This phenomenon will usually emerge when we respond to tasks with inadequate paradigms of how we learn ... What happens is that politics, arrogance and ignorance provide effective blocks to healthy learning and, in turn, to incompetence. Very often, we are not aware of this going on inside ourselves and in the lives of the people we are working with, as Ralph Stacey said: 'The real causes of poor strategic management – the learning process, the political interaction and group dynamic – remain stubbornly undiscussable.'

Table 37 Covey's four management paradigms

Need	Metaphor	Paradigm	Principle
Physical, economic	Stomach	Scientific, authoritarian	Fairness
Social, economic	Heart	Human relations (benevolent authoritarian)	Kindness
Psychological	Mind	Human resources	Use and development of talent
Spiritual	Spirit (whole person)	Principle-centred leadership	Meaning

Writers have stressed over time that effective leaders need to be flexible and adaptable. Hickman (1992) illustrates the management/leadership matrix, showing the range of styles available (see Table 38).

To contrast with Hickman's (1992) approach, and to see how leadership styles cover a range of different perspectives, Rolls (1995) offers her analysis of the work of the transformational leader and the appropriate *followership* expectations. Clearly, such an approach would be very attractive to many training leaders (see Table 39 on page 196).

Combining much of this work on management and leadership, Hickman (1992) gives an extremely effective view of management/leadership types by using the framework of the popular Myers-Briggs Personality Type Indicator® (see Table 40 on page 197). This helpful extension to the well-known MBPTI offers an easy entrance to a study of the management/leadership continuum. And Table 41 on page 198 gives you another way of looking at the MBPTI.

Table 38 *Hickman's management/leadership matrix*

Success factors	Management-dominated	Leadership-driven	Conflict-oriented	Vacillation-prone	Balanced and integrated
Competitive strategy/ advantage	Pursue same-game strategies	Formulate new-game strategies	Develop both same- and new-game strategies	Follow reactive strategies	Implement changing-game strategies
Organisation-al culture/ capability	Perpetuate cultures	Create cultures	Change and provoke cultures	Confuse cultures	Renew cultures
External/ internal change	Strive for stability	Thrive on crisis	Force stability and crisis together	Shift between stability and crisis	Blend stability and crisis
Individual effectiveness/ style	Prefer a structured approach	Favour an unstructured approach	Choose a loose/tight approach	Exhibit an uncertain approach	Promote a dynamic approach
Bottom-line performance/ results	Focus on tangible short-term results	Seek for intangible long-term results	Want both tangible short-term and intangible long-term results	Obtain marginal or negative results	Balance tangible short-term and intangible long-term results.

PAUSE FOR THOUGHT

Examine Hickman's management/leadership matrix in Table 37 and apply it to your own organisation. What conclusions can you draw?

Then, by way of summarising this whole section on management and leadership in the training and development function, explore some of the similarities and differences. Complete a Venn diagram for each:

1. MANAGING LEADING

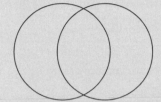

3. MANAGER LEADER

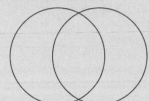

2. MANAGEMENT LEADERSHIP

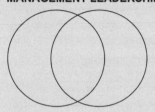

THE MANAGEMENT AND MARKETING OF TRAINING ACTIVITIES – IN PRACTICE

Ensuring effective management and marketing of training

Based on the results of research using two surveys, Fitz-enz (2000) tabulates some of the reasons for outsourcing the training function, and their relative success rates (see Tables 42 and 43 on pages 199–200). From these we can see how the performance of training managers could be assessed.

Against this backdrop of the nature and function of the role of the training manager, it is important to note that the research by Darling and her colleagues (1999) revealed the changing nature of the training market:

- a reduction in direct training, with a greater emphasis on facilitation and advisory/consultancy work
- a shift towards organisational development as a more strategic approach to training
- the need for organisations to constantly improve performance while still valuing people
- the expectation that line managers should take more responsibility for developing their staff through coaching, mentoring etc
- more cross-departmental working and working in multidisciplinary teams
- changes to training delivery which was becoming ever-more customer-focused and flexible
- more outsourcing of training to external consultants
- increasing globalisation: for one respondent this meant, for example, that 'you might never meet the people you manage – someone in the UK could be managing people in Barcelona or Moscow.'

Table 39 *Leadership and fellowship*

The five disciplines	Leadership competencies	Followership expectations
Systems thinking	Expansionist thinking Understanding of connectivity Intuition Perspective integration	Understanding the whole
Personal mastery	Compassion Self- and other-acceptance Shared power Authenticity Nurturance of spirit Moral leadership Sensitivity Humility Mastery Growth-oriented Risk-taking Self-directed Tolerance Value-ambiguity Trust Spirituality Ego-subordination	Encouragement Acceptance Empowerment Trust Self-discovery Someone worth working for Dignity Autonomy Fulfilled potential Growth Supported choice Independence Space to make mistakes Support in transition Learning Responsibility Self/other connection Ownership of results
Mental models	Insight Introspection Challenge assumptions Innovation	Innovation Meaning Challenge assumptions
Shared vision	Principles Personal/organisational values alignment Inspiration Goals Vision Vitality Mobilise commitment	Sense of purpose Personal/organisational values alignment Motivation Clarity Co-develop vision Engagement Commitment
Team learning	Co-operation Dialogue Listening Creativity Promote harmony Encourage relationship	Co-design Self-expression Contribution Creativity Social unity Relationship

Table 40 *Manager / leader types*

MANAGER ←――――――――――――――――――――――――――――→ **LEADER**

ISTJ	ISFJ	INFJ	INTJ
RESPONSIBLE MANAGER	ACCOMMODATING MANAGER	INSPIRATIONAL LEADER	PERFECTING LEADER
Does things right	*Serves people*	*Inspires others*	*Improves everything*
ISTP	ISFP	INFP	INTP
SOLUTION MANAGER	OBSERVANT MANAGER	IDEALISTIC LEADER	HOLISTIC LEADER
Addresses expedient needs	*Is sensitive to all*	*Seeks to transform society*	*Pursues logical purity*
ESTP	ESFP	ENFP	ENTP
REALISTIC MANAGER	ENTHUSIASTIC MANAGER	OPPORTUNISTIC LEADER	INVENTIVE LEADER
Gets things done	*Makes work enjoyable*	*Discovers possibilities*	*Finds new insights*
ESTJ	ESFJ	ENFJ	ENTJ
ACHIEVING MANAGER	FACILITATING MANAGER	PERSUASIVE LEADER	CONQUERING LEADER
Accomplishes objectives	*Provides help*	*Articulates values*	*Drives towards goals*

Table 41 *Half full ... or half empty ...?*

ISTJ	ISFJ	INFJ	INTJ
'It's half empty now, and it wouldn't surprise me if it dried up completely.'	Thinks: 'I bet my friend would like to have some water right now . . .'	Thinks: 'This glass of water is a metaphor for my life.'	Thinks: 'Glass is made from silicon dioxide, heated to a temperature of . . .
ISTP	**ISFP**	**INFP**	**INTP**
'So? It's water. Big deal!'	Holds up glass of water, tilts it from side to side, wiggles finger in it, licks finger, grins slightly, moves on.	'But look! A crystalline vessel, filled with shimmering, life-giving nectar!	Thinks: 'The glass is full ... half water, half air!'
ESTP	**ESFP**	**ENFP**	**ENTP**
'You call that a glass of water! Why, back where I come from ...'	'There's a glass of water! You know, it's really healthy to drink a lot of water! Why, I remember when I was growing up, ...'	'Whoopee! Water fight!'	'Voilà! 0.157 litres of dihydrogen oxide, prepared by micrognomes.'
ESTJ	**ESFJ**	**ENFJ**	**ENTJ**
'Hey! Whose job was it to fill up this glass?'	'I can't believe someone would leave this dirty glass out here! Clean up this mess right now!'	'There's more than enough for friends to share.'	'Hey! This is a beer glass, not a water glass!'

Source: 1996 Outsourcing Survey, Hewitt Associates.

Table 42 *Reasons for outsourcing the training function*

Reason	Met objectives (%)	Did not meet objectives (%)	Too soon to tell (%)
Improve cost-effectiveness	82	5	13
Reduce administrative costs	75	8	17
Capitalise on technological advancement/expertise	82	7	11
Improve customer service	70	19	11
Redirect HR focus toward strategy and planning	66	15	19
Allow company to focus on core business	63	21	16
Reduce corporate overhead	82	9	9
Provide seamless delivery of services	47	38	15
Lack of sufficient staff	69	27	4
Increase level of participant satisfaction	54	27	19
Improve response time to requests	59	29	12
Control legal risk, improve compliance	53	29	8
Increase flexibility in handling special needs	41	38	11
Increase level of accuracy	49	41	10
Make administrative costs more definable	45	44	11
Implement total quality management	17	71	12

Source: 1999 Outsourcing Survey, Hewitt Associates.

Table 43 *Rationale for outsourcing the training function*

Rationale	%
Most common reasons for outsourcing: ■ improve HR service delivery or quality ■ access to technology ■ access to expertise/innovation	 91 74 70
Secondary reasons for outsourcing: ■ predictable HR costs ■ increase flexibility ■ reduce administrative headcount	 36 34 31
Least important criteria for outsourcing: ■ reduce risks ■ redeploy and refocus HR resources ■ reduce administrative headcount	 44 42 41
Top criteria incorporated into service agreement: ■ predictable HR costs ■ improve HR service delivery/quality ■ access to technology	 76 70 54

Source: 1999 Outsourcing Survey, Saratoga Institute and Andersen Consulting, V. Yeh, editor.

PAUSE FOR THOUGHT

In the light of changes to the training market, how should training managers market their programmes?

Compare your answers with these tips from Hodges (2002):

- Ensure the programme objectives are aligned with the organisational mission.
- Take steps to get the future participants excited about the programme.
- Build transfer of training into supervisory performance standards.
- Set specific programme expectations.
- Brief participants on the importance of the training and on course objectives, content, process, and application to the job.
- Select programme participants carefully.
- Offer rewards and promotional preference to participants who demonstrate new behaviours.
- Arrange conferences with prior trainees.
- Review instructional content and materials.

We can see the need for an alignment between the needs of the individual, the strategy of the organisation, and provision by the training function. According to Harrison (2002), where line managers carry the main responsibility for the learning and development function in their units, there may still be a small central learning and development unit. If there is, its role will usually be one of ensuring overall strategic direction and of monitoring and co-ordinating the learning and development process across the organisation.

Harrison (2002) believes that there are four principles that should always be observed when handing over primary responsibility for the learning and development process to line manager.

- Have a clear learning and development corporate vision and strategy that is in line with overall HR and business goals and strategy.
- Have strategic learning and development objectives that are carried through by divisional and unit managers into detailed, practical plans for implementation of the policies that serve those objectives.
- Have an organisational structure and company-wide systems and procedures to ensure that all who carry learning and development roles and responsibilities have a clear understanding of their tasks.
- Have a system of training, guidance, monitoring, appraisal and rewards related to performance development and recognition of all those who carry learning and development roles and responsibilities.

The legal and ethical responsibilities of training managers

What are some of the issues in organising and managing that have a clear ethical dimension? Stewart (1999) outlines a number of areas of significance for all training professionals:

- employees
  - hiring and firing
  - right to liberty eg freedom of speech
  - right to privacy
  - right to fair wages
  - quality of working life
  - information/confidentiality
- customers
  - product quality and safety

- pricing policies
- advertising
- communities
  - pollution
  - physical environment
  - closure of operations
- government
  - compliance with legislation
  - implementation of regulations
  - tax returns
- shareholders
  - honesty
  - providing a return
- other organisations
  - acting honestly and fairly
  - honouring contracts.

PAUSE FOR THOUGHT

Review carefully the list (above) of ethical issues that affect organising and managing. How well does your organisation measure up to these criteria? Organise a meeting to discuss these issues. What were the outcomes, and why?

The legal and ethical responsibilities of training managers – some resources

Codes of practice

Code of Professional Practice for Trainers
http://www.aitd.com.au/downloads/part2_code_of_professional_practice.pdf
This document comes from the Australian Institute of Training and Development.

Management Responsibilities – Training and Reference Guide
http://www.utsa.edu/Audit/WEB_PAGES1/Mgnt-Resp-trai-Guide.htm

HRM Training Database
http://www.appl003.lsu.edu/hrm/hrmtraining.nsf/$Content/Non-Managers?OpenDocument
These two policies and procedures are taken from the universities and as such would be most useful for training managers.

Code of Professional, Social and Ethical Responsibility for Professional and Managerial Staff
http://www.union-network.org/UNIsite/Groups/PMS/publications/Code_e.PDF
This policy comes from the Swiss-based Union Network International, a global union for skills and services, with 1,000 affiliates and 15 million members.

Code of Conduct of the Global Knowledge Economics Council
http://www.gkec.org/code_of_conduct_of_the_GKEC.htm

Portals on business and management ethics, responsibilities and rights
Training managers and employees
http://www.business-humanrights.org/Training-managers-employees.htm

Online ethics centre – responsibilities of a team leader
http://onlineethics.org/corp/leader.html

Managing ethics in the workplace: a practical guide for managers
http://www.managementhelp.org/fp_progs/etx_mod/ethics.htm

Ethical corporation
http://www.ethicalcorp.com/

E-centre for business ethics
http://www.e-businessethics.com/orgcitizen2.htm

SUMMARY

We have seen in this chapter that the role and function of those with responsibility for the managing and marketing of learning events is constantly changing. Old paradigms and constructs will no longer suffice. There is a continuing migration towards embracing leadership, and to the consideration of followers. In addition, training professionals should welcome the infinite possibilities afforded to learners to connect with one another in their new-found roles as knowledge workers.

QUESTIONS

1. Argue the case for the creation of a new post of learning and development director in an organisation with which you are familiar.
2. An organisation has recently been heavily fined for repeated and significant breaches of health and safety at work legislation. Show how the management of learning and development could help to prevent a repetition of such faults.
3. Discuss the benefits and drawbacks of having a centralised learning and development department.

The continuing professional development (CPD) of the training practitioner

> To teach a man how he may learn to grow independently, and for himself, is perhaps the greatest service that one man can do another.
>
> **Benjamin Jowett**

LEARNING OUTCOMES

- Describe models and research relating to the core competencies and behavioural characteristics of effective trainers.

- Demonstrate techniques of self-assessment and continuing self-development for the training practitioner.

CHAPTER OUTLINE

- Models of core competencies of effective trainers. Continuous professional development and

  - regularly updating expertise and knowledge

  - identifying and making appropriate use of good practice and innovation related to training tasks and the training process.

- Practitioner guidelines for trainers, including

  - matters relating to the training and effectiveness of training professionals

  - training practice and problems, and their implications for the development of training practitioners.

INTRODUCTION

In this final chapter, we get an opportunity to spend some time thinking about ourselves. Too often, in my experience, training professionals spend their time and expertise on the training and development of others – *at their own expense*! Rarely do trainers take time to seriously consider their own development needs and plans. And so in this chapter there will be a number of very practical tasks to undertake, in order to give you a chance to reflect on your past learning, to assess your current skills, and to plan your future progress.

THE CONTINUING PROFESSIONAL DEVELOPMENT (CPD) OF THE TRAINING PRACTITIONER – IN THEORY

Core competencies of effective trainers

At one extreme, Stewart (1999) argues that training practitioners need to develop political and influencing skills, and that these should become a focus for their CPD. And at the other extreme, Rae (2002a) outlines the 17 skills that an effective trainer needs to develop:

- organisational knowledge
- management roles and functions
- training knowledge
- programme presentation skills
- technological and e-technology skills
- sensitivity to programme feedback
- people skills
- resilience
- commitment
- mental agility
- creativity
- self-development
- self-awareness
- sharing
- credibility
- humour
- self-confidence.

On the other hand, training officer capabilities have been synthesised by Pepper (1984) into just five main groups:

1. understanding situations
2. working with and through people
3. analysis and design
4. administration
5. the management of learning.

In commenting on competencies and workplace learning, Garavan and McGuire (2001) find that:

> Core competencies derive from within the realm of strategy and competitive advantage and some would argue that it is stretching it somewhat to call the strategic resources of the organisation core competencies ... Such a preoccupation reflects the strong positivistic assumptions that characterise the general discourse on competencies. A view prevails that, until there is a satisfactory resolution of the measurement problem, the competency approach will be subject to questions concerning its validity. Others question the futility of a positivist perspective and suggest that scepticism will exist as to whether or not it is entirely possible to condense jobs into a series of clearly defined competencies or attributes. An alternative, interpretivist paradigm argues that the notion of competence and competencies should be studies in a specific context, where the interaction issues of worker and work can be fully considered.

Self-assessment and self-development for trainers

Let's now move on to self-assessment and self-development for trainers. The CIPD has taken a lead in the last few years when it comes to CPD. Many other professions have had systems of CPD for a while; for example, accountants and solicitors, doctors and surveyors, engineers, nurses and teachers, have all had to undertake CPD in order to maintain their accreditation or their license to practise. In most of these examples, the CPD requirement is stated in terms of *inputs* rather than *outcomes* – the minimum number of hours that are spent on training courses or programmes; qualifications achieved; or certificates of attendance received.

The CIPD on the other hand has insisted from the outset that CPD, if it means anything at all, must be centred on *outcomes*. As training professionals, we must be concerned not with the courses, programmes, workshops or conferences that we have attended, but the learning that we have achieved and applied. It is also currently voluntary by nature, which is an important component of learning. But the CIPD has stressed that learning needs to be seen to take place everywhere and anywhere: reading a magazine or journal, watching a video, going to a meeting, discussing a situation with a colleague, attending a workshop or a lecture, or attending a branch meeting. All of these are golden opportunities for learning to be developed. And if these are then aligned to performance management systems or appraisal systems and linked with an individual's personal development plan or career development plan, then it's easy to see how the individual employee can decide beforehand how they want to develop and in what ways they're going to learn in the future.

It can be most instructive if you decide beforehand what you want to get out of a task group, how you want to learn from a conference, or in what ways you're going to develop if you're meeting your mentor, rather than merely reflecting afterwards on what has happened.

Self-development and self-assessment are becoming increasingly important for all employees, and therefore trainers must be models of good practice and good behaviour. Because of the ways in which organisations have changed dramatically over the last few years, it is less likely that the organisation will be concerned with the career path of the individual employee. It may have succession plans, although the sustainability of even those are questionable in many organisations. And so it is important for the employee to take responsibility not just for their learning, but also for their future development. Trainers especially need to fashion a career for themselves. Whether this is to include developing their professional expertise, their technical competence, or their specialist understanding; whether it's to go back into line management, or to stay within training and development; these questions must be addressed by the trainer themselves. Of course there will be conversations and discussions with line managers, HR professionals, possibly career development specialists within the organisation or in an outsourced consultancy, but the initiative and the motivation must come from the trainers themselves.

Self-assessment is difficult (see how you get on with the exercise on the next page), because it is unusual and there are problems of lack of time, or opportunity or inclination. But it is also uncomfortable because of the obvious limitations of subjectivity. Nevertheless, if you are to achieve your full potential, it is important to establish goals and targets – which must be specific, measurable, appropriate, realistic and timely – and are also apposite for the particular phase in your career. It's important to diarise opportunities to reflect, review and assess to what extent those targets have been achieved. And this will be complementary to, and outside of, your normal organisational performance management systems, because it is unlikely that the organisation will do it for you.

Trainers must see themselves as learners, and therefore model all the best practices of effective learners in, firstly, identifying their needs, then helping to design and be involved in the learning event, and finally assessing and evaluating the outcomes of those interventions. But the trainer needs to take the initiative, as a learner, in effecting those learning events.

PAUSE FOR THOUGHT

McGoldrick *et al* (2002) posit a number of questions to help the training practitioner focus on their 'being', that is to say, their engagement in a particular field. Take a few minutes now to reflect on these questions for yourself. How do you respond?

Efficacy questions	Responses
■ Am I familiar with the field and its literature? ■ Am I actually involved with the relevant data? ■ Have I got appropriate qualifications for dealing with the relevant matters? ■ Do I have dependable work habits? ■ Am I intelligent enough and intellectually tough enough? *'Self and other' questions* ■ Am I aware of my own motives? ■ Am I questioning my involvement with the field? ■ What relationship with others do I set up by my way of being? ■ Can I listen to others? *Political and power questions* ■ Am I aware of the social implications of my daily practice? ■ Am I aware of the sources of the money that supports me? ■ Am I aware of the social pressures that Influence my actions? ■ Am I sexist? Racist? Classist? Ageist? ■ Do I see life in terms of domination and submission? Competition and acclaim? Struggle for recognition? ■ Am I aware of the patriarchal patterns that surround me? *Dialectical questions* ■ Do I look for the contradictions underlining daily experience? ■ Do I take responsibility for my own life? ■ Do I perceive the world in terms of conflicts and their resolution? ■ Do I see the paradox of rhythm and the rhythm of paradox? *Legitimacy questions* ■ Is a client involved? If so, is there honesty or deception or lack of communication between the client and me? ■ Who provides the problem? Who defines what the problem is? Who owns the problem? Who legitimates the problem? ■ Who is the client? And who is the real client? *Relevance questions* ■ Am I choosing a problem that is relevant to my life? My career? A client? Ordinary people? Questioning patriarchy? The advancement of science? A class of problems? My unconscious? ■ What am I really trying to do?	

Edwards (1999) argues in favour of self-assessment on two counts. Firstly, self-assessment encourages greater individual responsibility for learning. Therefore, the learning is deeper, richer and more relevant. Secondly, the learner is in the best position to judge what learning has actually taken place. Naturally, self-assessment can be criticised for a lack of validity or reliability, but such criticism can be overcome through peer assessment. Furthermore, triangulating views from several other people through stakeholder analysis, 180- or 360-degree appraisal, will go further still in achieving a realistic assessment of performance.

As Irvine and Beard (1999) assert:

> The key to self-development is that learners take responsibility for their own learning.

They contend that there are historical precedents for self-development that predate modern changes in business practice. Successive Indian civilisations, for example, have apparently developed – over many centuries – various methodologies for self-discovery, self-improvement and self-development.

How can training specialists meet their development needs? Stewart and Tansley (2002) suggest ways in which specialists can gain knowledge about the services and support available for trainers via their professional body, to help their varied learning requirements and to support their needs for relevant professional information, knowledge and contacts:

- being prepared to respond to high job demands and address difficulties in managing their CPD
- forming networks, partnerships or discussion groups, whether virtual or otherwise, in order to provide both employed and self-employed training professionals with informal learning opportunities.

Leadbetter (2001) proposes an innovative approach to equipping ourselves to take ownership for our work, which could be particularly relevant to training practitioners, and which he calls *authorship*:

> Although a sense of authorship may be developed and learned, it has to come from within. It cannot be taught and delivered from without. And it takes time, trial, error, and experimentation, as much in the 'real world' of work as in the classroom. Learning about yourself, what you really want to do, and what you are good at, probably never ends. Learning does not prepare people for work so much as provide an essential ingredient of work.

So learning and work become inseparable. As learners, we must take responsibility for our own learning!

Figure 44 shows a model of work and learning. If we now overlay this view of personal development on to Kolb's classic model of learning, we create Figure 45 on page 210. And finally, this puts us in a position to illustrate the drivewheel in the cycle of personal development, as in Figure 46 on page 211.

The motive force for this development will come from a combination of:

- yourself
- your peers
- your mentor
- your manager
- your subordinates
- your learning network.

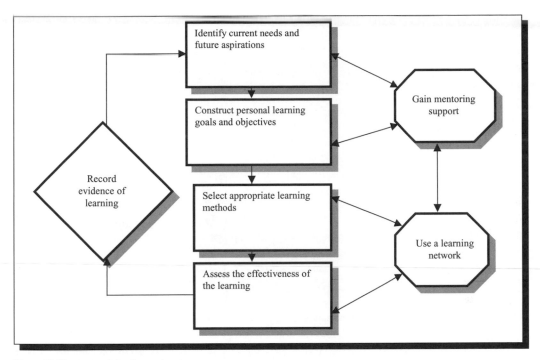

Figure 44 *The personal development cycle*

THE CONTINUING PROFESSIONAL DEVELOPMENT (CPD) OF THE TRAINING PRACTITIONER – IN PRACTICE

Core competencies of trainers

A number of writers have looked at the role of the trainer and the way this has changed over the years, both in response to the nature of training, and the character and speed of change. Consequently, the core competencies of effective trainers have changed. And while training practitioners still need the skill and the ability to present information effectively to different sizes of groups, in different locations, and in different situations, such competence is perhaps less important than it once was. Increasingly, trainers are also being required to demonstrate success in areas of facilitation, empowerment, coaching, mentoring, problem-solving, internal consultancy and change agency.

In the past, writers have made lists of what they consider to be the core competencies of trainers. However, for the training professional in the twenty-first century, I think we need to address a different set of knowledge, skills and attitudes. I feel these differ from those that are set out for NVQ purposes, by the Employment National Training Organisation and even the CIPD itself.

The study by Campbell (1996) identified a competency skill set for human resources practitioners:

- people skills
- understanding of the business
- credibility
- leadership
- comfort with change (and ambiguity)
- consultative approach
- establishment of mutual faith and trust 10 years from now.

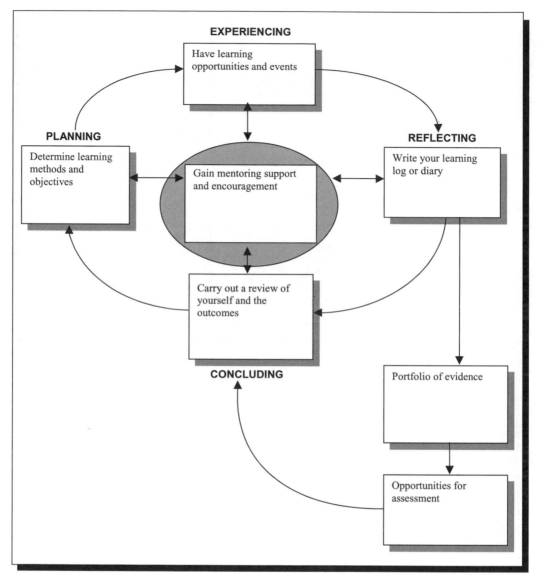

Figure 45 *Personal development and experiential learning*

If we are to become the change-makers and transformational leaders of tomorrow, then we need to espouse these competencies with enthusiasm.

Perhaps a fuller set of competencies is required. For example, the ASTD research reported by Wilson (1999) identified 35 areas of competence for those involved with HRD in the USA: (*core competency)

Technical competencies
1. adult learning understanding*
2. career development theories and techniques understanding
3. competency identification skill*
4. computer competence
5. electronic systems skill

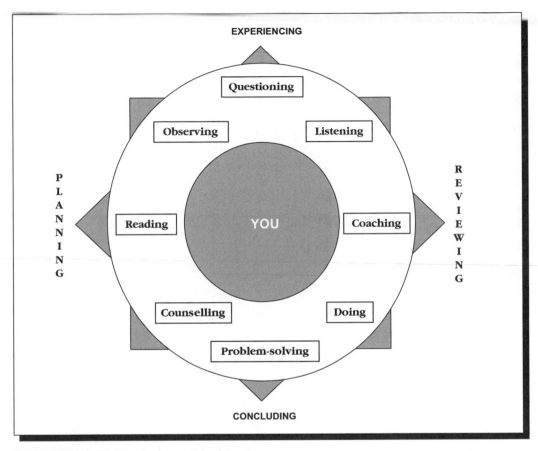

Figure 46 *Drivewheel in the cycle of personal development*

6. facilities skill
7. objective preparation skill*
8. performance observation skill
9. subject-matter understanding
10. understanding of training and development theories and techniques
11. research skill

Business competencies
12. business understanding*
13. cost–benefit analysis skill
14. delegation skill
15. industry understanding
16. organisational behaviour understanding*
17. understanding of organisational development theories and techniques
18. organisational understanding
19. projects-management skill
20. records-management skill

Interpersonal competencies
21. coaching skill
22. feedback skill*

23. group process skill
24. negotiation skill
25. presentation skill*
26. questioning skill*
27. relationship building skill*
28. writing skill*

Intellectual competencies
29. data-reduction skill
30. information search skill*
31. intellectual versatility*
32. model-building skill
33. observing skill*
34. self-knowledge
35. visioning skill.

How do you feel about such a list? Is it daunting or exhilarating? Is it irrelevant to your situation or a good measure for you to use currently?

In a quite different form of study, Darling and her colleagues (1999) found a number of skills required by different training professionals, including:

- training managers and team leaders
    - understanding of the business
    - good product knowledge (what the business offers)
    - people management
    - teamwork
    - juggling funding
    - passing on information
    - analysis and interpretation of information
    - developing profiles/forecasts
    - interpersonal skills
    - listening to the customer
    - influencing
    - enjoying going out to meet people
- training advisers and internal consultants
    - understanding the business/technical area
    - counselling skills
    - technical knowledge in professional area
    - taking responsibility
    - negotiating
    - assertiveness (particularly for team leaders)
    - interpersonal skills
    - curriculum design

- diagnostic/analytic skills
- contracting
- generating income
- research.

On the other hand, Dean (2001) asserts that in order to become an effective change professional, HRD professionals need to develop a number of *skills*:

- business understanding
- change-facilitation skills
- interpersonal skills
- employee-relations skills
- conflict-resolution skills
- conceptual skills
- negotiating skills
- technical skills
- consensus- and commitment-building skills
- analytical skills
- objectivity
- intuition
- project-management skills
- change alignment
- forthrightness
- organisation subordination
- ambiguity.

The researcher goes on to say that HRD professionals need to develop several areas of *expertise* to be successful organisation change professionals, including:

- establishing and managing client relationships
- conducting analyses
- identifying root causes
- recommending and implementing solutions
- evaluating results
- facilitating learning
- building partnerships
- facilitating change.

Stewart and Tansley in their 2002 research find that the training needs of training specialists have changed considerably, and now include items such as:

- maintaining a high level of specialist knowledge, not only in training and development, but also in business strategy and practice

- maintaining awareness of changing employment structures for themselves and their clients
- becoming reflective practitioners in the way they encourage their clients to do.

Similarly, Lynton and Pareek (2000b) recall a personal example to illustrate one of the key characteristics of effective trainers:

> Standing after the final session with some participants whose departure was delayed, one of the authors felt free to inquire: 'Why did you give Mel [a trainer] such a hard time?' After listening to their complaints, he added: 'But when I made similar mistakes, you helped me.' 'Oh,' came the rejoinder, 'that's different. You like us.' In a recent survey of 1,000 college students in America aimed at eliciting what characteristics in their instructors they found most helpful, even a 'steady temper' rated low. Top score went to enthusiasm.

Self-assessment and self-development for trainers

Reid and Barrington (2000) helpfully suggest a fresh approach to the tasks of self-assessment and self-development. They give several examples of questions to promote what they call 'reflection in action'. These are shown in Table 44.

Table 44 *'Reflection in action' (Reid and Barrington, 2000)*

Situation	Questions
New experience	■ Is this likely to happen again? ■ If so, should I behave differently? ■ Do I need to be better informed for a repeat?
New information	■ Will I need this information in the future? ■ If so, how can I ensure access to it then?
New problem	■ Has anyone else experienced this? ■ Is this problem analogous to …? ■ How can I share the problem with others?
Clash of opinions	■ What are the assumptions underlying each? ■ How fundamental is the difference?
Request for advice	■ Am I the best adviser? ■ How can I advise without creating dependency?
All situations	■ Do I need to communicate this to others?

Clearly, as professionals in the field, we need to model good practice by regularly completing our own learning logs and personal development plans (PDPs).

According to Floodgate and Nixon (1994), PDPs help people:

- adopt a structured way to analyse their strengths and development needs
- articulate this knowledge to their line manager/personnel manager in an objective manner which then results in their getting exposure to the learning activities they require

- keep a tangible record of their achievements against learning targets (a critical factor in measuring success in their performance review)
- identify the skills, knowledge and abilities they have and be able to express themselves in this way rather than just by their job title and grade
- see the PDP as a living document which is for their benefit and not simply another return to be completed for head office.

SUMMARY

So, we have travelled together a long way, on this road of self-assessment and self-development. As trainers, we need to set a good example to our learners and our colleagues in taking seriously the need we have to determine our futures.

As a closing thought, I would just like to add that you don't *have* to accept any 'life script' that may have been imposed on you in your life. There may have been a parent, a teacher, a spouse, or some other significant person in your life who has said something negative about you often enough for you to believe it. In my own case, at the very impressionable age of about 12, I remember sitting in the art class, working really quite hard on a particular painting. Art had never been my first love, but on this occasion I really wanted to do my best. The teacher approached my table, took one look at my labours, and demanded: 'What on earth is that?' When I replied it was a picture of a bird with her chicks in a nest, he just burst out laughing, and said: 'You'll never be any good at art!'

For many years, I believed him. However, I have enjoyed, with considerable satisfaction, my efforts with photography, and I have decided in the near future to learn how to do wood sculpture.

I have also really enjoyed the creative process of putting together this book for you. I hope you have enjoyed – and learnt something from – reading it.

Because it has been, it does not mean it has to be.

QUESTIONS

1. In what ways are performance management and training linked?
2. Argue the case for the introduction of personal development plans in an organisation with which you are familiar.
3. Critically evaluate the application of a competency framework to learning and development for your organisation.

Liverpool Community College

Bibliography

ADVANCED EDUCATION AND CAREER DEVELOPMENT (1995) *Vision for Change: A concept paper for the development of a virtual learning system.* Berrett-Koehler, San Francisco.

ARMSTRONG, M. (1996) *A handbook of personnel management practice.* London, Kogan Page.

BAHAR, A. *et al.* (1996) Managing training and development in Bahrain: the influence of culture. *Journal of Managerial Psychology* Vol. 11 No. 5.

BARCLAY, J. (1996) Learning from experience with learning logs. *Journal of Management Development*; Vol. 15 No. 6.

BEECH, N. *et al.* (2000) Transient transfusion; or the wearing-off of the governance of the soul? *Personnel Review*; Vol. 29 No. 4.

BILLETT, S. (2000) Guided learning at work. *Journal of Workplace Learning* Vol. 12 No. 7.

BLOOM, B. *et al.* (1956) *Taxonomy of educational objectives.* New York, David McKay.

BOAM, R. and **SPARROW, P.** (1992) *Designing and achieving competency.* London, McGraw-Hill.

BOURNER, T. and **FLOWERS, S.** (1997) Teaching and learning methods in higher education: A glimpse of the future. *Reflections on Higher Education*; Vol. 9.

BOYDELL, T. and **LEARY, M.** (1996) *Identifying training needs.* London, CIPD.

BRIERLEY, P. (1989) *Vision building.* London, Hodder and Stoughton.

BROCKBANK, A. *et al.* (eds.) (2002) *Reflective learning in practice.* Aldershot, Gower.

BROOKFIELD, S. (1986) *Understanding and facilitating adult learning.* Buckingham, Open University Press.

BROOKS, J. (ed.) (2000) A glossary of UK training and occupational learning terms. Stockport, ITOL.

BURACK, E. *et al.* (1997) The new management development paradigm. *Human Resource Planning;* Vol. 20 No. 1.

BURDEN, R. and **PROCTOR, T.** (2000) Creating a sustainable competitive advantage through training. *Team Performance Management*; Vol. 6 No. 5.

BURN, B. and **PAYMENT, M.** (2000) *Assessments A – Z.* San Francisco, CA, Jossey-Bass / Pfeiffer.

CAMPBELL, K. (1996) A 21st-Century Vision of Strategic Human Resource Management. *Human Resources Management;* Vol. 382 No. 2.

CHAWLA, S. and **RENESCH, J.** (1995) *Learning organization.* Portland, Productivity Press.

CHEETHAM, G. and **CHIVERS, G.** (2001) How professionals learn in practice: an investigation of informal learning amongst people working in professions. *Journal of European Industrial Training;* Vol. 25 No. 5.

COCKERILL, T. and **HUNT, J.** (1995) 'Managerial competencies: fact of fiction?'. *Business Strategy Review*; Vol. 6 No. 3.

COHEN, E. and **TICHY, N.** (1997) How leaders develop leaders. *Training & Development;* Vol. 51 No. 5.

COLE, G. (1993) *Management: theory and practice.* London, DP Publications.

COLEMAN, J. and **KLEINER, B.** (1999) How to orient employees into new positions successfully. *Management Research News;* Vol. 22 No. 10.

COWLING, A. *et al.* (1999) Developing a competency framework to support training in evidence-based healthcare. *International Journal of Health Care Quality Assurance; Vol. 12 No. 4.*

CRAIG, M. (1994) *Analysing learning needs.* Aldershot, Gower.

CRIPPS, P. (2001) *Blackhall guide to employee development: developing people to develop your company.* Stillorgan, Blackhall Publishing.

CRONBACH, L. (1963) Course improvement through evaluation Teachers college Records; Vol. 64.

DARLING, J. *et al.* (1999) *The Changing Role of the Trainer.* London, CIPD.

DAVIS, V. *and* **KLEINER, B.** (2001) How to orient employees into new positions successfully. *Management Research News;* Vol. 24 No. 1

DIJKSTRA, S. *et al.* (eds.) (1997a) *Instructional Design: International Perspectives Vol. 1: Theory, Research and Models.* New Jersey, Lawrence Erlbaum Associates.

DIJKSTRA, S. *et al.* (1997b) *Instructional Design: International Perspectives Vol. 2: Solving Instructional Design Problems.* New Jersey, Lawrence Erlbaum Associates.

DUNN, J. (1995) *The effective leader: a biblical guide.* Eastbourne, Kingsway Publications.

EASTERBY-SMITH, M. (1986) *Evaluation of management education, training and development.* Aldershot, Gower.

EDWARDS, C. (1999) 'Evaluation and assessment' in WILSON, J. (ed) Human resource development. London, Kogan Page.

EFFAH, P. (1998) The training and development of academic librarians in Ghana. *Library Management;* Vol. 19 No. 1.

FITZ-ENZ, J. (2000) *The ROI of Human Capital: Measuring the Economic Value of Employee Performance.* New York, AMACOM.

FREDERICKS, J. *and* **STEWART, J.** (1996) 'The strategy – HRD connection' in STEWART, J. and MCGOLDRICK, J. (eds) Human resource development: perspectives, strategies and practice. London, Pearson.

FREEL, M. (1999) Where are the skills gaps in innovative small firms? *International Journal of Entrepreneurial Behaviour and Research;* Vol. 5 No. 3.

GARAVAN, T. *and* **McGUIRE, D.** (2001) Competencies and workplace learning: some reflections on the rhetoric and the reality. *Journal of Workplace Learning;* Vol. 13 No. 4.

GARAVAN, T. (1991) Strategic human source development. *Journal of European Industrial Training;* Vol. 15 No. 1.

GARAVAN, T. *et al.* (1995) The emergence of strategic human resource development. *Journal of European Industrial Training;* Vol 19 No. 10.

GARBUTT, D. (1969) *Training costs with reference to the Industrial Training Act.* London, Gee.

GILLEY, J. *and* **COFFERN, A.** (1994) *Internal Consulting for HRD Professionals: Tools, Techniques and Strategies for Improving Organisational Performance.* New York, McGraw-Hill.

GILLEY, J. *and* **MAYACUNICH, A.** (1998) *Strategically Integrated HRD: Partnering to Maximise Organisational Performance.* New York, Addison-Wesley.

GILLEY, J. *et al.* (2001) *Philosophy and practice of organizational learning, performance and change.* Cambridge, MA, Perseus.

GILLEY, J. *et al.* (2002) *Principles of human resource development.* Cambridge, MA, Perseus.

GUEST, D. (2002) *Managing excellence and high performance.* Milton Keynes, Open University Press.

GUILE, D. *and* **FONDA, N.** (1999) *Managing learning for added value*. London, CIPD.

HAMBLIN, A. (1974) *Evaluation and control of training*. London, McGraw-Hill.

HAMLIN, B. and **DAVIES, G.** (1996) 'The trainer as change agent: issues for practice' in *Stewart, I.* and *McGoldrick, J.* (eds) *Human resource development: perspectives, strategies and practice.* London, Pearson.

HAMLIN, R. *et al.* (eds.) (2001) *Organisational change and development*. Hemel Hempstead, Pitman.

HANDY, C. (1997) *The hungry spirit*. London, Random House.

HARRISON, R. (2001) *Learning and development*. London, CIPD.

HESSELING, P. (1996) *Strategy of evaluation research in the field of supervisory and management training*. Anssen, Van Gorcum.

HICKMAN, C. (1992) *Mind of a manager, soul of a leader*. New York, John Wiley.

HIGSON, M. *and* **WILSON, J.** (1995) Implementing personal development plans: a model for trainers, managers and supervisors *Industrial and Commercial Training;* Vol. 27 No. 6.

HODGES, T. (2002) *Linking learning and performance*. Woburn, MA, Butterworth-Heinemann.

HOFSTEDE, G. (2001) *Culture's consequences*. Thousand Oaks, CA, Sage.

HONEY, P. *and* **MUMFORD, A.** (1986) *Manual of learning styles*. Maidenhead, Peter Honey.

HONEY, P. *et al.* (1998) *A declaration on learning*, Maidenhead, Learning declaration group.

HONEY, P. (2003) Peter Honey on e-learning. *Organisations and people;* Vol. 10 No. 1.

HORWITZ, F. (1999) The emergence of strategic training and development: the current state of play. *Journal of European Industrial Training;* Vol. 23 No. 4/5.

HYLAND, P. (2000) Learning strategies and CI: lessons from several small to medium Australian manufacturers. *Integrated Manufacturing Systems;* Vol. 11 No. 6.

IRVINE, D. *and* **BEARD, C.** (1999) 'Management training and development: problems, paradoxes and perspectives' in WILSON, J. (ed) *Human resource development.* London, Kogan Page.

JACKSON, P. (1969) *Organisational change and supervisory effectiveness.* Unpublished Ph.D. Thesis, Birkbeck College, University of London.

JARVIS, P. (1984), Andragogy: a sign of the times *Studies in the Education of Adults*, No. 16.

JOHNSON, G. *and* **SCHOLES, K.** (1997) *Exploring corporate strategy*. London, Prentice Hall.

JOHNSON, R. (1993) The role of distance learning in continuing education and professional development *International Journal of University Adult Education*; Vol. XXX No. 11/2.

JONES, J. *and* **MOXHAM, J.** (1969) Costing the benefits of training. *Personnel Management;* Vol. 1 No. 4.

JONG, de J. *et al.* (1999) HRD tasks of first-level managers. *Journal of Workplace Learning;* Vol. 11 No. 5.

KELLEHER, M. (1996) 'New forms of work organisation and HRD' in STEWART, I. and MCGOLDRICK, J. (eds) Human resource development: perspectives, strategies and practice. London, Pearson.

KNOWLES, M. *et al.* (1998) *The adult learner*. Houston, TX, Gulf.

KOHN, V. *and* **PARKER, T.** (1969) Some guidelines for evaluating management development programmes. *Training and Development Journal;* Vol. 23 No. 7.

KOLB, D. (1981) Experiential learning theory and the learning style inventory. *Academy of Management Review* 6.

KOLB, D, (1984) *Experiential learning*. Englewood Cliffs, NJ, Prentice Hall.

LANGE, T. and **PUGH, G.** (1997) High-tech investment and learning-by-doing: an alternative training strategy. *Education and Training;* Vol. 39 No. 8.

LANNOM, J. (1998) *Untapped Potential: Turning Ordinary People into Extraordinary Performers.* Nashvllle, Thomas Nelson Publishers.

LAWLESS, N. *et al.* (2000) Face-to-face or distance training: two different approaches to motivate SMEs to learn. *Education and Training;* Vol. 42 No. 4.

LECKY-THOMPSON, R. (1997) Tales of the city (London training policies). *People Management;* Vol. 3 No. 2.

LEE, C. and **CHON, K.** (2000) An investigation of multicultural training practices in the restaurant industry: the training cycle approach. *International Journal of Contemporary Hospitality Management;* Vol. 12 No. 2.

LEE, R. (1996) The 'pay-forward view of training. *People Management;* Vol. 2 No. 3.

LEWIN, K. (1951) *Field theory in social science.* London, Tavistock.

LEWIS, P. and **THORNHILL, A.** (1994) The Evaluation of Training: An Organizational Culture. Approach *Journal of European Industrial Training;* Vol. 18 No. 8.

LUCAS, B. (1999) A date for your diary. *People Management;* Vol. 5 No. 9.

LYNTON, R. and **PAREEK, U.** (2000a) *Training for organizational transformation: Part 1.* New Delhi, Sage.

LYNTON, R. and **PAREEK, U.** (2000b) *Training for organizational transformation: Part 2.* New Delhi, Sage.

LYONS, L. (2000) Management is dead. *People Management;* Vol. 6 No. 21.

MAIN, J. (1992) How to steel the best ideas around. *Fortune,* 19 October.

MANN, S. and **ROBERTSON, I.** (1996) What should training evaluations evaluate? *Journal of European Industrial Training;* Vol. 20 No. 9.

MARCHINGTON, M. and **WILKINSON, A.** (2002) *People management and development.* London, CIPD.

MARTIN, M. and **JACKSON, T.** (2002) *Personnel Practice.* London, CIPD.

MAYO, A. (2000) *Creating a Training and Development Strategy.* London, CIPD.

MAZOUÉ, J. (1999) The essentials of effective online instruction. *Campus-Wide Information Systems* Vol. 16 No. 3.

McCARTHY, A. and **GARAVAN, T.** (1999) Developing self-awareness in the managerial career development process: the value of 360-degree feedback and the MBTI. *Journal of European Industrial Training;* Vol. 23 No. 9.

McCLELLAND, D. (1973), Testing for competence, rather than intelligence. *American Psychologist;* Vol. 28.

McCRACKEN, M. and **WALLACE, M.** (2000) Towards a redefinition of strategic HRD. *Journal of European Industrial Training;* Vol. 24 No. 5.

McGOLDRICK, J. *et al.* (2000) *Understanding human resource development.* London, Routledge.

McLAGAN, R. (1989) *Models of HRD Practice.* Alexandria, VA, ASTD Press.

MEGGINSON, D. *et al.* (1993) *Human resource development.* London, Kogan Page.

MIRABILE, R. (1997) Everything you need to know about competency modelling. *Training & Development* August.

MOORE, S. (1999) Understanding and managing diversity among groups at work: key issues for organisational training and development. *Journal of European Industrial Training;* Vol. 23 No. 4

MULLINS, L. (2002) *Management and organisational behaviour.* London, Pearson.

NELSON, J. (ed.) (1999) *Leading, managing, ministering.* Norwich, Canterbury Press.

NEW, G. (1996), Reflections: a three-tier model of organisational competencies. *Journal of Managerial Psychology;* Vol. 11 No. 8.

NOEL, J. *and* **DENNEHY, R.** (1991) Making HRD a force in strategic organisational change. *Industrial and Commercial Training;* Vol. 23 No. 2.

O'DONNELL, D. *and* **GARAVAN, T.** (1997) Viewpoint: Linking training policy and practice to organizational goals. *Journal of European Industrial Training;* Vol. 21 No. 9.

O'DWYER, M. *and* **RYAN, E.** (2000) Management development issues for owners/managers of micro-enterprises. *Journal of European Industrial Training;* Vol. 24 No. 6.

OPPENHEIM, A. (1966) *Questionnaire design and attitude measurement.* London, Heinemann.

PALMER, R. (1999) 'The identification of organizational and individual training and development needs' in WILSON, J. (ed) Human resource development. London, Kogan Page.

PARSONS, R. (2002) *The Heart of Success.* London, Hodder & Stoughton.

PEDLER, M. *et al.* (1991) *The learning company.* London, McGraw-Hill.

PEPPER, A. (1992) *Managing the training and development function.* Aldershot, Gower.

PETTIGREW, A. *et al.* (1982) *Training and development roles in their organisational setting.* Sheffield, MSC.

PHILLIPS, J. (2002) *How to Measure Training Success: A Practical Guide to Evaluating Training.* New York, McGraw-Hill Education.

PHILLIPS, J. *and* **JACOBS, R.** (2002) *Implementing on-the-job learning.* Alexandria VA, ASTD.

PHILLIPS, J. *and* **STONE, R.** (2002) *How to measure training results.* New York, McGraw-Hill.

PISKURICH, G. *et al.* (eds.) (2000) *The ASTD handbook of training design and delivery.* New York, McGraw-Hill.

PYM, D. (1968) Organisational evaluation and management training. *Journal of Management Studies;* Vol. 5 No. 2.

RAE, L. (2002a) *Assessing the value of your training.* Aldershot, Gower.

RAE, L. (2002b) *Trainer assessment.* Aldershot, Gower.

READ, C. *and* **KLEINER, B.** (1996) Which training methods are effective? *Management Development Review* Vol. 9 No. 2.

REID, M. *and* **BARRINGTON, H.** (2000) Training interventions. London, CIPD.

REITMAN, A. *and* **WILLIAMS, C.** (2002) *Career moves: take charge of your training career now.* Alexandria, VA, ASTD.

REYNOLDS, J. *et al.* (2002) *How do people learn?* London, CIPD.

ROBINSON, A. *and* **STERN, S.** (1995) Strategic national HRD initiatives: lessons from the Management Training Program of Japan. *Human Resource Development Quarterly;* Vol. 6 No. 2.

ROGERS, C. (1961) *On becoming a person.* Cambridge, MA, Houghton Mifflin.

ROLLS, J. (1999) 'Transformational leadership' in NELSON, J. (ed) (1999) Leading, managing, ministering. Norwich, Canterbury Press.

SADLER-SMITH, E. (1996) Learning styles: a holistic approach. *Journal of European Industrial Training;* Vol. 20 No. 7.

SAWDON, D. (1999) 'Making the most of consultancy: perspectives on partnership' in Wilson, J. (ed) Human resource development.

SENGE, P. (1990) *The fifth discipline.* New York, Doubleday.

SHAW, M. *and* **GREEN, H.** (1999) Continuous professional development: emerging trends in the UK. *Quality Assurance in Education;* Vol. 7 No. 3.

SIMMONDS, D. (1998) *Evaluation Toolkit.* Ely, Fenman Training.

SIMMONDS, D. (2000) *Learning Methods Toolkit.* Ely, Fenman Training.

SLOMAN, M. *and* **ROLPH, J.** (2003) *E-learning: the learning curve.* London, CIPD.

SPENCER, L. *and* **SPENCER, S.** (1993), *Competence at Work: Models for Superior Performance.* New York, Wiley.

STEAD, V. *and* **LEE, M.** (1996) 'Intercultural perspectives on HRD' in STEWART, J. MCGOLDRICK, J. (eds) Human resource development: perspectives, strategies and practice. London, Pearson.

STEWART, J. *and* **McGOLDRICK, J.** (eds.) (1996) *Human resource development: perspectives, strategies and practice.* London, Pearson.

STEWART, J. *and* **TANSLEY, C.** (2002) *Training in the knowledge economy.* LONDON, CIPD.

STEWART, J. (1999) *Employee development practice.* London, Pitman.

STOREY, J. (2001) *Human Resource Management: A Critical Text.* London, Thomson Learning.

SWANSON, R. (2001) *Assessing the financial benefits of human resource development.* Cambridge, MA, Perseus.

SWANSON, R. *and* **HOLTON, E.** (2001) *Foundations of human resource development.* New York, McGraw-Hill.

THOMAS, V. (1999) *Future Leader.* Carlisle, Paternoster Press.

THOMSON, R. *and* **MABEY, C.** (1994) *Developing human resources.* Oxford, Heinemann.

TORRACO, R. *and* **SWANSON, R.** (1995) The strategic roles of human resource development. *Human Resource Planning;* Vol. 18 No. 4

TREGASKI, O. *and* **DANY, F.** (1996) A comparison of HRD in France and UK. *Journal of European Industrial Training;* Vol. 20 No. 1.

TYLER, R. *et al.* (1967) *Perspectives of curriculum evaluation.* Chicago, Rand-McNally.

VARTANIAN, F. (1997) Development of human resources for medical research. *Health Manpower Management;* Vol. 23 No. 1.

VERMEULEN, W. *and* **CROUS, M.** (2000) Training and education for TQM in the commercial banking industry of South Africa. *Managing Service Quality;* Vol. 10 No. 1.

WALTER, D. (2002) *Training on the job.* Alexandria, VA, ASTD.

WALTON, J. (1999) *Strategic human resource development.* London, Pitman.

WARR, P. *et al.* (1970) *Evaluation of management training.* Aldershot, Gower.

WEST, C. (2002) *Continuing Professional Development for Trainers: The Practical Toolkit for Planning and Recording Your Personal Learning.* Ely, Fenman Training.

WILSON, D. *et al.* (2001) *The future of learning for work.* London, CIPD.

WILSON, J. (ed.) (1999) Human resource development. London, Kogan Page.

WOODALL, J. *and* **WINSTANLEY, D.** (1998) *Management development: strategy and practice.* Oxford, Blackwell Publishers.

WOODRUFFE, C. (2000) Keep X on the files. *People Management;* Vol. 6 No. 15.

WOODS, J. *and* **CORTADA, J.** (2002) *ASTD training and performance yearbook.* New York, McGraw-Hill.

Index